An Employment-Targeted Economic Program for South Africa

A project of The Poverty Group of the Bureau for Development Policy,
New York and the International Poverty Centre in Brasilia (IPC),
United Nations Development Program

An Employment-Targeted Economic Program for South Africa

Robert Pollin
Gerald A. Epstein
James Heintz
Léonce Ndikumana

*Department of Economics and Political Economy Research Institute (PERI),
University of Massachusetts-Amherst, USA*

COUNTRY STUDY SUPPORTED BY THE INTERNATIONAL POVERTY CENTRE
OF THE UNITED NATIONS DEVELOPMENT PROGRAM
*This is an independent report produced by a team of international and national
consultants supported by the International Poverty Centre in Brasilia (IPC). Initial
support for this report was provided by the Poverty Group of the United Nations
Development Program in New York. This report is part of a wider global research
program encompassing several other countries. The views in this report are the authors'
and not necessarily IPC's. However, the IPC regards this report as an important
contribution to the debate on economic policies and employment programs in South
Africa as well as in other countries in Africa.*

Edward Elgar
Cheltenham, UK • Northampton, MA, USA

Published by
Edward Elgar Publishing Limited
Glensanda House
Montpellier Parade
Cheltenham
Glos GL50 1UA
UK

Edward Elgar Publishing, Inc.
William Pratt House
9 Dewey Court
Northampton
Massachusetts 01060
USA

A catalogue record for this book
is available from the British Library

Library of Congress Cataloguing in Publication Data

An employment-targeted economic program for South Africa / Robert Pollin ... [et al.].
    p. cm.
  Includes bibliographical references and index.
  1. Full employment policies—South Africa. 2. Unemployment—South Africa.
I. Pollin, Robert.
  HD5842.A6E47 2007
  331.12'042—dc22
                          2006023667

ISBN 978 1 84720 118 8

Printed and bound in Great Britain by MPG Books Ltd, Bodmin, Cornwall

Contents

Tables

Figures

Acknowledgments

Between August 23–September 1, 2004, we conducted more than 30 interviews in Johannesburg, Pretoria, and Cape Town with people offering us a wide range of knowledge and insight about the workings of the South African economy. We could not have even thought to pursue this project had these people not given so generously of their time. It isn't possible for us to mention all of the people we met with, but a partial list of those we wish to thank includes Stephen Hanival and Dirk van Seventer of TIPS; Rashad Cassim and Simon Roberts of the University of Witwatersrand; Miriam Altman of HSRC; Wiseman Nkuhlu of NEPAD; Lumkile Mondi, Gerhard Kuhn, Chifipa Mhango, and Christo van Zyl of IDC; Herbert Mkhize, along with representatives of business, government, labor and community constituencies at NEDLAC; Bhenki Langa, Guy Mhone, Tim Hinks, and Afeikhena Jerome at NIEP; Brian Kahn of the SARB; Rudolph Gouws of the Rand Merchant Bank; Kenneth Andoh, Astrid Coyne-Jensen, and Momammed Mwamadzingo of ILO; Neil Coleman, Oupa Bodibe, and Ravi Naidoo of NALEDI; Murray Liebbrandt, Nicoli Nattras, Melvin Ayogu, Cecil Mlatsheni, Lawrence Edwards, and Samson Muradsikwa of the University of Cape Town; Stan du Plessis and Servaas Van Der Berg of the University of Stellenbosch; Sean Phillips of the Department of Public Works; Alan Hirsch of the Office of the Presidency; Elias Masilela, Kuben Naidoo, and Kevin Fletcher of the National Treasury; Kgalema Mothanthee of the ANC; Nanda Ndalane, Rob Davies, and Jeremy Cronin of the Parliament of South Africa; and Mandisi Mpahlwa of the DTI.

Robert Pollin presented an earlier draft of this study in January 2005 at a conference in Brasilia on "Strengthening the Employment Nexus between Growth and Poverty Reduction," sponsored by the UNDP International Poverty Centre there. He benefited greatly from the discussion of this work at that conference and from the more general conference discussions.

Our full team returned to South Africa March 11–16, 2005 to present a preliminary draft of this study before a series of seminars at the University of Cape Town, and in public meetings in Cape Town, Pretoria, and Johannesburg. We are grateful to all seminar participants for their interest and spirited comments. We especially benefited from the formal comments by David Kaplan, Lumkile Mondi, Stephen Gelb, Wiseman Nkhulu, Rob Davies (from South Africa), Rob Davies (from Zimbabwe), and Ben Smit. We also received highly constructive and characteristically challenging written comments on earlier drafts from Keith Griffin, Aziz Khan, Laurence Harris, Terry McKinley and Charles Meth. Between our preliminary March 2005 draft and this current version, we also were fortunate to have been able to present parts of our findings before seminars at the International Labour Offices in Geneva, at the 2006 Allied Social Science Association meetings, and at seminars at York University as well as our home institution, University of Massachusetts-Amherst. We benefited substantially from all of these interchanges.

We owe a special debt of gratitude to the South African economists who have served as our consultants on this project. They are Anna McCord of the University of Cape Town; Stephen Gelb of the EDGE Institute and University of Witwatersrand; and Julian May, Vishnu Padayachee, and Imraan Valodia of the University of KwaZulu-Natal.

We are greatly appreciative of the support of our sponsors in the UNDP system—at both the Poverty Group of the Bureau for Development Policy, New York, and the International Poverty Centre in Brasilia (IPC). We especially single out the efforts of Terry McKinley and Selim Jahan. We also are grateful for the support from UNDP officers in South Africa, including John Ohiorhenuan, John Wayem, Philip Browne, and Lusanda Monale.

Our research assistants, Ozgur Orhangazi, Fiona Tregenna and Andong Zhu, all made significant contributions to this project, for which we are very appreciative. Kim Weinstein has done her customary excellent work in laying out this study. Against formidable odds, Judy Fogg continues to keep this project and everything else at PERI in order.

Brief Highlights of Major Proposals

The focus of our study is the severe problem of mass unemployment in South Africa today, and the corresponding problem of mass poverty. Depending on whether one considers the "official" or "expanded" definition (the expanded definition including discouraged workers), unemployment in South Africa stood at between 26.5–40.5 percent as of March 2005. The ANC-led government has committed itself to cutting the unemployment rate in half by 2014, i.e. bringing the official unemployment rate down to roughly 13 percent as of 2014. Our proposed program is designed to produce major reductions in unemployment and poverty and a general spreading of economic well-being; and to achieve these ends in a manner that is sustainable over a longer-term framework. Our program is certainly consistent in intention with the preliminary presentations of the government's forthcoming Accelerated and Shared Growth Initiative for South Africa (ASGISA). It also shares several specific features in common with the preliminary version of the ASGISA.[1]

UNEMPLOYMENT AND POVERTY IN SOUTH AFRICA TODAY

South Africa's problem of mass unemployment can be usefully conceptualized in simple accounting terms, as the result of two factors:

1. *Insufficiency in the rate of output growth*, i.e. the economy's production of goods and services. Between 1994–2004, the average GDP growth rate was 3.1 percent. This is superior to the last decade of apartheid. But given the growth rate of the population of slightly under 2 percent per year, it is still inadequate for generating a significant expansion of employment opportunities.
2. *Declining labor intensity of production in the formal economy.* Between 1994–2001, the number of workers utilized per unit of output—i.e. a basic measure of labor intensity—fell by an average of nearly four percent per year, an acceleration of a longer-term trend decline between 1967–2001 of roughly one percent per year.

Employment projection to 2014

If South Africa proceeds along this approximate growth pattern for the next decade, we estimate—using a series of reasonable assumptions about labor force growth and the ratio of informal/formal employment—that official unemployment will have risen to roughly 33 percent as of 2014.

Economic Growth and Poverty

We observe that—at least between the years 1995 – 2000, for which we have adequate data—economic growth was associated with declining incomes across households at all income levels, but with the sharpest income declines occurring among the least well off.

Supply-Side Interventions to Expand Employment

The fact that South Africa is experiencing both high unemployment and rising capital intensity of production suggests to some analysts that businesses are convinced that the costs of hiring more workers exceed the benefits. From this perspective, the solution to mass unemployment is to lower unit labor costs, in particular through reducing wages. But we argue that the evidence linking mass unemployment to high labor costs is generally not convincing. At the same time, we do support measures to maintain wage increases in line with productivity growth and to improve the efficiency of the country's industrial relations system.

MAIN FEATURES OF PROPOSED EMPLOYMENT-TARGETED PROGRAM

To establish the framework for introducing our overall employment program, we divide the South African economy into two broad categories—activities that will receive large-scale credit subsidies and those that will be unsubsidized.

Subsidized activities

These would include small-scale agriculture, small and medium-sized enterprises, and larger-scale businesses that either operate at high levels of labor intensity or can generate substantial employment multipliers. We would expect firms that receive the credit subsidies to account for roughly 20–25 percent of all investment activity in South Africa's economy. We propose that government policy aim to enable these activities to expand at roughly 8 percent per year through 2014.

Unsubsidized activities

For the remaining 75–80 percent of South Africa's economy, we propose that economic growth accelerate to roughly 4.5 percent per year through 2014.

Alternative Employment Projection for 2014

Combining an 8 percent growth stimulus for the subsidized activities and a 4.5 percent growth rate for the rest of the economy generates an overall average annual growth rate of 5.3 percent. At this growth rate, as well as making reasonable assumptions about labor market trends, we estimate that unemployment could decline to about 15.4 percent as of 2014.

Alternative Employment Projection and Poverty Reduction

Given that unemployment will remain very high even with an aggressive employment-targeted program, other measures besides employment growth are needed to improve living conditions for the poor over the next decade. We therefore support measures to increase spending on social services and income supports for the poor. We outline the revenue sources that would be needed to pay for program expansions on the order of R10–20 billion per year.

TOOLS FOR IMPLEMENTING THE EMPLOYMENT-TARGETED PROGRAM

Achieving Sustained 4.5 Percent Growth for Unsubsidized Share of Economy

1. *Fiscal Stimulus.* The government is presently projecting a structural fiscal deficit through 2008–09 in the range of 2 percent of GDP. However, as of 2004, it had increased its deficit projections to about 3 percent of GDP. We think this higher deficit/GDP ratio is an appropriate and sustainable level of structural fiscal stimulus consistent with the government's employment goals.
2. *Monetary stimulus.* We propose that the Reserve Bank lower lending rates to stimulate growth, especially by encouraging higher levels of investment and consumption spending. For example, lowering the prime lending rate from, say, 11 to 7 percent, and holding rates at that lower level for five years, will increase average growth from 3 to 3.6 percent over the five-year period. At the same time, the impact on inflation and the exchange rate will be relatively mild, i.e. raising inflation from, say, 5 to 6 percent as a five-year

average, and lowering the value of the rand from, say, R6.3 per dollar to R7.1 per dollar by the end of the five-year period.

We believe that these combined relatively modest fiscal and monetary stimuli will be able to bring the average growth rate in the range of 4.5 percent, as long as effective controls are maintained at keeping inflation within a moderate range and maintaining a relatively stable exchange rate.

Achieving 8 Percent Growth Stimulus for Subsidized Activities

The key mechanism through which we propose to generate the 8 percent growth stimulus for the subsidized activities is the provision of credit at concessionary rates to these industries. We propose a formula for determining appropriate subsidized credit rates based on 1) the proportion of a loan being guaranteed; and 2) the differential between market rates and default-safe government bond rates.

We propose three main policy tools to channel credit to the targeted industries at concessionary rates.

1. *Major expansion in lending activity and developmental focus of the country's eight currently operating development banks.*
2. *Asset reserve requirements.* These requirements would establish that financial institutions hold, for example, 20 percent of their assets in loans to subsidized activities. We propose measures to operate this system flexibly, for example, allowing banks that hold more than 20 percent of their loans with subsidized firms to sell permits to institutions whose loans to subsidized firms are below the 20 percent minimum threshold.
3. *Major expansion of the government's system of loan guarantees.* We propose that the government underwrite roughly R40 billion in loans to subsidized activities. We calculate the budgetary costs of this program as being roughly R4.5 billion/year, assuming a 75 percent underwriting and a 15 percent failure rate on guaranteed loans.

The idea of subsidizing firms that either operate at high levels of labor intensity or that generate large employment multipliers builds on the approach of the current Expanded Public Works Program (EPWP), which is specifically targeted at promoting labor-intensive production techniques in some public infrastructure projects. But the EPWP in its current form will provide only very modest gains in employment expansion. The ASGISA is focused on a major expansion in public investment, including in labor-intensive areas. But as yet we have not seen proposals as to how this new public investment spending will be financed. The method of financing will be crucial for determining the net employment effects of the program.

CONTROLLING INFLATION
AND THE EXCHANGE RATE

Inflation Control and Economic Growth

We review the current literature on the relationship between economic growth and inflation. Researchers differ widely in their conclusions. But there is virtually no evidence demonstrating that developing countries experience slower GDP growth through inflation within a single-digit range. This is especially true if inflation is generated through increasing overall demand, as opposed to supply shocks, exchange rate shocks, or monopolistic pricing practices. If inflation in South Africa were to reach double-digit rates, we propose two policy measures other than raising interest rates as control measures: 1) policies to weaken monopolistic price mark-ups; and 2) incomes policies—that is, wage and price restraint that is negotiated on an economy-wide basis between the organized sectors of labor and business.

Capital Controls and Exchange Controls

Capital controls, exchange controls and other capital management techniques have been utilized as mechanisms for reducing the sensitivity of domestic financial markets, including exchange rates, to macroeconomic policy. South Africa has a long history of utilizing these policies. We argue that these controls can be successful in supporting efforts by the Reserve Bank to lower nominal interest rates within the relatively small range of about 4 percentage points that we are proposing. In addition, severe bouts of exchange rate volatility will be less likely when capital management policies are deployed to prevent such episodes.

GOVERNMENT SPENDING PROGRAMS
AND TAX POLICY

Increased Spending

The programs we are advocating would entail annual increased government expenditures of roughly R20–30 billion (in 2004 prices):

1. Public investment/infrastructure: R5–7.5 billion
2. Income transfers and social support: R10–20 billion
3. Credit subsidies to businesses to promote accelerated employment growth: R 5–7.5 billion

Increased Revenues

These programs should be paid for in two roughly equal parts. About R14 billion would come through increasing the structural fiscal deficit from approximately 2 to 3 percent of GDP. The remainder R16 billion would be paid for through raising taxes, such that the tax revenue/GDP ratio would rise from roughly 25 to 26 percent. The increased revenues should come from these sources:

1. R6 billion from the three major revenue sources: personal income tax, corporate profit tax, and VAT.
2. R10 billion from three additional sources:
    a) R6 billion from extending the Uncertified Securities Tax to bond trading. At present, the tax only covers stock trading.
    b) R2.5 billion from enacting the Mineral and Petroleum Royalty Bill drafted by the National Treasury in 2003.
    c) R1.5 billion from raising economic growth to 5.3 percent from 3 percent and from lowering poverty rates, which in turn reduces demand for social service spending.

Additional Policies for Productive Sectors

In addition to the targeting of industries based on their employment multipliers, we also propose two other areas of sectoral policy:

1. *Administered pricing.* More effective measures to control price setting in monopolistic and oligopolistic markets, including the administered pricing of parastatals and import parity pricing in the domestic steel industry.
2. *Promoting some capital-intensive industries with low employment multipliers.* We discuss the motor vehicle industry and sectors of capital goods production, because of their potential to enhance productivity and capacity to produce import-competing capital goods.

NOTE

1. We have seen the acronym for the Accelerated and Shared Growth Initiative for South Africa presented in two ways: as all capital letters, ASGISA, the more conventional way of presenting acronyms; and as AsgiSA. For consistency with other acronyms in the study (such as GEAR), we are using the conventional style throughout.

Summary of Major Findings and Proposals

This volume outlines a pro-poor, employment-focused economic policy framework for South Africa. Its specific focus is the severe problem of mass unemployment in South Africa today. Unemployment in South Africa was between 26.5 and 40.5 percent as of March 2005, depending on whether one uses the "official" or "expanded" definition of unemployment (with the expanded definition including so-called "discouraged workers"). Our concentration on the problem of mass unemployment is fully consistent with the stated goals of the current African National Congress (ANC) government. At the Growth and Development Summit in 2003, President Thabo Mbeki singled out "more jobs, better jobs, and decent work for all" as one of the country's four key economic challenges. Currently, the preliminary presentations of the Government's new economic policy framework, the "Accelerated and Shared Growth Initiative for South Africa" (ASGISA), affirms its commitment to cutting the unemployment rate in half by 2014.

Following an introductory first chapter, the main body of this work consists of two short chapters that lay out basic concerns, then two substantially longer chapters presenting the framework for policy analysis and specific policy proposals.

Chapter 2 presents evidence on the scope of the unemployment problem in South Africa today, considering the unemployed by gender, race, region, length of joblessness and age. It then examines how the country's problem of mass unemployment can be usefully conceptualized in simple accounting terms—namely, as the result of 1) insufficiency in the rate of output growth, i.e., the economy's production of goods and services; and 2) a declining number of jobs being created per unit of output.

Chapter 3 examines supply-side perspectives on employment expansion. The fact that the South African economy is experiencing both high unemployment and rising capital intensity of production suggests to some analysts both an explanation for high unemployment and a solution to the problem. For these analysts, the explanation for the problem is straightforward: businesses will not hire more workers because they are convinced that the costs of doing so will exceed the benefits. Businesses therefore choose either to 1) maintain their operations at a lower level than they would if the benefits of hiring more workers exceeded the costs; or 2) increase the use of machines in their operations as a substitute for employing workers as their preferred means of expanding their operations. Seen from this perspective, the solution to the problem of unemployment is also straightforward: lower the costs that businesses face in hiring more workers.

In general, there are four possible ways in which the costs to businesses of hiring workers could fall: 1) workers receive lower overall compensation, including wages and benefits; 2) the industrial relations system and labor market regulations—including laws and regulations regarding workers' rights to organize, conflict resolution, and hiring and firing—operate with more flexibility for business; 3) workers perform their workplace operations at a higher level of productivity; or 4) the government absorbs some portion of the costs of hiring workers. In most discussions that consider the sources of unemployment from this business cost-oriented perspective, the focus generally is on the first way to reduce business costs, i.e., to lower wages and benefits for workers relative to both other input costs and the prices at which businesses can sell their final products.

This study argues that the evidence linking mass unemployment to high labor costs is not persuasive. We also argue that wage cutting as a policy approach is certain to elicit strong resistance, which in turn will worsen the country's investment climate. At the same time, we do support measures to maintain wage increases in line with productivity growth and to improve the efficiency of the industrial relations system. This study also introduces a proposal for a hybrid program of credit and employment subsidies as a means through which the government will effectively absorb a share of businesses' labor costs.

Chapter 4 considers the demand-side forces in South Africa's economy that will need to be mobilized to achieve faster economic growth and greater labor intensity. In terms of growth, the report discusses all four components of the conventional national income identity that, taken together, define economic growth—i.e., private investment, private consumption, net exports, and government spending. The report places particular stress in this section on the growth-enhancing effects of expanding public infrastructure investments. Indeed, public investment could expand both output and private sector productivity, and could correspondingly increase private investment and export competitiveness. It is significant that the ASGISA program also emphasizes the need for expanded public investment.

In considering ways to increase the labor intensity of growth, the report examines two basic approaches. The first is the Expanded Public Works Program (EPWP) now being implemented by the national government. The second approach is to encourage accelerated growth in business activities within South Africa that are capable of generating large increases in employment. The report examines the relative labor intensity of various industries in South Africa

Figure S.1 Real Growth Rate of South Africa GDP, 1984–2004

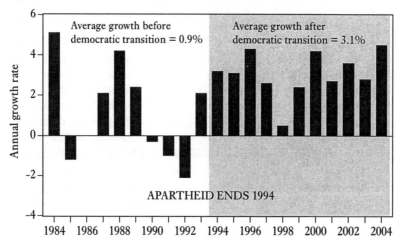

Sources: South Africa National Accounts; South African Reserve Bank Quarterly Bulletin, December 2005.

as well as the "employment multipliers" of industries, i.e., their capacity to generate relatively large numbers of new jobs through their upstream links with other business firms in the country.

Chapter 5, which concludes the study, considers specific policy tools that can be deployed to promote faster growth, rising labor intensity and poverty reduction. It considers policy interventions in the following areas: fiscal policy, monetary policy, credit subsidies, and development banking; capital market and exchange rate controls; inflation control; and sectoral policies in the areas of 1) monopolistic pricing and 2) promoting growth of selected productivity-enhancing and import-substituting capital-intensive industries on grounds other than employment benefits.

MAJOR FINDINGS AND RECOMMENDATIONS

Proposals and Objectives

1. Between 1994 and 2004—i.e., since the end of apartheid—the South African economy grew at an average annual rate slightly above 3 percent. As we see in Figure S.1, this is a major improvement over the country's dismal 0.9 percent average growth rate over the last decade of apartheid. At the same time, a 3 percent growth rate is only about 1 percent faster than South

Africa's average rate of population growth. As such, a 3 percent growth rate by itself is not nearly adequate to deliver major improvements in average living standards.

In addition, average labor intensity of production—as measured by the ratio of employment per R1 million in output—has been falling sharply in South Africa. The average decline between 1994 and 2001 was nearly 4 percent per year, a substantial acceleration over the longer trend decline of about 1 percent per year from 1967 to 2001. We can see this long-term pattern in Figure S.2. If the South African economy proceeded along approximately this growth path for the next decade, it would not be possible for the government to achieve its stated goal of reducing unemployment by half by 2014. Making reasonable assumptions about labor force growth and the proportionate rise of informal versus formal employment, the report projects that continuing for the next decade at a 3 percent growth rate and a 1 percent annual decline in labor intensity would produce an official unemployment rate by 2014 in the range of 33 percent.

2. For the government to achieve a 50 percent reduction in unemployment by 2014 will require an aggressive employment-targeted program that increases both the rate of economic growth and the labor intensity of growth. However, even under an aggressive program such as this report describes, the unemployment rate as of 2014 is still likely to be in the range of 15 percent. This means that other measures besides employment growth are needed to improve living conditions for the poor. We therefore support significant increases in government social expenditures and income transfers, even while recognizing the large fiscal commitments that the Government is already making in these areas. We show how increased spending in these areas can be achieved through only modest increases in the conventional sources of tax revenue.

3. The logic of the employment-targeted program that we propose is as follows. It divides the South African economy into two broad categories—subsidized and unsubsidized activities. The subsidized activities will be eligible to receive credit on highly concessionary terms, based on both a large expansion of the government's current development banking activities and a large-scale program of loan guarantees administered by the private banking system. Overall, these subsidized activities should account for roughly 20–25 percent of all new investment spending in the South African economy. Small-scale agriculture, small and medium-sized businesses, and cooperative businesses would all be eligible for this subsidy program. In addition, any other businesses could qualify for this subsidy if they could demonstrate their capacity either to raise the labor intensity of output or to generate large employment multipliers. Some of the activities that are likely to qualify for such subsidies are within the industries identified by the pre-

Figure S.2 Ratio of Formal Employment to GDP in South Africa, 1967–2001 (number of formal jobs per R1 million in output)

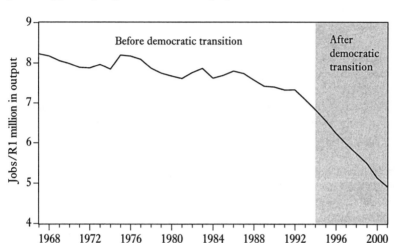

Source: Reserve Bank of South Africa.

liminary presentations of the ASGISA program as "priority" areas. These include agro-processing (such as biofuels) and tourism. We estimate that sectors receiving large credit subsidies should be capable of growing at an average annual rate of about 8 percent through 2014.

The idea of providing subsidies for activities that are either labor intensive or capable of generating large employment multipliers builds on the approach of the current EPWP program. But the EPWP in its current form is too modest in scale. According to one estimate, the public infrastructure component of the program that is scheduled to receive 75 percent of the program's total budget will generate roughly 80,000 net new jobs per year. As of March 2005, creating a net increase of 80,000 new jobs would have led to a reduction in the unemployment rate from 26.5 to 26.0 percent.

4. For the 75–80 percent of business activities in South Africa that would not receive credit subsidies, the report proposes that growth of output should be accelerated to an average annual rate of roughly 4.5 percent through 2014. This is a rate that could be achieved through a fairly small relaxation of the government's fiscal and monetary stances—that is, a relaxation that will not create significant problems either in terms of inflation or the exchange rate. If we combine the 8 percent growth rate for subsidized activities with a 4.5 percent growth rate for the remaining 75–80 percent of the

economy, the result would be an overall average growth rate of 5.3 percent between 2005 and 2014. We note that this average growth path over 2005–2014 is nearly identical to that being projected in the preliminary presentations of the ASGISA initiative. Assuming this growth projection can be sustained over the next decade, and also making reasonable assumptions about labor market growth and the ratio of formal to informal economy jobs, this report estimates that South Africa's official unemployment rate could fall to roughly 15.4 percent by 2014. Table S.1 below provides the basic assumptions, data and calculations through which we generated our alternative estimates of the unemployment rate as of 2014.

The report utilizes a series of conventional policy tools to achieve these objectives. These measures will promote growth, employment expansion and poverty reduction while maintaining stability of inflation and the exchange rate.

Policy Tools

Fiscal Stimulus

Because of the high levels of government debt incurred during the apartheid era, the ANC government understandably chose to establish a tight fiscal stance in the initial years of post-apartheid democracy. The deficit as a share of GDP fell to a low of 1.1 percent in 2002. According to its 2005 Medium Term Budget Policy Statement (MTBPS), the National Treasury has projected a fiscal deficit in the range of 2 percent of GDP through 2008-09. However, in its 2004 MTBPS, the Treasury had projected a more relaxed fiscal stance, in the range of 3 percent of GDP through 2006/2007, and somewhat higher figures still for the full Public Sector Borrowing Requirement. This earlier proposal for a more expansionary, but still prudent, fiscal stance would contribute positively to economic growth, since it would mean an additional injection into the economy of roughly R14 billion per year (in 2004 prices) relative to the baseline of a deficit at 2 percent of GDP. At the same time, even with a three percent deficit/GDP ratio, South Africa would still remain within the range of performance of other lower-middle income countries. The average fiscal deficit for these countries over 1990–2001 was 2.6 percent of GDP.

Monetary Stimulus

The South African Reserve Bank and ANC-led government have been committed to tight monetary policies since assuming office in the historic transition of 1994. This commitment was strengthened through the adoption, in two stages between 1998 and 2000, of an inflation-targeting regime, with the CPIX inflation target being set at 3–6 percent per year.[1] The preliminary presentations of the ASGISA program confirm continued support for a 3–6 percent inflation target.

Table S.1 Total Employment and Unemployment Rate in 2014 under Alternative Scenarios for Economic Growth and Labor Intensity

	(1) Labor force	(2) Formal employ- ment	(3) Informal employ- ment	(4) Total employ- ment	(5) Total unemploy- ment	(6) Unemploy- ment rate (= columns 5/1)
Scenario 1: Steady state from current economic trends *1) 3% annual growth rate* *2) 1% annual decline in* *employment/output*	19.5 million	9.8 million	3.2 million	13.0 million	6.5 million	33.3%
Scenario 3: Accelerated growth; credit subsidies to promote labor intensity *1) 4.5% growth for* *non-subsidized activities* *2) 8% growth for* *subsidized activities* *3) 5.3% combined average* *growth for subsidized and* *non-subsidized activities* *4) Employment/* *output constant*	19.5 million	12.4 million	4.1 million	16.5 million	3.0 million	15.4%

Additional assumptions:
1. Labor force growth is 1.9 percent per year.
2. Informal employment/total employment = 27 percent.

Source: Calculations based on data in Table 4.5.

The primary policy instrument that the government utilizes to control inflation is adjusting interest rates and, more precisely, raising interest rates to dampen the inflationary pressures that might result from more rapid economic growth. However, the South African economy has been paying a significant price in terms of slower growth of output and employment through its commitment to high interest rates. Both business investment and household consumption could increase if interest rates were allowed to fall.

Considering these and other channels of influence in a vector autoregression econometric model, the report finds, overall, that lowering the nominal prime lending rate by one percentage point and holding it at that lower level for five years would increase GDP growth by about 0.15 percentage points per year. For example, starting from a GDP growth rate of 3 percent and a nominal prime rate of 11 percent, if the prime rate fell to 10 percent and were held at that level for five years, the average rate of GDP growth over the five-year period would rise to 3.15 percent. At the same time, the corresponding rise in inflation would be relatively modest, increasing inflation from, say, a base rate of 5 percent to 5.2 percent. The rand would also depreciate over this five-year period but, again, only by a modest amount, namely, falling on average by about 0.6 percent per year relative to the dollar.

Based on these rough estimates, the report proposes that the Reserve Bank maintain lending rates at four percentage points below their current levels, which would then raise the average GDP growth rate from the base of three percent to somewhere around 3.6 percent over a five-year policy timeframe. The resulting effects on inflation and the exchange rate would remain relatively modest.

However, the four percentage point decline in lending rates would not, by itself, induce an adequate increase in economic growth for the 75–80 percent of the economy that is not receiving credit subsidies. But in our judgment, allowing the fiscal deficit to rise to roughly 3 percent of GDP should provide the remaining stimulus to move the unsubsidized segments of the South African economy to the target 4.5 percent growth path.

Public Credit Allocation and Development Banking

The key mechanism through which the report proposes to generate an 8 percent growth stimulus for 20–25 percent of the economy is to provide credit on a subsidized basis. We develop a formula for establishing an appropriate subsidized interest rate, based on 1) the proportion of a loan that the government is guaranteeing; and 2) the difference between market interest rates and government bond rates that have no default risk.

The report proposes three main policy tools to channel credit to the targeted industries at concessionary rates.

1. *A major expansion in the lending activity and developmental focus of the country's currently operating development banks.* The Industrial Development Corporation is South Africa's largest development bank. Its 2005 Annual Report reported that through its lending activity over 2004–05, it anticipated creating 16,700 jobs. This is far too modest a contribution for such an important institution, given that the official statistic of 4.3 million unemployed people in 2005 is 257 times larger than this 16,700 figure. The capitalization of these banks therefore needs to increase and they should be allowed to assume a higher level of risk on behalf of an employment-targeted growth agenda.

2. *The establishment of so-called "asset reserve requirements" for private banks and other financial institutions.* Asset reserve requirements require that financial institutions hold a designated proportion of their assets in loans to priority areas or else hold the same proportion of their total assets in a

sterile cash reserve account. For example, applying our subsidy policy would stipulate that banks should hold 25 percent of their loan portfolio in designated subsidized activities. If the subsidized activities did not account for at least 25 percent of the banks' total loan portfolio, the banks would then need to cover this gap by holding cash. Features of this proposal are comparable to the system of "prescribed assets" that operated in South Africa from 1956 to 1989. However, this report proposes measures to operate this system more flexibly—for example, through allowing banks that hold more than 25 percent of their loans in subsidized activities to sell permits to institutions whose targeted industries account for below the 25 percent minimum of subsidized loans.

3.   *A major expansion of the government's system of loan guarantees.* For the government's current loan guarantee program, the accruals on its contingent liabilities—i.e., the amounts that the government actually pays when loans default—has been a trivial cost, amounting, on average, to 1/100 of 1 percent or less over the recent past. We examine a program of the following magnitude: the government underwrites about R40 billion per year in loans, i.e., a figure approximately equal to 25 percent of fixed capital formation as of 2004. We then assume a default rate on these loans of 15 percent and loan guarantees that cover 75 percent of the principal on defaulted debts. Under this scenario, it follows that the accruals to the government would amount to R4.5 billion/year (i.e., R40 billion x .15 x .75). This is a crucial result. It shows that the government has the capacity to underwrite a major loan guarantee program, equivalent to roughly 25 percent of productive investment in the economy, with a financial commitment of no more than 1-2 percent of its fiscal budget.

Controls on Exchange Rates and Capital Flows
Exchange rate variability can create significant problems for monetary policy. Excessive depreciations could raise inflation rates, while excessive appreciations could generate lost output, profits and employment in some industries. Variability itself can also be harmful by generating more uncertainty and thereby possibly discouraging private investors.

All of these issues will become central if South Africa commits itself to a more expansionary set of fiscal, monetary and credit allocation policies—i.e., a set of measures that could effectively support an employment-targeted program. Policymakers will of course have to take seriously the possibility that financial market investors might react negatively to such a program, and might sell off their holdings of rand. Such a reaction could occur entirely as a result of a shift in investors' perceptions, regardless of whether the fundamental indicators of economic stability—such as fiscal deficits and the inflation rate—may change by only the relatively modest amounts this report is projecting.

Capital controls, exchange controls and other capital management techniques have been utilized as mechanisms for reducing the sensitivity of domestic financial markets, including sensitivity of exchange rates, to macroeconomic policy. For South Africa, such measures could potentially serve, at least, to partially insulate the economy against any negative reactions by financial markets to an employment-targeted economic program. The key question for South Africa then is: to what extent and under what conditions can capital management interventions enhance the autonomy of macroeconomic policy, including by helping to manage exchange rates?

In our view, such measures are capable, at least, of supporting efforts by the Reserve Bank to lower nominal interest rates within the range of about four percentage points that we are proposing. In addition, severe bouts of exchange rate volatility will be less likely when capital management policies are deployed to prevent such episodes. The fact that South Africa has a long history of operating exchange and capital controls enhances the prospect that such measures could be used effectively to support a more expansionary set of fiscal, monetary, and credit allocation policies. At the same time, in part because such measures are again becoming increasingly common as a form of macroeconomic management, they would not suggest that South Africa is moving away from its generally open interactions with global markets.

Inflation Control and Economic Growth

The government clearly appears committed to the idea that maintaining a low inflation environment is a necessary foundation for attacking poverty and unemployment in a sustainable way. We certainly do not advocate a high inflation rate or a relaxation of the inflation-targeting regime as ends in themselves. However, the primary tool that the government utilizes to control inflation is to maintain high interest rates. By contrast, we have advanced measures to lower interest rates—both across the board, and also through providing concessionary borrowing rates for industries with high employment multipliers. This report anticipates that a likely effect of such measures will be for inflationary pressures to develop beyond the recent levels common under the inflation-targeting regime.

The question that the report therefore examines is: how severe would be the costs to the South African economy of allowing the inflation rate to rise above its current target range of 3–6 percent? Recent research on this general issue had been pioneered by the late Michael Bruno, who had served both as Governor of the Bank of Israel and Chief Economist of the World Bank. In his 1995 World Bank study, Bruno analyzed the relationship between inflation and economic growth for 127 countries between 1960 and 1992. He found that average growth rates fell only slightly as inflation rates moved up to 20–25 percent. Of particular importance for policymaking in South Africa, Bruno found that during 1960–72, economic growth on average increased as inflation rose from negative or low rates to the 15–20 percent range. This is because, as Bruno explained, "in the 1950s and 1960s, low-to-moderate inflation went hand in hand with very rapid growth because of investment demand pressures in an expanding economy," (1995, p. 35). That is, demand-pull inflation, resulting from a process of economic expansion, was positively associated with growth as long as the inflation rate remained moderate.

Many researchers have subsequently examined the issue, a minority challenging Bruno's findings. This study developed its own model of the growth-inflation relationship, whose results broadly affirm Bruno. And while a consensus has not been established on the issue, a few basic conclusions from the range of studies, including the one for this report, do seem warranted. One is that, regardless of whether researchers observe a negative growth-inflation relationship emerging in the *double-digit* range for developing countries, there is only negligible evidence showing a negative relationship between growth and *single-digit* inflation. In addition, no researcher has challenged Bruno's point that the relationship between inflation and growth will be different depending on *what is causing* the economy's inflationary pressures. Thus, if South Africa pursues an aggressive employment-targeted program, one would expect that the inflationary pressures that might then emerge would not be harmful to growth, as long as policies maintain inflation at a moderate level.

But what happens if inflation accumulates momentum, such that a rise to, say, a 10 percent inflation rate leads to still greater inflationary pressures? Should South Africa then revert to raising interest rates, i.e., its standard policy tool at present for controlling inflation? In fact, two other policy tools are available for use. The first tool would be to pursue measures that weaken the monopolistic pricing power that now characterize some sectors of the economy. The second tool would be to pursue so-called "incomes policies." Incomes policies have been developed in various ways across countries, but the basic idea is straightforward: wage and price increases are negotiated over an economy-wide basis between the organized sectors of labor and business. Incomes policies can also be beneficial more generally in improving the efficiency of the country's industrial relations system and the implementation of its labor-law regulations.

The most basic critique of incomes policies is that in order for the approach to have any chance of success, it is necessary that workers achieve a high level of organization and that there be some reasonable degree of common ground for negotiations between workers and business. Otherwise, there would be no realistic prospect for economy-wide bargaining that could yield results that would be honored widely. In the case of South Africa, a high degree of organization does exist both among sectors of the working class and among business. However, the relationship between unions and business is highly contentious. This could possibly diminish to the extent that both sides recognize the obvious benefits of a program of accelerated economic growth and employment expansion.

Government Spending Programs and Tax Policy

Beyond providing a fiscal stimulus, the government obviously would play a crucial role in an employment-targeted program through its spending priorities and tax programs. The programs that this report is advocating would entail annual expenditures of R20-30 billion (in 2004 prices), broken down as follows:

1. Public investment in infrastructure: R5–7.5 billion
2. Income transfers and social support: R10–20 billion
3. Credit subsidies to businesses to promote accelerated employment growth: R5–7.5 billion

This report supports the idea of raising the structural fiscal deficit from 2 percent to 3 percent of GDP. If the Treasury did operate with this higher deficit, that alone would cover about R14 billion/year, i.e., roughly half of the total spending increase implied by our high end figure of R30 billion. Raising the additional R16 billion would have to come primarily from more revenue. This would raise South Africa's tax revenue/GDP ratio from the 2004 rate of 24.7 percent to roughly 25.8 of GDP.

An increase to a roughly 26 percent ratio would still place South Africa well below the ratios for lower-income OECD countries, such as Greece (45.1 percent) and Poland (41.8). It would also put South Africa roughly in line with a group of rapidly growing Asian economies, including Singapore (29.0 percent), Republic of Korea (28.4 percent) and Malaysia (22.2 percent). None of these other countries necessarily provides a particularly appropriate comparison to South Africa. But the key point is that neither the nearly 25 percent ratio at which South Africa currently operates nor an increase to 26 percent would establish South Africa as a significant outlier either among the OECD or Asian comparison groups.

Of the R16 billion/year that would need to be raised through additional revenue, the report argues that about R6 billion could be raised through increasing rates modestly on the government's three major revenue sources, the personal income tax, the corporate profit tax and the VAT. However, the other R10 billion could be raised through three other sources. The first would be to extend the current Uncertified Securities Tax, which now applies only to stock trading, to the bond market as well. This is done in several comparison countries such as Brazil, Chile, Malaysia, and Morocco. We conservatively estimate that such a tax could raise roughly R6 billion per year. A second source would be enacting the Mineral and Petroleum Royalty bill that was drafted by the Treasury in 2003. We estimate that this royalty would generate another R2.5 billion.

Finally, assuming that the economy's growth would rise from a 3 percent trend to a 5.3 percent trend through an employment-targeted program, we conclude that tax revenues of about R6.5 billion would result because of higher incomes. Such a rise in incomes will also bring reductions in the government's expenditures on income support payments, given that employment will increase and poverty will decline. But in our calculations we allow for only a modest net fiscal contribution since the Treasury has already factored in a significant growth dividend in its fiscal projections through 2008–09.

Policies for Productive Sectors

In addition to subsidizing activities for the expressed purpose of accelerating employment growth, this report considers two other concerns within the realm of sectoral policy. The first deals with the costs incurred through monopolistic pricing power and the administrative determination of prices. The administrated prices of the parastatals—the publicly-owned utilities and economic services industries—are a case in point. Enterprises such as Eskom (electricity), Transnet (transportation), and Telkom (telecommunications) provide essential inputs and services to sectors throughout the South African economy. However, prices are poorly regulated and are not effectively coordinated with national policy objectives. Prices are often the outcome of a process of negotiation rather than an integrated regulatory framework. For example, large industrial users of electricity are able to negotiate more favorable rates than smaller commercial enterprises. This effectively subsidizes the costs of production for larger firms, at the expense of smaller-scale users.

Such pricing practices therefore act to counter efforts to promote small enterprises and cooperatives. Similar problems with administered prices exist for other critical segments of the economy. For example, the practice of "import parity pricing" enables steel producers to set prices at the international price plus tariff and transportation costs rather than at the price that would reflect domestic production conditions. Such practices raise barriers to the success of an employment-targeted program. At the same time, common blanket solutions, such as privatization, are not likely to resolve these problems. Many of these industries are "natural monopolies" that require regulation regardless of who owns the assets. Thus, establishing a coherent set of such regulations will be critical to the long-term viability of an employment-targeted program.

The second concern that the report addresses is that of promoting some industries even when their employment multipliers are weak. Such measures relate to both the motor vehicles industry and the capital goods industry. While neither industry should be targeted for accelerated expansion on the basis of its employment multipliers, there are other grounds on which they should be promoted. In particular, it would clearly be crucial over the next decade for the South African economy to continue enhancing productivity and the capacity to produce import-competing capital goods. This is so even if policymakers remain focused on employment creation as their primary objective. Indeed, implementing an effective employment-targeted program should indeed enhance the capacity of policymakers to advance a broader economic policy agenda, since they can pursue other objectives—such as building a competitive capital goods industry—without neglecting the imperatives of job creation and poverty reduction.

NOTE

1. The CPIX consumer price index excludes interest rates on mortgage bonds, which are included in the CPI measure. The CPI measure is the so-called "headline" inflation rate.

1. Introduction

Following the overarching programmatic commitments of the United Nations Development Program in the field of economic policy, our project is an effort to outline a pro-poor economic policy framework for South Africa today.[1] We aim to develop a program that will be coherent and workable within the current political and economic framework, while also being effective as a tool for expanding job opportunities, reducing poverty, and spreading well-being as broadly as possible.

The specific focus of our study is the severe problem of mass unemployment in South Africa today. Depending on whether one considers the government's "official" or the "expanded" definition of unemployment, the unemployment rate stood between 26.5 and 40.5 percent as of March 2005. The difference between the official and expanded definitions of unemployment is that the expanded definition includes "discouraged" workers—i.e. people who self-identify as wanting work and are available for work but who had not taken active steps to find work in the four weeks prior to having been surveyed by the government. From March 2004 to March 2005, the official unemployment rate did fall, from 27.9 to 26.5 percent. This decline in official unemployment is certainly a meaningful development. But these gains are, of course, modest, and the problem of mass unemployment remains.

Our concentration on the problem of mass unemployment is fully consistent with the stated goals of the current African National Congress (ANC)-led government. Thus, at the Growth and Development Summit in 2003, President Thabo Mbeki singled out "more jobs, better jobs, and decent work for all," as one of the country's four key economic challenges (the other three being expanding investment, advancing equity, and building local-level capacity; *Growth and Development Summit* summary pamphlet, Department of Labor, p. 3). More specifically, according to presidential economic advisor Alan Hirsch, the government has committed itself, as its first economic priority, to reducing unemployment by half as of 2014 (Hirsch 2004).

Employment is the most important source of potential income for the majority of South Africans. This fact establishes a fundamental link between unemployment and poverty: that joblessness is the single greatest cause of mass poverty and, correspondingly, reducing unemployment would be the single most effective means of reducing poverty. This does not mean that a program of job creation alone will be sufficient as a tool for fighting poverty in South Africa. As we will discuss below, substantial increases in social welfare spending are also needed at present to eliminate the most extreme forms of destitution, and to provide the impoverished with the minimum means—in terms of nutrition levels, among other things—to effectively participate in the labor force. However, increased social welfare spending, on its own, is also not capable of carrying the burden of effectively fighting poverty. Indeed, social welfare spending becomes increasingly effective when employment opportunities expand for the poor, since, with expanding employment opportunities, the burden of fighting poverty will lighten for any kind of cash transfer program.

And thus, toward the aim of advancing a "pro-poor" economic policy approach in South Africa, we return to the imperative of developing an effective program of employment creation as one of the two most important policy interventions that the government should pursue. The other fundamental policy concern is to attack the country's HIV/AIDS pandemic. But our study does not focus on the many pressing issues related to HIV/AIDS.

The program we advance can be termed "employment targeted." Our notion of an "employment targeted" economic program stands in clear contrast with the ascendant approach, in South Africa and elsewhere, of formulating economic policy, macroeconomic policy in particular, within a framework of "inflation targeting." We fully recognize the need to prevent excessive inflationary pressures from gaining momentum in South Africa and elsewhere. At the same time, we observe that establishing the primacy of inflation control as a policy goal is inhibiting the growth of decent job opportunities and the possibility of seriously reducing poverty. Thus, our "employment targeted" approach seeks to strike a workable balance between inflation control and the imperative of creating more jobs and reducing poverty. As we try to show, major gains in employment opportunities and poverty reduction are attainable in South Africa without threatening the onset of a destructive inflationary spiral. And as we also show, if the South African economy continues to operate with its existing policy package along its current trajectory, the likelihood is high that the official unemployment rate will be substantially above 30 percent by 2014.

As we write, the government of South Africa is developing its own plan for an ambitious new economic program, the "Accelerated and Shared Growth Initiative for South Africa," (ASGISA). We are familiar with the still preliminary plans for this program through early public presentations and discussions with officials at the National Treasury.[2] To our knowledge, the ASGISA, at least in its preliminary form, remains committed to halving the unemployment rate as of 2014. It also projects a sustained increase in South Africa's average GDP growth rate, to 4.5 percent between 2005–2009 and to 6.0 percent between 2010–2014. These overall goals are certainly consistent with the program we develop here. Moreover, as we will discuss, there are major common elements between our program and specific features of the ASGISA, in its preliminary form.

Following this introductory Chapter 1, the study consists of two short chapters that lay out basic concerns, then two substantially longer chapters presenting our framework for policy analysis and our specific policy proposals. In Chapter 2, we present evidence on the scope of the unemployment problem in South Africa today, considering the unemployed by gender, race, region, length of joblessness and age. We also examine how the country's problem of mass unemployment can be usefully conceptualized in simple accounting terms—as the result of 1) insufficiency in the rate of output growth—i.e. the economy's production of goods and services; and 2) a declining number of jobs being created per unit of output. We show the importance of both increasing the rate of output growth and raising the ratio of jobs created per unit of output—what is termed the labor intensity ratio—as the basis for any significant reduction in South Africa's unemployment rate. We finally also present evidence showing that the South African economy's growth path—at least between the years 1995–2000 for which we have adequate data—has been associated with a broad decline in incomes, with the most severe income declines having been experienced by the less well-off.

In Chapter 3, we examine supply-side perspectives on employment expansion. The fact that the South African economy is experiencing both high unemployment and rising capital intensity of production suggests to some both an explanation for high unemployment and a solution to the problem. The explanation for the problem is straightforward: businesses won't hire more workers because they are convinced that the costs of doing so will exceed the benefits. Businesses therefore choose either to 1) maintain their operations at a lower level than they would if the benefits of hiring more workers exceeded the costs; or 2) increase the use of machines as a substitute for employing more workers as their preferred means of expanding their operations. Seen from this perspective, the solution to the problem of unemployment is also straightforward: to lower the costs businesses face in hiring more workers. However, we argue in this chapter that the evidence linking mass unemployment to high labor costs is not convincing. We also argue that wage cutting as a policy approach is certain to elicit strong resistance, which in turn will worsen the country's investment climate. At the same time, we do support measures to maintain wage increases in line with productivity growth and to improve the efficiency of the industrial relations system. We also introduce here our proposal for a hybrid program of credit and employment subsidies as a means through which the government will effectively absorb a share of businesses' labor costs.

In Chapter 4, we consider the forces in South Africa's economy that will need to be mobilized to achieve three ends: 1) faster economic growth; 2) greater labor intensity of growth; and 3) poverty reduction. In examining the factors that could contribute to faster economic growth, we discuss all four components of the conventional national income identity which, taken together, define economic growth—i.e. private investment, private consumption, net exports, and government spending. In considering ways to increase the labor intensity of growth, we examine two basic approaches: the Expanded Public Works Program (EPWP) now being implemented by the national government; and promoting accelerated growth for those sectors of the South African economy that would generate relatively large numbers of new jobs, both within their own sectors and throughout the country more broadly. In terms of poverty reduction, we briefly consider measures to expand social expenditures and income transfers. The importance of such direct poverty-reduction measures is underscored by the fact that, even under a highly favorable employment growth scenario over the next decade, such as that projected by the ASGISA, there would still be somewhere between 13–20 percent of the workforce who are unemployed as of 2014.

In the concluding Chapter 5, we then consider specific policy tools that can be deployed to promote faster growth, rising labor intensity and poverty reduction. We consider policy interventions in six areas: 1) fiscal policy; 2) monetary policy; 3) credit allocation and development banking; 4) capital market and exchange rate controls; 5) inflation control; and 6) interventions tied to specific sectors of the economy.

NOTES

1. For an outstanding survey of recent research sponsored by the UNDP on pro-poor economic policies around the world, see Khan (2004).
2. The preliminary documents which we have examined are the November 2005 Power Point presentation by Joel Netshitenzhe, "A Growing Economy that Benefits All" and an undated paper titled "Accelerated and Shared Growth Initiative for South Africa (ASGISA)." Beyond these two documents, our project consultants Anna McCord and Stephen Gelb have held several discussions on the program with various officials of the National Treasury. This study has also benefited from the April 2006 TIPS Working Paper by Davies and van Seventer, "An Economy-Wide Impact Assessment of the Economic Infrastructure Investment Component of the Accelerated & Shared Growth Initiative (ASGISA)." We will refer to these documents further below.

2. The Nature of Mass Unemployment in South Africa Today

WHO ARE THE UNEMPLOYED?

As noted at the outset, there are two basic ways in which unemployment is defined in South Africa today, through which we derive the divergent figures of 26.5 percent versus 40.5 percent for the March 2005 unemployment rate. The official definition of unemployment, which is based on the international standard developed by the International Labour Organization ((ILO), refers to people within the economically active population who 1) did not work during the prior seven days; 2) want to work and are available to start work within a week; and 3) have actively looked for work during the past four weeks. The expanded definition includes those people who have not searched for work during the past four weeks. Focusing for the moment on the more narrow official definition, what is behind the 26.5 percent unemployment rate are these underlying facts: among the country's 46.8 million people, 16.2 million, or 34.6 percent, are counted as "economically active." Of these, 11.9 million have jobs and 4.3 million are unemployed.[1]

As we see in Table 2.1, the severity of unemployment differs by gender and population group.[2] Women consistently experience substantially higher rates of joblessness than do men. Among different population groups, Whites have the lowest unemployment rates (an average of 5.1 percent) and Africans have the highest unemployment rates (an average of 31.6 percent). The unemployment rates for the Coloured and Indian/Asian populations are significantly higher than those of Whites (averaging 19.8 and 19.0 percent respectively).

The burden of unemployment also differs geographically, with the highest concentration of unemployed workers being in rural areas. Table 2.2 presents unemployment as of March 2005 by province using the official definition. It also includes figures on discouraged workers as a percentage of the working-age population as of March 2005. It finally also shows the percentage of the population in each province that is rural. As we see in the table, the official unemployment rate for the provinces ranged from 17.6 in the Western Cape to 32.4 percent in Limpopo, a difference of 14.8 percentage points. Western Cape is the second most heavily urbanized province in the country while Limpopo is the

Table 2.1 Official Unemployment by Gender and Population Group, March 2005

	Male	Female	TOTAL
African	26.7%	37.6%	31.6%
Coloured	18.6%	21.2%	19.8%
Indian/Asian	15.4%	22.6%	19.0%
White	4.4%	5.9%	5.1%
TOTAL	22.4%	31.4%	26.5%

Source: Statistics South Africa, 2005 Labour Force Survey.

Table 2.2 Unemployment, Discouraged Workers, and Rural Population by Province

	LFS, March 2005		2001 Census
	Official unemployment	Discouraged workers	Percent rural population
Limpopo	32.4%	21.9%	86.7%
KwaZulu-Natal	31.7%	13.1%	54.0%
North West	28.8%	15.6%	58.2%
Free State	30.6%	8.3%	24.2%
Gauteng	22.7%	11.4%	2.8%
Mpumalanga	27.4%	13.8%	58.7%
Eastern Cape	27.1%	13.9%	61.2%
Northern Cape	29.4%	11.5%	17.3%
Western Cape	17.6%	6.3%	9.6%
TOTAL	26.5%	13.0%	42.5%

Note: Discouraged workers are presented as a working-age population.
Sources: Labour Force Survey March 2005 (Pretoria: Statistics South Africa, July 2005) and *Investigation into Appropriate Definitions of Urban and Rural Areas in South Africa*, Statistics South Africa, Report 03-02-20, 2003, Table 3.1-1, p. 8.

most rural. The differences between the regions are still sharper in considering discouraged workers. Thus, in the Western Cape, only 6.3 percent of the working-age population are discouraged, whereas in Limpopo, discouraged workers account for 21.9 percent of the working-age population. Overall, the figures in Table 2.2 suggest that discouraged workers are even more heavily concentrated in rural areas than are the official unemployed.

The long-term unemployed constitute a sizeable share of the jobless population in South Africa, as we see in Table 2.3. Of all the officially unemployed individuals who have worked in the past, nearly 60 percent have been seeking

Table 2.3 The Officially Unemployed by Duration of Job Seeking, March 2005

	Worked before (41% of the unemployed)	Never worked* (59% of the unemployed)
Less than a month	9.2%	6.0%
1 month to 3 months	12.2%	9.3%
3 months to 6 months	9.7%	7.5%
6 months to 1 year	10.4%	8.9%
1 year to 3 years	22.9%	26.2%
More than 3 years	35.7%	42.1%

Note: * Of all unemployed persons who have never worked before, 76% of them are aged 15 to 30 years.
Source: Labour Force Survey March 2005 (Pretoria: Statistics South Africa, July 2005).

work for more than one year. Of those who have never worked before, approximately 68 percent have been looking for work for more than one year. Past employment experience greatly increases the probability of being employed. Only 41 percent of the unemployed have worked before, compared to 59 percent who have never worked. Of all the unemployed who have never worked in the past, 76 percent are aged 15 to 30 years old.

The fact that many of the unemployed who have never worked are young and that many of these young people remain unemployed for long periods of time is representative of South Africa's serious problem of youth unemployment. Many young South Africans are caught in an unemployment trap. They need labor market experience to get a job, but they need a job to gain labor market experience. According to the March 2005 Labour Force Survey, individuals aged 15 to 34 years account for 74.9 percent of all unemployed people in South Africa (official definition), but only 59.6 percent of the working age population 15 to 65 years old.

Differences exist among data series as to whether there has been an increasing or decreasing trend in unemployment over the past decade, and it is therefore difficult to determine whether the employment problem is getting worse or better. Either way, what is clear from these figures is that the problem of mass unemployment is a structural one, not simply a cyclical phenomenon. Moreover, the employment figures alone do not adequately capture conditions for people in the labor market. For example, all workers engaged in so-called "informal" activities are counted as among the employed. Informal employment is generally defined as the set of remunerative activities that exist outside of the formal system of state regulation. This group includes street traders, domestic laborers, industrial outworkers, small-scale manufacturers, and people self-employed in agriculture. As of March 2005, those in informal, non-agricultural employment accounted for a full 24.5 percent of all employment.[3] As another indicator of quality of employment opportunities, one study which finds employment levels to have risen 1995–2003 still also concludes that average real monthly earnings fell by more than 20 percent over this period (Casale, Muller and Posel 2004).

By definition, the problem of mass unemployment has both supply- and demand-side causes. But in terms of effectively addressing the problem in the short-term as well as the long-term, the focus of our study will be on the demand side of the labor market, i.e. on measures that will substantially increase the demand for the South African workers who are in the labor pool today.

This is not to neglect the crucial issues on the supply-side of the market. Two supply-side issues are central. The first is the low level of formal education, vocational training and job experience among the workforce. The second is the contention that labor costs in South Africa are too high, especially relative to countries that are its trade competitors.

In terms of the issue of education and training, we support the government's initiatives aimed at aggressively expanding and improving the country's educational opportunities and encourage more such measures (though we do not examine this issue in this study). At the same time, there is also a clear link through which expanding job opportunities—the demand for labor—will also enhance the benefits of an improved system of education and training. Thus, workers in South Africa were long deprived of opportunities to acquire a decent education, skills, or to gain entrepreneurial initiative. The most effective way of creating such opportunities now is in the context of an expanding economy, which offers opportunities for on-the-job training and other forms of learning-by-doing, including learning how to establish one's own small or medium-sized enterprise. Such efforts will clearly be enhanced over time to the extent that opportunities grow for a decent formal education.

The issue of labor costs in South Africa being too high has been widely debated. The two interrelated questions considered are the extent to which: 1) excessively high wages are themselves responsible for mass unemployment; and 2) the industrial relations system and labor market regulations are inefficient, discouraging business from expanding employment. We review the literature on these questions at some length in Chapter 3 of our study. As we show, the available evidence suggests that these factors are not likely to have been major causes of South Africa's current employment problems. Yet, there is a separate question as to whether reductions in labor costs for business and improvements in the industrial relations system might support an agenda for employment expansion and economic growth into the future. We do endorse measures both to reduce the costs of hiring workers and to improve the labor negotiating environment. Specifically, we describe a large-scale hybrid program of employment and credit subsidies to reduce the costs of hiring more workers. We also discuss the introduction of so-called "incomes policies" as a means of improving the environment for labor

Figure 2.1 Real Growth Rate of South Africa GDP, 1984–2004

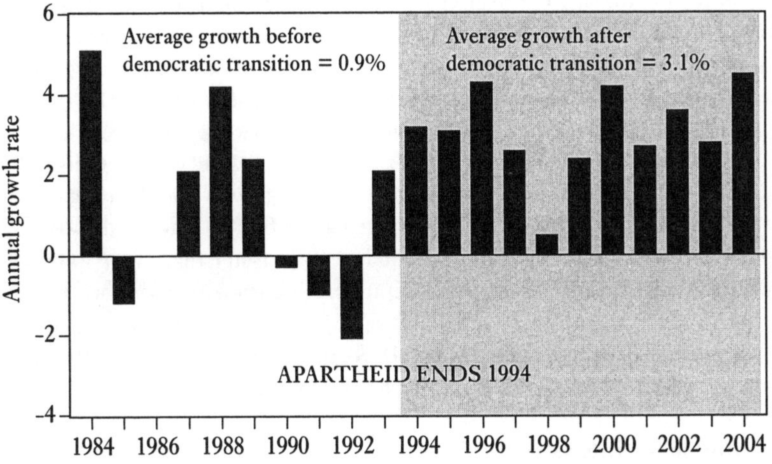

Sources: South Africa National Accounts; 12/05 South African Reserve Bank Quarterly Bulletin.

negotiations. We describe these measures both in Chapter 3, briefly, and then at greater length in Chapter 5. At the same time, we develop both of these proposals within the context of a broader program aimed at expanding the demand for labor and the rate of economic growth. Given the evidence we review in Chapter 3, we are persuaded that supply-side measures on their own are not likely to generate large employment growth and welfare gains.

THE LABOR DEMAND PERSPECTIVE

Thus, we now turn our attention to examining the issue of employment from the perspective of labor demand. Within this perspective, the problem of mass unemployment can be seen clearly in terms of a simple identity. That is, the insufficiency of demand for labor results from a combination of two factors: 1) insufficiency in the rate of output growth; and 2) a ratio of labor demand per unit of output—i.e. the degree of labor intensity under current production methods—that is too low. In fact, we can observe from the data both the problem of insufficient levels of output growth and a decreasing level of labor intensity.

Slow economic growth

In Figure 2.1, we see the pattern of GDP growth between 1984–2004, i.e. including both the decade prior to the 1994 end of apartheid and the subsequent

11 years of democratic transition. As we see, GDP growth has improved significantly in the democratic era relative to the last decade of apartheid. Thus, the average growth rate was 1.1 percent between 1983–93, and 3.1 percent between 1994–2004. The gains in growth since 1994 should of course be recognized, especially the strong economic performance in 2004 itself, when GDP grew at 4.5 percent. We do not yet have sufficient evidence that the 2004 growth experience represents a new, higher growth trend. The Treasury itself in its 2005 Medium Term Budget Policy Statement anticipates growth "moderating to just above 4 percent for 2006," (p. 2). Considering the full 11 years of democracy, output has been expanding at only about 1 percent faster than the population growth rate, and even this rate of per capita income growth is somewhat overstating the positive growth picture, because population growth has been slowed by a rising death rate, due to the HIV/AIDS crisis.[4] Output growth at this pace cannot be expected to be a major engine of employment growth.

Declining labor intensity

In Figure 2.2, we present figures on employment relative to GDP—specifically the number of jobs in the formal South African economy relative to R1 million in output from 1967–2001.[5] This is one broad indicator of the extent of the labor intensity of output in South African production. As we can see, this employment/output ratio has been trending downward steadily since the 1960s. However, the rate of decline has continued, and indeed accelerated sharply, after 1994. As the figure shows, as of 1967, an estimated 8.2 formal economy workers were employed in South Africa for every R1 million in output. By 2001, the figure had fallen to 4.9 workers/R1 million in output—that is, 40 percent more people were employed in the formal economy in 1967 than 2001 for a given level of output. Even since 1994, this employment/output measure has fallen by 28 percent. In just seven years, in other words, formal economy businesses in South Africa were hiring nearly 30 percent fewer people for a given amount of goods and services they produced.

All major sectors of the South African economy outside of agriculture—i.e. government, mining, manufacturing, construction, trade, and finance—have experienced declining labor intensity from the 1970s onward. But the sharpest declines have been in mining and manufacturing over the 1990s. For mining, declining labor intensity is a result of the diminishing ore grades available for extraction, and, thereby, the need to deploy increased mechanization to profitably reach these ores. In the case of manufacturing, the decline in labor intensity corresponds with a broader pattern throughout middle- and low-income countries, in which manufacturing production has become increasingly mechanized in the context of maintaining pace with global competition. Considering this broader global pattern, Ghosh (2003), for example, finds that while manufacturing output has risen in the

Figure 2.2 Ratio of Formal Employment to GDP in South Africa, 1967–2001 (number of formal jobs per R1 million in output)

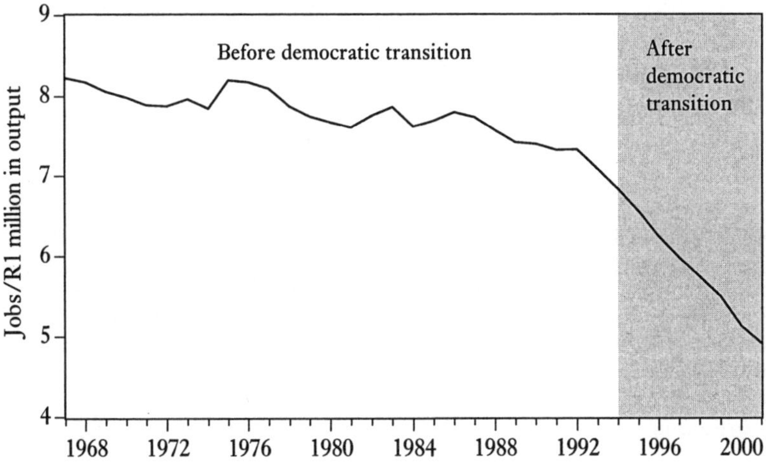

Source: Reserve Bank of South Africa.

south, employment growth has stagnated because of 1) a rise in import competition; and 2) low employment elasticities of new production.

Based on these trends, it is clear that, at its core, any successful employment program for South Africa will have to do two things: raise the average rate of output growth; and increase the labor/capital ratio of the overall level of output.

IMPACT OF SLOW GROWTH AND DECLINING LABOR INTENSITY

We can see how crucial this is through the simple hypothetical exercise presented in Table 2.4. In the table, we consider alternative assumptions as to the rate of economic growth and the change in labor intensity over the decade 2005–2014. The starting point for the exercise is the actual levels of economic growth, employment, and labor intensity in 2004, as presented in Panel A of Table 2.4.

We begin by making two assumptions about economic growth. The first is that the economy's growth rate over 2005–2014 is 3 percent, i.e. essentially equal to the growth rate that was achieved over 1994–2004. We then consider an acceleration in the average growth rate to 5 percent, somewhat less than the average rate the government has set for its goal under the ASGISA, which, as

Table 2.4 South Africa Employment Growth 2005–2014 under Alternative Economic Growth and Labor Intensity Assumptions

A) ACTUAL LEVELS OF ECONOMIC ACTIVITY IN 2004

Total output (GDP)	R1.4 trillion
Total employment	12 million
Employment/output ratio	8.6 jobs per R1 million in output

B) TOTAL EMPLOYMENT IN 2014 UNDER ALTERNATIVE ASSUMPTIONS

	3% Growth	5% Growth
Employment/output remains constant	16.2 million	19.6 million
Employment/output10% lower in 2014 (declining labor intensity)	14.6 million	17.6 million
Employment/output 10% higher in 2014 (rising labor intensity)	17.8 million	21.6 million

C) DIFFERENCES IN EMPLOYMENT GROWTH SCENARIOS

3% growth with constant output/employment vs. 5% growth with constant output/employment	3.4 million jobs
3% growth with 10% fall in employment/output vs. (declining labor intensity) 3% growth with 10% rise in employment/output (rising labor intensity)	3.2 million jobs
3% growth with 10% fall in employment/output vs. (slower growth and rising labor intensity) 5% growth with 10% rise in employment/output (faster growth with rising labor intensity)	7 million jobs

we have seen, averages to about 5.3 percent over 2005–2014 (i.e. 4.5 percent between 2005–2009 and 6 percent between 2010–2014). We then consider three alternatives for labor intensity: that the employment/output ratio—the measure of labor intensity that we are using here—remains the same; that the employment/output ratio is 10 percent lower as of 2014; and that the employment/output ratio is 10 percent higher in 2014.

The next two panels of the table show the results of these alternative scenarios in terms of employment in 2014. As we see in Panel B, under the assumption that growth remains at its current pace, and that labor intensity remains constant, there will be 16.2 million people employed, both formally and informally, in South Africa in 2014, 4.2 million more than the 12 million employed in 2004. However, if economic policies are successful in raising the average growth rate to 5 percent, a total of 19.6 million people will be employed in 2014, a gain of 7.6 million over the actual 2004 level, as well as an improvement of 3.4 million over what would result in 2014 from a 3 percent average growth rate.

The improvements in overall employment are lower, of course, if we assume that the employment/output is 10 percent lower in 2014. A fall in the employment/output ratio of at least this magnitude is consistent with the experience over the past decade, and will almost certainly occur unless policymakers actively intervene to promote labor intensive activities. The importance of pursuing such policies in addition to growth-promotion policies can be seen in the second row of Panel C. As we see there, if we assume a constant average growth rate of 3 percent over the decade, but allow labor intensity to be either 10 percent lower or higher as of 2014, the more labor intensive employment growth path will alone generate an additional 3.2 million jobs.

Finally, in the last row of Panel C, we observe the effects of both accelerating growth from an average of 3 percent to 5 percent, *and* allowing labor intensity to be 10 percent higher rather than 10 percent lower as of 2014. In combining both the growth and labor intensity effects, the overall difference in job creation amounts to an increase in employment of *7 million jobs*—i.e. an amount that is more than half of the total number of employed people in South Africa as of 2004.

Based on this simple exercise, it is clear why the focus of an employment-targeted policy for South Africa needs to be on both raising the trend rate of economic growth and increasing the relative labor intensity of growth.[6]

It is also crucial to emphasize that the country's current economic path of relatively slow growth and declining labor intensity has increased inequality and, in particular, has been harmful to the well-being of the poor. It is not surprising that this is so, given that, as we have seen, the unemployed are concentrated most heavily among Africans, traditionally the most disadvantaged population group in South Africa; and among those living in relatively poor regions of the country.

In Figure 2.3, we present summary data from a 2005 study by Liebbrandt, Levinsohn and McCrary (2005), "Incomes in South Africa Since the Fall of Apartheid." The data are for changes in total individual income between 1995 and 2000 for different income percentiles within the South African population. The income figures include both labor and pension income. The authors also present data broken down by gender in their paper and emphasize the importance of the distinct patterns of income change for men and women. However, for our purposes here, the overall pattern, combining both men and women, is sufficient.

Figure 2.3 Total Real Income Changes for Different Income Groups in South Africa, 1995–2000

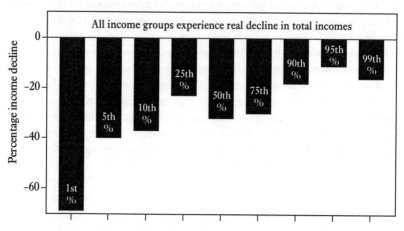

Source: Liebbrandt, Levinsohn and McCrary (2005).

The first thing that is striking about these results is that Liebbrandt et al. find that *all* income groups in South Africa, from lowest to highest, experienced a decline in total income between 1995–2000. This pattern of overall income decline is not consistent with the national income account figures, which show an overall modest increase in national income over this period. As the authors note, such discrepancies between household survey data and national income accounting figures are not unusual with data for other countries as well. But this discrepancy aside, what is also clear from the data is that the most severe declines in real income were experienced by those in the lower-income percentiles. For example, the poorest 1 percent experienced a 69 percent decline in income, those in the 5th income percentile experienced a 40 percent real income decline, and those in the 10th percentile experienced a 37 percent decline. Meanwhile, for the 90th percentile, the decline was a much lower 18 percent, and those in the 95th percentile saw their incomes decline by a still lower 11 percent.

These results from Liebbrandt et al. are consistent with the results obtained by Hoogeveen and Ozler of the World Bank in their 2004 study, "Not Separate, Not Equal: Poverty and Inequality in Post-Apartheid South Africa." Hoogeveen and Ozler examine the same data sets and time period—i.e. a comparison of 1995 and 2000—as Liebbrandt et al., but consider the data in terms of household expenditures rather than individual incomes. They find that annual per capita growth of household expenditures between 1995 and 2000 was

0.5 percent, as they put it, "very much in line with the GDP growth and the growth of final consumption expenditure by households," (p. 6). In other words, their calculations on changes in household expenditures between 1995 and 2000, unlike the Liebbrandt et al. results, are not inconsistent with the national income data.

Hoogoveen and Ozler examine the poverty and inequality trends through a number of measures. Among these, they develop a new poverty line based on what they term the "cost of basic needs." They offer a range of values for this of between 322 and 593 Rands per month in 2000 prices (this is equal to a range of about R400–734 in 2004 prices, a set of figures to which we return later in the study). They report poverty using their own lower-bound figure as well as the more standard $1 and $2 per day poverty lines. Their lower-bound figure is close to the $2 per day poverty threshold.

Weighing evidence from these various measures, they find that growth was not pro-poor, but rather that poverty and inequality increased sharply between 1995 and 2000. As they conclude:

> The depth and severity of poverty increased as a result of declining expenditures for those at the bottom of the expenditure distribution, and inequality among Africans rose sharply. By 2000, there were approximately 1.8 million more South Africans living with less than $1/day and 2.3 million more with less than $2/day (p. 28).

In a recent paper, van der Berg, Burger, Burger, Louw and Yu (2006) have challenged the evidence showing that poverty increased substantially in the initial post-Apartheid period up to 2000. According to their own estimates, poverty did still worsen between 1993–2000 according to all the various measures they report. But the severity of the decline was more mild than suggested either by Liebbrandt et al. or Hoogoveen and Ozler.

Van der Berg et al.'s study is notable especially in terms of what it finds for the years since 2000—that poverty in South Africa actually declined significantly over these more recent years. For example, using a poverty line of R3000 in annual per capita income, they find that the poverty headcount ratio fell from 41.3 percent in 2000 to 33.2 percent in 2004. They similarly found that the number of people living in poverty fell from 18.5 to 15.4 million.

If these results are accurate, they clearly suggest that the problems that produced rising poverty in South Africa from the end of apartheid through 2000 had been successfully addressed from 2001–2004. Van der Berg and his co-authors argue that the primary source of declining poverty was the increase of more than 70 percent in real terms in social grants to the poor, most notably the child support grant for impoverished households containing children less than 15 years of age, and the deracialization of the means-tested social old age pension. But the authors also conclude by emphasizing that, for the future, additional reductions in poverty will have to come primarily through improving job opportunities rather than continuing to rely so heavily on social grants. They write, "More rapid job creation is required to make further progress in combating poverty, since the social grant system—while having made a large contribution to the recently observed decline in poverty—is currently nearing the limits of its poverty alleviation capacity," (p. 29).

However, their more optimistic assessment of the conditions of the poor in South Africa does itself raise significant questions. The first, and most basic, is with the accuracy of their methodology and findings. Meth (2006) has advanced a substantial critique of both their methodology and findings. Applying an alternative estimation technique, Meth finds that headcount poverty at a R3000 annual per capita poverty line was rather at least 18 million and possibly as high as 19 million in 2004—i.e. roughly 3 million more people than estimated by van der Berg and colleagues. Meth's findings for 2004 are clearly more in line with the estimates for 1995–2000 of Liebbrandt et al. and Hoogoveen and Ozler.

This is not the place to attempt to adjudicate a methodological debate between competing experts in this area.[7] Suffice it to say that, even if we allow that van der Berg and colleague are right, it is still clear, as they themselves emphasize, that any further substantial reduction in poverty will have to come primarily through economic growth and job creation rather than expanding social grants alone. In other words, even if one takes the van der Berg findings as the baseline for considering a forward-looking policy agenda, we are still faced with the imperative of advancing a program that can dramatically increase employment opportunities for South Africans over the next decade.

Overall, one must of course honor the enormous gains that the government of South Africa has made since 1994 in terms of health care, access for the poor to public services and infrastructure, and most especially in dismantling apartheid. But one also cannot escape the conclusion that over the first decade of non-racial democracy, the South African economy has followed a path that has led to slow economic growth and a sharp decline in the labor intensity of output even while unemployment hovers around 30 percent.

WHY IS THERE EMPLOYMENT STAGNATION IN THE FORMAL ECONOMY?

Apartheid was a system that, among other things, systematically excluded the African majority from opportunities for a decent working life. Just on the issue of employment creation alone, the problems inherited by the ANC-led government on taking office in 1994 were therefore immense.

With this fundamental reality as background, it is also the case that the ANC-led government had moved toward embracing tight fiscal and monetary policies since first taking office in the historic transition of 1994. This approach was formalized with the introduction of the GEAR (Growth, Equity, and Redistribution) program in 1996, which outlined an explicit program of macro stringency as the foundation for a stable long-term growth path. In his recent book *Season of Hope: Economic Reform Under Mandela and Mbeki* (2005), Presidential economic policy advisor Alan Hirsch offered some candid views as to how the GEAR program was developed in response to pressures from the International Monetary Fund (IMF) and international financial investors. Hirsch writes:

> Another motivation for fiscal and monetary conservatism was the ANC's fear of giving up South Africa's limited economic sovereignty to the International Monetary Fund and/or the World Bank as the result of a financial crisis ... The irony was that in order to stave off the power of international finance, the ANC committed itself to policies approved by these same financiers. In order not to get too indebted to those who could turn their debt against them, they had to be conservative and pander to some of their prejudices (2005, p. 69).

The ANC also faced additional pressures at the time it implemented the GEAR. As Professor Stephen Gelb (2004) discusses, the government inherited an extremely difficult fiscal position on taking office. Due to politically-related spending commitments of the outgoing apartheid government, the fiscal deficit rose from an average of 4.2 percent of GDP between 1988–91 to 9.3 percent in 1992 and 10.1 percent in 1993. Government debt had risen from 29.0 percent of GDP in 1990/91 to 47.0 percent in 1994/95. This level of deficit spending was considered unsustainable given the high public debt servicing costs that threatened to crowd out social spending, and the government committed itself to a policy of fiscal tightness.

It was equally committed to a program of monetary tightness to maintain a low-inflation environment and to protect the value of the rand. The new government did inherit relative price stability following the severe recession of 1989–93. It wanted to maintain inflation at this low level, and formalized this commitment even beyond the GEAR program in mid-1998 by establishing "inflation-targeting" as the single aim of central bank policy. The first target, set in February 2000, was to bring inflation within a range of 3–6 percent by April 2002. Adjusting interest rates was established as the primary mechanism for controlling the inflation rate.

The commitment to macroeconomic stringency is also part of a broader package of measures consistent with aspects of the neoliberal policy approach advanced by the IMF, even while the ANC-led government itself has not professed a broad-based commitment to a neoliberal approach. These other measures include liberalizing trade and capital flows and minimizing regulation of businesses.

Within its internal logic, this policy approach does not by any means dismiss the importance of stimulating output and employment. Rather, it sees the foundation for building a sustainable growth path as relying on the ability to establish credibility among domestic and especially foreign investors, and thus to rely on private investment as the principal engine of growth. Moreover, trade liberalization is a means of enabling the economy to expand its exports, with export growth then serving as a crucial additional source of output and employment growth.

The justifications for this stringent approach to macroeconomic management cannot be dismissed lightly. There were reasonable grounds for the ANC to have accepted this policy approach when it did. Nevertheless, these policies have now been in operation for a decade, during which time there has been ample opportunity to demonstrate their effectiveness. And while this approach has indeed succeeded in lowering both the fiscal deficit and the inflation rate and in improving South Africa's external balance in terms of the current account and foreign exchange reserves, it has not succeeded in significantly reducing unemployment or poverty.

Moreover, there are logical reasons why this economic policy approach would not be successful in reducing unemployment or poverty. This is the case even while many of the policy initiatives of the ANC-led government did clearly address the needs of the poor. These policies include expansion of child maintenance grants and other social grants, large-scale investments in low-cost housing, land restitution, and investments in social infrastructure such as water taps.

Perhaps especially in recognition of these significant initiatives, it is also important to briefly consider the difficulties presented by the economic policy framework pursued under the GEAR strategy. The key points are as follows:[8]

1. The government's commitment to macroeconomic tightness—through minimizing fiscal deficits and maintaining high real interest rates—inhibited economic growth, and thereby employment growth. Weak economic growth and high interest rates in turn discourage private investment. The problem is compounded when high unemployment creates social unrest, which only destabilizes the outlook for potential private investors.

2. Even as a means of promoting private investment, public sector investment and employment can serve crucial functions in terms of a) stabilizing aggregate demand and employment; and b) promoting productivity growth. Thus fiscal tightness further weakens the opportunities for private investment because of reducing expenditures in public investment.

3. The unregulated flows of portfolio capital have been highly volatile, reflecting the more general volatility of unregulated financial markets, in advanced economies as well as developing economies. This has increased the overall speculative element in the country's financial markets, such that as-

set trading in financial markets has grown exponentially since the early 1990s, especially relative to the growth of real investment. Consequently, even though South African policymakers frequently refer to the country's "first world" financial system, the positive benefits of this financial system to the country's development goals have been insufficient.

4. Export promotion has had some success, especially in the automobile sector. But despite its huge labor surplus, South Africa is most competitive as an exporter in more capital intensive industries such as automobiles relative to other countries in sub-Saharan Africa, or very low labor cost countries, especially China. Thus, the promotion of exports has only strengthened the economy's trend toward increased capital intensity. Moreover, in terms of import competition, eliminating tariff barriers can generate rapid losses and bankruptcy for domestic firms that are unprepared, at least in the short-run, to compete with foreign multinational firms.

5. Foreign investors have many developing countries in which to choose to locate, with China currently being the most favored site by far. As such, even with South Africa having succeeded in creating a low inflation, low-regulation environment, this did not ensure that it would succeed in attracting foreign investors. The evidence to date suggests that multinational firms have little interest in locating in sub-Saharan Africa.

The problem is compounded by the fact that foreign investors are interested in a stable social environment; a well-functioning physical and educational infrastructure; and a growing domestic market. But the commitment to macroeconomic stringency undermines social cohesion by worsening problems of poverty and underemployment; weakens the public infrastructure through cutting government spending and revenue collection; and slows the expansion of domestic markets through deliberately constraining aggregate demand.

At present, the government is committed to the ASGISA framework, aiming at raising the average growth rate to 4.5 percent between 2005–2009, and again to 6.0 percent between 2010–2014. Moreover, from preliminary documents and correspondences on the ASGISA, it is clear that the government intends to take aggressive positive steps in the areas of expanding public infrastructure and the provision of social services, as well as promoting the growth of priority sectors, such as tourism, agriculture and agro-processing (biofuels). All of these measures will support a process of accelerated and shared economic growth. At the same time, it also appears from the preliminary documents on the ASGISA that the government remains committed to maintaining tight fiscal and monetary postures and to reducing taxes. It is therefore not clear where the financial resources will come from to promote this highly desirable growth initiative. It is in this context that we now turn to considering some of the specific questions involved in promoting growth, increasing labor intensity, and reducing poverty. We turn first to examining supply-side measures to reduce unit labor costs, then move on to discussing demand-side issues.

NOTES

1. In Appendix 1, we provide details on the construction of employment statistics in South Africa and the ways in which we use these data. The population estimates are taken from "Mid-Year Population Estimates, South Africa, 2005" from Statistics South Africa. This document notes that the population estimates as of mid-year 2005 are lower than had been previously published. Statistician-General Pali J. Lehohla explains that "this is primarily a result of additional information about mortality now available to Statistics South Africa," including an explicit accounting for HIV/AIDS. This document reports HIV-prevalence at approximately 10 percent of the population.
2. "Population group" refers to the historic apartheid-era racial classifications. There has been a movement away from using these categories in South Africa. However, since they remain socially meaningful for analyzing such issues as the distribution of employment opportunities, poverty, and inequality, they will be used in this report to illustrate on-going inequities.
3. Informal employment includes those employed in the non-agricultural informal sector and those employed as domestic workers.
4. For example, population growth between 2004–2005 was approximately 0.9 percent, significantly lower than the longer-term annual population growth rate of nearly 2 percent.
5. This data series ends in 2001 because of a change in the sampling frame in the Employment and Earnings enterprise survey of Statistics South Africa after 2001. The more recent sample is more comprehensive in the range of enterprises surveyed. Nevertheless, a gap still exists between the Employment and Earnings survey estimates (enterprise-based) and the Labour Force Survey estimates (household-based). The household surveys report higher levels and greater increases in employment than the enterprise surveys. Throughout this report, we use the enterprise survey estimates for estimating time-series trends or relative comparisons between detailed industrial sectors. However, we use the Labour Force Survey estimates as a more accurate assessment of *current levels* of employment—both formal and informal—in South Africa.
6. We also note, finally, that one observes an even more serious problem of declining labor intensity through estimating an employment elasticity of output growth—i.e. the percentage growth in jobs associated with one percent increase in output—over this 1967–2001 period. These estimates are not highly reliable, given the inconsistencies in the time series data and the fact that there are no time-series data at all for agricultural employment. Within these severe constraints, it may still be worth noting that our best estimate of the non-agricultural employment elasticity in this period is 0.28, meaning that a one percent increase in non-agricultural output increases non-agricultural employment by slightly less than 0.3 percent. We note that this employment elasticity figure is far below the 0.8 figure that is presented in a preliminary November 2005 policy document describing the employment goals of the ASGISA program. A fuller description of our employment elasticity estimate is presented in Appendix 1.
7. The different findings in the estimates result from how the various researchers handle problems of under-reporting of income and expenditures in household surveys and censuses. The approach taken by van der Berg et al. (2006) was to harmonize income data between the national income accounts and the survey data provided by their preferred source, the All Media and Product Surveys (AMPS) group. To do so, they raised the racial mean incomes derived from the AMPS surveys to the means estimated from the national accounts. Meth (2006) offers an extended critique of this approach and advances an alternative methodology.
8. Pollin (2006) presents a survey of these problems within the broader context of globalization.

3. Supply-Side Perspectives on Employment Expansion

The fact that the South African economy is experiencing both high unemployment and rising capital intensity of production suggests to some both an explanation for high unemployment and a solution to the problem. The explanation for the problem is straightforward: businesses won't hire more workers because they are convinced that the costs of doing so will exceed the benefits. Businesses therefore choose either to 1) maintain their operations at a lower level than they would if the benefits of hiring more workers exceeded the costs; or 2) increase the use of machines in their operations as a substitute for employing workers as their preferred means of expanding their operations. Seen from this perspective, the solution to the problem of unemployment is also straightforward: to lower the costs businesses face in hiring more workers.

There are four possible ways in which the costs to businesses of hiring workers could fall:

1. Workers receive lower overall compensation, including wages and benefits;
2. The industrial relations system and labor market regulations—including laws and regulations regarding workers' right to organize, conflict resolution, and hiring and firing—operates with more flexibility for business;
3. Workers perform their workplace operations at a higher level of productivity; or
4. The government absorbs some portion of the costs of hiring workers.

In most discussions that consider the sources of unemployment from this business cost-oriented perspective, the focus generally is on the first way to reduce business costs, i.e. to lower wages and benefits for workers relative to both other input costs in production and to the prices at which businesses can sell their final products. Indeed, the idea that excessive wage demands are the basic source of unemployment is embedded in the classical analysis of labor markets and unemployment. That basic idea has been extended in recent years to encompass the idea of inflexible labor markets: that legal and institutional constraints in wage bargaining prevent wages from being set at a market-clearing level and also inhibit firm managers from organizing the workplace in the most efficient way.

These two considerations on lowering labor costs are highly influential in debates on mass unemployment in South Africa. We will focus on these two considerations in this chapter of our study. But we also provide some brief discussion in this chapter on raising productivity and government employment subsidies—i.e. using government subsidies as a way of reducing labor costs for business. We then also take up these latter two concerns in more depth later in the study. Specifically, in Chapter 5, our discussion of incomes policies considers the issue of industrial relations and productivity, while our proposals on credit allocation look at such measures as a means of government subsidizing labor costs.

WAGE CUTTING AND LABOR MARKET FLEXIBILITY

The classical explanation for unemployment

Under the pure classical model, as well as its contemporary "new classical" variant, there is fundamentally never a problem of involuntary unemployment. If unemployment exists beyond the frictional adjustments that always take place in labor markets, it is because workers are unwilling to accept jobs at wages that employers are willing to pay. Moreover, because business owners operate to maximize their profits, they will always be willing to pay workers a wage equal to the contribution the workers can make to the firm's profitability. Thus, according to the classical model, if workers are searching for employment but aren't being hired, this can only be so because workers are seeking to be paid an amount beyond what would be profitable for business owners, given the other production costs businesses face and the prices at which they can expect to sell their final products. This then means that if workers were willing to lower their wage demands to a point that is acceptable to businesses, then businesses would be willing to hire them.

Various observers have presented evidence consistent with some variant of this classical model to explain mass unemployment in South Africa. For example, Jeffrey Lewis' major study for the World Bank (2001) presents two kinds of evidence on this score, concerning, first, wage rates themselves; and second, the inflexibilities in the South African labor market that prevent the labor market from clearing at something close to full employment.

High wages
The main points that Lewis raises here are straightforward.

1. Unemployment is concentrated among the semi-skilled and unskilled. There is almost no unemployment among skilled and highly skilled workers in South Africa.
2. Real remuneration from 1970–99 was basically stagnant for highly skilled and skilled workers, but increased by 250 percent for unskilled and semi-skilled workers.

Based on this evidence, Lewis writes,

While there are numerous factors that contribute to the differential patterns of unemployment by skill group, the pattern of wage growth appears particularly significant ... The neoclassical conclusion that unskilled and semi-skilled labor has to a large extent been priced out of the market seems unavoidable, (2001, p. 14).

Labor Market Inflexibility

Since 1995, several legislative and regulatory measures have been enacted to redress the injustices to non-White workers wrought by apartheid. Lewis says these measures have contributed to making the South African labor market inflexible. These include the Labor Relations Act (LRA), focusing, among other things, on workers' right to organize; the Basic Conditions of Employment Act (BCEA) of 1997, focusing on workplace conditions; the Employment Equity Act, seeking to correct racial imbalances through, among other things, affirmative action; and the Skills Development Levy of 1998, seeking to develop more worker training.

Lewis acknowledges that it is difficult to quantify the impact of these initiatives on the South African employment situation. However, he is clear that these measures have at least contributed, as he says, "to the impression of inflexibility." As Lewis writes,

South African business leaders cite labor regulations and union activities as discouraging employment creation. The World Economic Forum's Global Competitiveness Report ranks South Africa *at the bottom* of its fifty-nine nation comparison on whether labor regulations on wages, hours or dismissals favor flexibility. The Competitiveness Report asks groups of domestic business leaders to rank their agreement or disagreement with statements such as, "Hiring and firing practices are flexibly determined by employers." On this question South African executives strongly disagreed. Relative to the rankings of business counterparts in other economies, South Africa came in dead last on most matters concerning flexibility, labor relations and the work ethic of the labor force (2001, pp. 14–15).

Given such evidence both on rising wages and apparent labor market rigidities, South Africa's unemployment problem does seem consistent with the classical theoretical framework of analyzing unemployment, at least at a first glance. However, it isn't necessary to rely on a classical approach to connect up

patterns of rapid wage growth and labor market rigidities with high unemployment. In fact, consistent with this same set of data, one could explain high
unemployment in South Africa through focusing primarily on the challenges of
global competitiveness.[1]

GLOBAL COMPETITIVENESS APPROACH

In a standard model of international trade, a major factor determining export
success will be a country's unit labor costs relative to those of its competitors. A
country with relatively high unit labor costs will not be able to compete in global
export markets.

Of course, the fact that a country is not highly successful as an exporter
does not mean it will necessarily face employment problems. Countries could
maintain a high level of employment derived predominantly from domestic
sources of labor demand. However, in the case of South Africa, as Edwards and
Golub (2004) put it,

> The restrained fiscal policies meant that the government placed its bets on exports
> and the private sector as the engine of growth. The liberalization of international
> trade and domestic markets is intended to spur output and employment through
> export-led growth and higher foreign direct investment. Given the emphasis on
> exports and foreign investment, international competitiveness became an important
> component of the strategy (p. 1323).

The Edwards and Golub study focuses on the empirical facts concerning
South Africa's unit labor costs. They measure unit labor costs in South Africa
relative to a set of developed countries; and, separately, relative to a set of developing countries. Their measure of relative unit labor costs is:

$$c_i = (a_i/a^*_i) (w_i/w^*_i e),$$

where a is the unit labor requirement in South African production for sector i
(the inverse of productivity); w is the wage rate in sector i; and e is the exchange
rate; a^* is the foreign unit labor requirement; and w^* is the foreign wage. According to the equation above, we can decompose relative unit labor costs into
relative productivity (a_i/a^*_i) effects, and relative wage effects measured in a common currency $(w_i/w^*_i e)$.

They report rankings for 24 industrial categories. They also report an average ranking over the 24 industrial groupings. According to their results, South
Africa has made substantial improvements in their relative unit labor cost position since the 1970s, both with respect to developed and developing countries.

Edwards and Golub do not discuss the sources of this improved performance. But as one obvious general factor, it is of course the case that the South African economy became much more open and engaged in global trade with the end of apartheid in 1994. More specifically, considering the developed countries, South Africa has improved from being 31 percent above average for 1970–79 to being 21 percent below average during 1995–98.

However, Edwards and Golub argue that the more significant relative ranking is with respect to other developing countries, since it is against other developing countries that South Africa will mainly compete for export markets and attracting foreign direct investment. Average unit labor costs were 65 percent above the full sample average in 1970–77. For 1995–98, they were 20 percent above average, an improvement of 45 percentage points. Nevertheless, according to Edwards and Golub, the most important fact is not that South Africa had dramatically improved its unit labor costs position relative to other developing countries, but rather, despite this improvement, that it remains 20 percent above the average unit labor costs of other developing countries. According to Edwards and Golub, this fact may be contributing to South Africa's high unemployment rate, even while it is not likely to be the only explanation for the South African situation.

EXAMINING THE EVIDENCE ON UNIT LABOR COSTS AND UNEMPLOYMENT

As we see then, we can reach the conclusion from a range of perspectives that high labor costs are a major determinant of mass unemployment in South Africa. As a theoretical matter, there is no doubt that, at some threshold point, high labor costs will significantly discourage businesses from hiring workers. This in turn will lead to reductions in employment levels, as businesses either substitute machines for workers in their business operations or scale back their operations. But at what wage level does the South African economy reach this threshold? This is an empirical question, not a matter that can be solved simply by theory. It is therefore crucial to examine the evidence that analysts have brought to bear on this question. As we will see, serious ambiguities are present in the major studies that find significant links between labor costs and mass unemployment in South Africa. We consider, in turn, the evidence in terms of wages, labor market rigidities, and trade competitiveness.

Data on Wage Elasticity of Demand

A standard study on the relationship between wages and employment in South Africa is that by Fallon and Lucas (1998), written under the auspices of the

World Bank. The most basic finding that Fallon and Lucas present is that of a wage elasticity of demand for black formal sector employees of -0.71. This means that a 10 percent increase in the real product wage of African formal sector workers will produce a 7.1 percent reduction in employment for these workers. Fallon and Lucas also report wage elasticities for 16 separate sectors of the South African economy, with values ranging widely, between -0.06 in tobacco to -2.9 for non-metallic minerals. The -0.71 figure is the weighted mean derived from the individual estimates for the 16 separate sectors.

But there are many questions to consider with this elasticity estimate. To begin with, the -0.71 figure represents a dramatic increase over an estimate of -0.28 that Fallon had himself generated only six years earlier. Fallon and Lucas report that their much larger revised elasticity estimate is closer in line with estimates of wage elasticities of other countries. And while this is true, the large shift in their own estimate underscores the difficulties in providing generalizations on this matter, given the remarkable historical and institutional changes that South Africa has undergone in the past 30 years—as well as the inadequacy of data on employment under the apartheid regime.

Fallon and Lucas also report "impact elasticities" in this latest 1998 study. This is the wage elasticity over a one-year period. They find that the impact elasticities are very weak, at -0.156. With an impact elasticity of -0.156, as they acknowledge, it would take 2.8 years for even half of the adjustment to a wage change to work its way through the economy. That is, in a best case scenario under the Fallon and Lucas estimates, a wage-cutting strategy would take a long time. Its effectiveness would also be highly uncertain. This is because many other things would be going on in the economy over the roughly six-year period as the effect worked its way through the economy.

Data on Real Wage Increases

According to figures reported in Lewis, the problem that could be contributing to unemployment is that wages for unskilled and semi-skilled workers rose by 250 percent from 1970–99. These are the same categories of workers that experience high rates of unemployment. This is in contrast to wages for highly-skilled and skilled workers that, according to Lewis, were essentially flat over the same 30-year period. There is almost no unemployment among the more skilled categories of workers.

There are several questions to raise with these figures. The first is a straightforward statistical issue. In fact, there are no time series data on wage rates by skill level in South Africa. Rather, Lewis took these figures from work by his World Bank colleague Claude van der Merwe, who extrapolated them from a variety of sources. In his memo on this topic van der Merwe states that "care should be exercised in interpreting remuneration by skill. As the data has been calculated using at most five observations over 30 years, only broad long-term trends can be recognized at the industry level."[2]

Just as a check on the extrapolation methodology used here, let us consider briefly the data from Statistics South Africa on Africans and whites in manufacturing—allowing Africans to roughly proxy for "unskilled" and "semi-skilled" workers while whites proxy for "skilled" and "highly-skilled."[3] According to Statistics South Africa, the African real wage in manufacturing rose by 85 percent from 1973–97, while wages for white manufacturing workers rose by 17 percent over this same period. The broad trend from these figures is therefore comparable to that reported by Lewis, allowing that our proxy figures—Africans and whites as opposed to various skill levels—are reasonably accurate. Nevertheless, the magnitude of the divergence between the two groupings of workers is much less pronounced; and, correspondingly, the rise in wages for Africans is substantially slower than suggested by Lewis's extrapolation.

But let us assume Lewis's figures are roughly accurate. Further questions still arise. The first question is about the pattern of real wages for the highly-skilled and skilled workers. Why were these wages flat for a full 30-year period, during which time average labor productivity rose by approximately 50 percent? If Lewis's figures are even broadly accurate, this absence of wage gains for skilled and semi-skilled workers would appear to be at least as serious a concern as the wage increases for semi- and unskilled workers.

As for the wages for the semi- and unskilled: the wage increases that they received over this period were of course from an extremely low level—from a level that could be fairly termed a poverty-level wage in the early 1970s to something, by the end of the 1990s, that is approximately twice a poverty line wage, but no more than that. And of course, the reason wages were so low in the early period is straightforward: apartheid helped create a well-disciplined workforce at very low wages. The real wage gains during this period were therefore an indicator of the effectiveness of the organized struggle against apartheid. Moreover, using the Statistics South Africa figures for manufacturing, the African wage equaled only 18 percent of the average wage for whites in 1973. The gap does diminish. But by 1997, the average African worker in manufacturing still only earns 29 percent of the wage of white workers in the same industry. This, again, is after wages rose rapidly for Africans but only very modestly for whites.

Based on these data, even if we were to allow that there has been a trade-off between employment and wages, it does not appear that the solution in this case would be to push African wages back down. The wage increases that did occur since the early 1970s—whether they are in the range extrapolated by Lewis of 250 percent, or the lower 85-percent range, as suggested by the official figures from the manufacturing sector—still leave African workers only modestly above a reasonable poverty line.

Data on Labor Market Rigidities

Significant issues arise in the data on labor market rigidities as well. First, on the issue of responsiveness of wages to inflation, Fallon and Lucas (1998) report that "rigidities in the determination of African real wages are also illustrated by their vulnerability to unanticipated levels of inflation," (p. 13). They explain these inflation-induced rigidities as follows:

> The results suggest that an unforeseen one percentage point increase in the inflation rate temporarily reduced the real African wage by about -0.27 to -0.42 percent, thus suggesting that nominal wage changes do not immediately adjust to inflation.

However, assuming their figures are accurate, the point they are demonstrating with these results is not the rigidity of real wages in South Africa, but precisely the opposite. If nominal wages of black workers do not rise in step with inflation, this means that real wages are indeed highly flexible in a downward direction due to inflation.

This is not to suggest that it is advantageous that real wages for blacks are downwardly flexible due to inflation. Indeed, Fallon and Lucas themselves state that the fact of insufficient wage indexation for blacks is a problem, not a desirable situation. It is simply to recognize the fact that, according to Fallon and Lucas's own evidence, real wages for blacks in South Africa are highly flexible in an inflationary environment.

Fallon and Lucas are also ambiguous as to how unionization contributes to labor market rigidities. They recognize several factors that would suggest that the effect of unions on employment is likely to be weak. These include the facts that:

1. Unions only cover roughly 30 percent of the total formal sector work force in South Africa (which means that they cover only 22 percent of all workers, including those in the informal economy);
2. Unions are committed to preventing retrenchment for their members. So they may be supportive of wage restraint when the only alternative is retrenchment; and
3. Union representation tends to be strongest where wage elasticities of employment demand are weakest, such as in mining.

At the same time, Fallon and Lucas also state that South African business people claim that the impact of unions serves as a general impediment to their business expansion plans. To the extent this is true, it would then mean that the union effect on employment is more negative than can be readily captured through statistical measures.

Given these various considerations, the overall result from Fallon and Lucas, as they concede, is that they can't state with confidence what the effects of unions are on unemployment. As they conclude, "It is hard to judge by how much union activity depresses formal African employment," (p. 18).

Lewis also acknowledges ambiguities in assessing the impact of rigidities on employment. He reports the results of a survey of large firms (50 or more employees) in Johannesburg conduced by the World Bank and Greater Johannesburg Metropolitan Council (GJMC) that included questions on how labor market rigidities affect employment (p. 32). The considerations the survey raised with respect to unions' impact on employment were 1) one-third of the largest firms in the group (greater than 200 employees) must deal with three or more unions; 2) 45 percent of the full sample of large firms are bound by collective bargaining arrangements; 3) 30 percent of the large firms experienced at least one strike during 1998; and 4) the average time required to retrench entry level workers was 2.7 months.

The findings of the survey respondents were that "around 70 percent of firms pointed out that *individual* regulations had no effect on employment decisions." The questionnaire also recognized that the firms may not be able to pinpoint the effects of these individual factors on employment. So they also asked whether there were *cumulative* negative employment repercussions from all of these four effects. In response to this, 60 percent responded that there were no cumulative effects — "that all labor legislation combined had no cumulative impact on their employment decisions," (p. 32).

Of course, these results do still suggest that for roughly 30 percent of large firms in Johannesburg, the individual factors do reduce employment and that for 40 percent, the overall effect is negative. However, there is nothing in the reported survey results that suggests by how much this minority of large firms is reducing their level of employment. It obviously matters a great deal whether these negative employment effects for the minority of firms are large or small. Beyond this, again, a very large majority of firms report no effects on employment by these factors. This result, moreover, is of a survey of employers themselves— i.e. the very group that would be most likely to report negative effects of unions.

Moreover, as Fallon and Lucas point out, the unionized sector of the South African labor market is roughly 30 percent of the total workforce. Assume we can generalize from these survey results of large firms in Johannesburg to the entire South African economy. Given this assumption, it would then mean that 40 percent of all firms with unionized employees react negatively in their employment decisions to the presence of unions. That in turn means that firms reacting negatively to unions employ roughly 12 percent of the formal workforce and nine percent of the total workforce, including informal workers.

Thus, at most, the World Bank survey results of businesses themselves suggest that rigidities imposed by unionization are affecting the businesses that employ roughly 10 percent of South Africa's labor force. This is not nearly extensive enough as to serve as a major explanation for mass unemployment in South Africa today.

Data on Trade Competitiveness

There is no doubt that relative unit labor costs are a significant factor in establishing trade competitiveness for South Africa or any other country. But the the evidence that Edwards and Golub present on this issue is also highly problematic.

As we have discussed, with respect to the developing countries, the crucial fact for Edwards and Golub is not that South Africa's unit labor costs have fallen substantially. It is rather that, despite this fall, South Africa still maintains relative unit labor costs that are 20 percent higher than the average for developing countries. However, Edwards and Golub (2004) do not show why this single threshold—being above a weighted average for 10 countries on a scale that averages 24 different product types—should be more important for establishing trade competitiveness than the general movement of South Africa's relative position— that is, the fact that South Africa did substantially improve its standing in unit labor costs relative to both the developed and developing world.

The problem with their relative unit labor cost threshold as a basis for anticipating export success becomes evident when we consider their own data at an industry-level disaggregated basis. Of course, when we move down into the details of how trade competitiveness actually occurs in global markets, South Africa, as an economic entity, does not compete with other countries as entities. Competition actually takes place at the level of specific products and firms. For testing the robustness of this Edwards and Golub indicator of trade competitiveness, it is therefore useful to see how well it holds up at a more detailed level. In particular, it is illuminating to consider the trajectory of competitiveness in four industries in which, according to Edwards and Golub's own figures, South African manufacturers did both improve dramatically in terms of relative unit labor costs, *and more importantly*, succeeded in moving from being well above average by the Edwards and Golub measure of relative unit labor costs from 1970–9 to being well below average in 1995–98.

These four sectors—leather products, footwear, industrial chemicals, and professional/scientific equipment—are shown in Table 3.1, along with 1) their relative rankings in the two periods 1970–79 and 1995–98 as reported by Edwards and Golub; and 2) the trade performance of these sectors in these two periods.

As we see in the table, with three of the four sectors, the growth rate of exports actually falls in 1995–98 relative to 1970–79, despite the dramatic improvements in relative unit labor costs in these sectors. Thus, with leather products, Edwards and Golub report that relative unit labor costs through 1970–79

Table 3.1 Relative Unit Labor Costs and Trade Performance of Selected South African Sectors, 1970–79 and 1995–98

	Edwards and Golub measure of South Africa unit labor costs relative to developing country sample		Sectoral export growth (real average annual figures)	
	1970–79	1995–98	1970–79	1995–98
Leather products	60% above	23% below	17.5%	7.9%
Footwear	93% above	53% below	4.3%	-21.1%
Industrial chemicals	54% above	12% below	9.1%	6.7%
Professional and scientific equipment	86% above	27% below	-6.7%	11.3%

Sources: Relative unit labor cost figures from Edwards and Golub (2004); sectoral export growth figures from Statistics.

were 60 percent above average for the sample of 10 developing countries, but improved to 23 percent below average over 1995–98. However, export growth in leather products averaged 17.5 percent for 1970–79 but then fell to 7.9 percent in 1995–98. The pattern is similar but more dramatic for footwear, while a more moderate version of the same pattern holds with industrial chemicals. The one exception to this pattern is professional and scientific equipment. Here, consistent with the Edwards and Golub postulate, relative unit labor costs fell from 86 percent above average in the first period to 27 percent below average in the second period. Along with this, sectoral growth rose from an average -6.7 percent in the first period to a positive 11.3 percent in the second period.[4]

The overall point from these data is clear: the measure on which Edwards and Golub have relied for establishing export success in South Africa is very blunt. The fact that they are operating with a blunt measure of export competitiveness is reinforced by their own econometric exercise. According to their econometric results, the ability of this measure to contribute to an explanation of South Africa's trade competitiveness has diminished dramatically over time. As they write:

> During 1970-79 and 1980-89 Relative Unit Labor Costs, relative wages, and relative productivity were significant in explaining the structure of exports. During the 1990s, however, these variables are incorrectly signed and fail to explain the structure of trade, as shown by the low F-statistic ... The weaker results during the 1990s suggest that other factors not related to labor costs are becoming more important in influencing the sectoral composition of South African exports. The 1990s were a period characterized by significant structural breaks such as the ending of sanctions, the

election of a new government, a new macroeconomic policy, new labor legislation, and the initiation of tariff liberalization. The impact of these structural breaks may affect exports in a way that is not necessarily related to RULC. For example, the reintegration of South Africa into the world economy since 1994 led to rapid increases in exports to various regions. Some of this export growth is due to increased market access and not changes in labor cost competitiveness. Structural changes in the economy have also affected RULC across sectors ... These changes in the sectoral structure of exports and RULC may obscure the long-run relationship between the two (pp. 1332–1333).

In short, the Edwards and Golub approach offers limited guidance for understanding how much lowering wages—or even unit labor costs more generally, through either a wage or productivity channel—would contribute to promoting employment.

POLICY APPROACHES TO REDUCING UNIT LABOR COSTS

Overall, then, we have considered in this chapter the evidence presented by Lewis (2001), Fallon and Lucas (1998), and Edwards and Golub (2004) on 1) wage elasticities of demand; 2) real wage increases; 3) labor market rigidities; and 4) relative unit labor costs and trade competitiveness. It is fair to conclude that, based on this evidence, the argument that excessive wages and labor market rigidities are one of the primary causes, if not *the* primary cause, of mass unemployment in South Africa is based on a weak empirical foundation. As noted above, these authors themselves acknowledge this point to some extent. Nevertheless, even if the evidence presented on behalf of these arguments is itself weak, it is still possible that reducing unit labor costs could be a central feature of policies to attack mass unemployment. As such, we next address some considerations with respect to the four ways of reducing unit labor costs, i.e. wage cutting, raising productivity, increasing institutional flexibility, and using government subsidies to absorb some of businesses' labor costs.

Wage Cutting

The government's stated goal is to cut unemployment in half in 10 years. In Table 3.2, we present some figures which provide a rough sense of what would be needed to achieve a reduction in unemployment through wage cutting alone, assuming a wage elasticity of demand of -0.7. As the table shows, there were 4.1 million unemployed officially as of September 2004 and 11.6 million officially employed in either formal or informal activity. Of those employed, 8.7 million either had formal jobs or worked in agriculture. Thus, based on this situation,

Table 3.2 Scenarios for Reducing Formal Unemployment by Half through Wage Cutting

Total employment	11.6 million
Formal employment and agriculture	8.7 million
Unemployment	4.1 million
Average real wage	R3800
Wage reduction needed to reduce unemployment in half	38.4%
Wage level after wage cut	R2340
Estimated midpoint poverty line for family of four	
(based on Hoogeveen and Ozler individual poverty threshold)	R2268

Note: Assume wage elasticity of demand for labor at -0.70.

to reduce unemployment by half would mean to create 2.1 million new formal jobs, i.e. an increase of 18 percent in the total number of jobs and 24 percent in formal plus agricultural forms of employment.

Assuming a wage elasticity of labor demand of -0.7, that would mean that a wage cut of 38.4 percent would be necessary to generate an additional 2.1 million jobs. According to recent research by Casale, Muller, and Posel (2004), the average wage in formal economy employment, expressed in 2004 prices, is about R3800 per month. Considering a wage-cutting scenario with formal jobs only, to cut the average formal worker's wages by 38.4 percent would mean that the new wage would be about R2340 per month.

What would this sort of wage cut imply with respect to living standards for average working families in South Africa? To address this, we can draw on the benchmark "cost of basic needs" poverty line developed by the World Bank economists Hoogeveen and Ozler, to which we have referred in Chapter 2. As we noted in Chapter 2, the Hoogeveen and Ozler (2004) cost of basic needs poverty line was between R400–734 per month in 2004 prices. For the purpose of our exercise, we work with the midpoint of their range as an individual poverty line, i.e. R567 per month. We then multiply this figure by four to establish a rough poverty line for a family of four (the details of the reasoning for this calculation are in the endnote).[5] That brings us to a four-person poverty line of approximately R2268/month. As we see from Table 2.2, this fall in the average wage would mean that the average wage would fall from being 70 percent above the poverty line for a family of four to being approximately equal to a poverty-line family income.

There would be both positive and negative ramifications of such a measure. On the positive side, of course, to begin with, 2 million more people would have jobs. Each of these workers would be able to support a family of four at a level roughly equal to a midpoint poverty line. This is clearly an improvement insofar as many, if not most, unemployed workers and their families currently live closer to a destitution level. Even a modest income from this job would improve their living standard and increase their degree of attachment to the formal economy.

On the negative side, nearly nine million workers—if we include those employed both in the formal economy and in agriculture—and their families would experience a sharp decline in their real incomes. To take the case of the family whose working member is earning the average wage of R3800, the experience would mean a nearly 40 percent decline in income. If this were also a family of four, they would now be living at roughly the mid-point Hoogeveen and Ozler poverty line. The policy would clearly be pushing millions of working families into, or at least close to, a state of poverty.

This would no doubt produce both demoralization and resistance among South African workers. Resistance would take the form of strikes and other activities that would disrupt normal business activities. This in turn would worsen the environment for investors, both foreign and domestic.

To the extent that the average worker has outstanding debts, this measure would of course make it more difficult for them to make payments on their debts, since their debt servicing costs/income ratio would become increasingly burdensome. For example, if we assume that the average worker paid out 10 percent of her income in interest and principal repayments, at the new wage average wage rate, this same debt level of R365 would now constitute 16 percent of income. This would in turn raise bankruptcy rates and make it more difficult for financial institutions serving the middle class to grow.

Overall then, this approach will most likely engender negative countereffects that are at least as powerful as the benefit of 2 million more people obtaining jobs at wages roughly equal to the Hoogeveen/Ozler poverty line. Weighing all of these factors, significant wage cutting might seem to be a viable option for reducing poverty and unemployment only if there were no other policy options available.

Productivity

Raising productivity could of course lower unit labor costs. However, by definition, it could not, on its own, increase employment, since a higher level of productivity would mean that the same amount of goods and services could be produced with fewer workers. Indeed, as we have seen, a rise in capital intensity has been a major factor pushing down the demand for labor. By contrast, the solution to unemployment, at least in part, will entail generating growth in industries and production technologies that have a higher level of labor intensity.

But there is an important corollary issue on the relationship between unemployment, wage cutting and productivity. This is that workers will tend to operate more efficiently—at a higher level of productivity—when their wages are increased. This is the so-called "efficiency wage" effect: that workers' morale and commitment to their job will rise when they are paid more. Lower job turnover and worker absenteeism will be among the explicit outgrowths of the rise in worker morale associated with a higher wage standard. In light of the current discussion, it is also important to recognize that this same efficiency wage effect will operate in reverse. That is, a strategy of wage cutting will engender reduced efficiency—more turnover, more absenteeism, lower morale on the job. Thus, through this negative efficiency wage channel as well, a wage-cutting strategy would seem to be a viable strategy for reducing unemployment only if no other options were available.

The only way raising productivity can be supportive of increased labor demand is if the rise in productivity also induces an increase in aggregate demand for products. This could occur through two channels:

1. The rise in productivity does increase export competitiveness to the extent that it expands South Africa's export market significantly.
2. Government infrastructure investments increase productivity, and also increase the opportunities for private investors. This creates a virtuous cycle of increased spending on public investment, leading to increases in private investment and overall productivity. Job growth would then rise with the increase in overall demand. However, note that even here, if productivity grows faster than overall demand, there will not be a net increase in job growth, but rather a further decline in employment for a given level of output.

Wage Restraint and Institutional Flexibility

We concluded from our review above of the evidence on labor market rigidities—from Fallon and Lucas as well as Lewis—that such rigidities are not likely to be a significant cause of mass unemployment in South Africa. Still, South Africa's employment situation can benefit significantly through operating wage-bargaining and labor regulations as efficiently as possible. What do we mean by this? For example, it is no doubt true that it is more difficult for a business to negotiate with three separate unions rather than one. It is also better that there be fewer, rather than more, work stoppages. Wage increases should also be roughly commensurate with productivity growth to maintain inflationary pressures within a moderate range. Increased flexibility along these lines could certainly be implemented in South Africa without being hostile to working people and unions.

Indeed, the union movement and unionized workers are likely to benefit disproportionately through recognizing the benefits of flexibility along the lines we describe here. In particular, when unions and business can conduct wage-setting negotiations in a relatively cooperative way as a means of avoiding a build-up of inflationary pressures, this in turn opens space for macroeconomic policy to be more expansionary. We take up this issue at greater length below in our discussion on incomes policies as an inflation-control measure. For now, we wish to emphasize one additional point on the issue of wage cutting as a strategy and building a flexible industrial relations system—that in fact, a strategy of wage cutting will undermine any effort to create more flexible and cooperative institutional arrangements. Indeed, pursuing a wage-cutting agenda will precisely strengthen resistance, and serve as a barrier to the development of institutions through which wages can be negotiated and regulations made to operate more flexibly.

Government Subsidizes Employment Creation

In principle, there are significant advantages to this method of lowering unit labor costs. The key advantage is that workers are not being asked to experience pay cuts in order to encourage businesses to hire more of them. In general, we share Jeffrey Lewis's (2001) favorable evaluation of employment subsidies when he writes, "employment subsidies can be used as a strategy for increasing employment without producing negative consequences for productivity and competitiveness."[6] Lewis makes clear that employment subsidies are a distinctively supply-side approach to expanding job growth through promoting more labor-intensive production methods. At the same time, Lewis holds that "employment subsidies and demand-side job creation policies are not mutually exclusive."

However, there are serious issues to address in attempting to implement an effective employment subsidy program. The two broad forms that these measures can take are either as a general or a marginal employment subsidy. A general employment subsidy would apply to all workers, both new and already employed. A marginal subsidy would apply only when new workers are hired from a previously established base of employees. A general subsidy program would obviously be much larger in scope, and correspondingly much more expensive, than a marginal subsidy program. It would also reward businesses simply on the basis of their existing employment levels. But a marginal subsidy program, which does not face these problems, would also be much more difficult to administer. Such programs require that there be some measurement of what employment would have been without the subsidy program. As such, they create incentives for firms to under-report employment. They therefore also would place large administrative demands on the government.

Given these and related concerns, we present in a later section of this study a kind of hybrid employment subsidy program. More specifically, the measure we propose is actually a credit subsidy program. But firms would be eligible to receive subsidized credit on the basis of their ability to increase their hiring of workers within their own operations and to generate large employment multipliers through their demand for inputs from other firms (i.e. their upstream employment linkages). Relative to more standard general and marginal employment subsidy measures, our proposal has these advantages: 1) it has features of both a general and a marginal employment subsidy program; 2) it is capable of operating on a large-scale basis without requiring large direct government expenditures; and 3) it can serve both to stimulate aggregate business investment—for small, medium, and large-scale enterprises—on the demand side, while also promoting more labor intensive methods on the supply side.

NOTES

1. There is also a more heterodox theoretical approach to explaining economic growth in developing countries advanced by Dani Rodrik and colleagues (see, for example, Rodrik 2004). This approach begins without theoretical presumptions about how the labor market should clear and why involuntary unemployment cannot exist in a fundamental sense. Instead, this approach is flexible in considering the factors that might be promoting or inhibiting economic growth in developing countries. The explanation for mass unemployment would then be found within the framework of identifying the barriers to a robust growth path. In situations where growth has been slow, this approach rather looks to an economy's structure of relative prices as providing crucial evidence as to the major barriers to achieving an accelerated growth path. Considering this approach within the South African context, one could argue that the fact that businesses are already substituting capital for labor while unemployment remains extremely high would suggest that the high price of employing labor relative to capital—and high wages in particular—is the fundamental barrier to a major employment expansion.
2. We are grateful to Dr. Lewis for sharing his private correspondence with van der Merwe on this topic.
3. Using these racial groupings to proxy for skill categories of course does not in any way imply that we believe that whites are intrinsically endowed with higher skill levels. For the purposes of this exercise, we are using these proxies simply in recognition that, under apartheid, whites in South Africa were given far more opportunities to develop their employment-related skills.
4. Furniture is the one other sector in the Edwards and Golub data set that shifts over the two periods from being above to below average in relative unit labor costs. But we are unable to obtain accurate data on trade growth at this level of sector specificity for these two periods. However, we do note that for the related Wood and Wood Products sector, we again see a decline, rather than increase, in export performance between the two periods, from a 28.6 percent average annual growth rate over 1970–79 to an 8.0 rate between 1995–98.
5. The reasoning for multiplying the midpoint Hoogeveen and Ozler line by four is as follows. The ratio of total population of South Africa relative to the total that are employed is approximately 3.8. This suggests that each employed person in the economy is, on average, supporting 3.8 people. As such, the wage to maintain a family at approximately the poverty line would be the individual poverty line income level multiplied by 3.8, rounded up to 4. It is true that households operate with economies of scale, such that the poverty line for a family isn't necessarily equal to that for an individual multiplied by the family size. But the Hoogeveen/Ozler threshold is within a broad band. As such, even allowing for economies of scale within a family, it is still reasonable that an appropriate four-person family poverty threshold would correspond to their individual threshold multiplied by the number of family members.
6. Lewis (2001), p. 35. Lewis's overall discussion of this issue is on pp. 34–39 of his study.

4. A Policy Framework on Growth, Labor Intensity, and Poverty Reduction

For South Africa to achieve its highly desirable goals in terms of employment growth and poverty reduction, it will need to pursue policies along three dimensions:

1. Increasing the rate of economic growth, i.e. the total amount of overall output produced in the economy each year;
2. Increasing the average labor intensity of output; and
3. Increasing the degree of inclusion of the poor in society, and particularly in the job market.

In this chapter, we identify the major types of policy interventions that will be needed to promote progress along all three dimensions—i.e to increase economic growth, labor intensity of output, and the social inclusion of the poor.

ECONOMIC GROWTH

By definition, the overall GDP of an economy can be broken down into four component parts: private investment, private consumption, net exports, and government spending. Thus, in considering ways of raising the average growth rate of the South African economy, we need to consider the prospects for accelerating growth in some combination of these four areas. We consider these in turn.

Private Investment

Private investment is correctly recognized as a foundation for successful long-term growth in South Africa. It is easy to understand why this should be so, since any economy that aspires to long-term improvements in productivity and average living standards must devise effective means of raising the quantity and quality of its capital stock.

The level of private investment activity in South Africa has been disappointing since the transition to democracy in 1994. We can see this in Figure 4.1. We see from the figure that investment/GDP had risen to a high point of 29.7 percent in 1976, but that it has been falling steadily ever since. Since 1994, the decline in the investment share has halted, but there has been no steady movement upward beyond this. As of 2004 investment accounted for only about 16.1 percent of GDP.

The government has been clear in targeting an increase in investment as among its highest priorities. President Mbeki listed "addressing the investment challenge" as one of the "four key challenges" in his address at the 2003 Growth and Development Summit. In the preliminary ASGISA documents and statements, it is clear that raising the rate of investment growth is a foundation of the program. The ASGISA aims to promote a 10 percent average annual increase in investment, which would in turn raise the investment/GDP ratio to 25 percent by 2014.

Sources of private investment growth

Alan Hirsch, the Chief Director of Economic Policy in the Office of the Presidency, considers in his 2004 paper the factors that are contributing to the slow rate of investment growth. It is worth citing his assessment in some detail:

> There are some objective reasons for the slow rate of investment. Both domestic and foreign investors are influenced by the relatively slow domestic growth rate, high interest rates (which encourage short-term flows), and the volatile exchange rate. More subjective judgments include the extent of inequality and the potential for social conflict, where decisions might be made by investors based on their assessment, or the assessment of their advisors, of the perceived will and capacity of government.
>
> Other factors influencing investment include the high degree of concentration and centralization of ownership in some market segments in South Africa, and shareholder pressure for short-term and certain returns.
>
> Some factors influencing investment are as much the product of mindset and perceptions as objective facts. One is a concern about the crime rate and its impact on doing business in South Africa, though the per capita incidence of crime is decreasing, and is no higher than in many of South Africa's competitors, which are often less open about their crime statistics. Another is a contrary view or misunderstanding of South Africa's role or potential role in Zimbabwe. Some potential investors believe that the labour market regime inhibits investments, while others are concerned about the expected or imagined effects of affirmative action on the employment prospects for whites.
>
> For a few there is an underlying pessimistic view that interprets every possible event as a sign of South Africa's inevitable failure. This in turn often derives from a lack of understanding and trust between the potential investors of capital and the political rulers. For unavoidable historical reasons, the cultural gap between political and economic leaders is unusually large in South Africa at this time.

Figure 4.1 Investment as a Share of GDP in South African Economy, 1970–2004

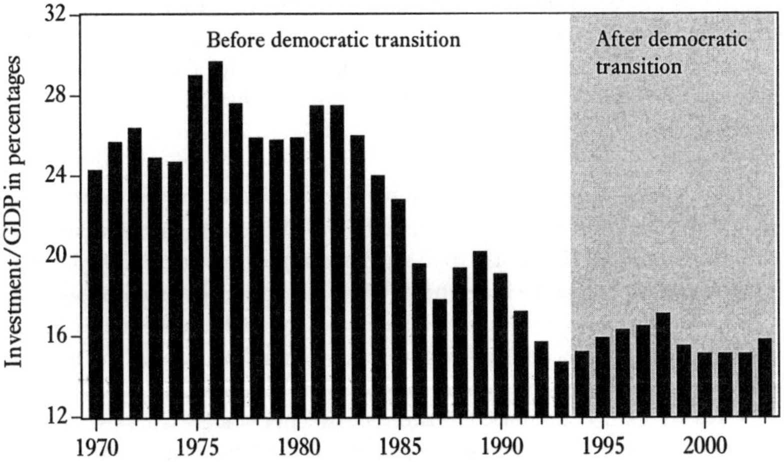

Source: Reserve Bank of South Africa.

Hirsh's assessment in fact corresponds closely with standard academic analyses of the determinants of investment, both in general terms and specifically with respect to South Africa. According to such standard models, there will be five basic factors—both "objective" and "subjective"—influencing investment.

1. The overall growth rate of the economy (the so-called "accelerator" effect);
2. The costs of capital, including here both interest rates and tax rates;
3. The expectations of profitability, based on past profit performances;
4. The confidence about the long-term stability of the economic environment and the broader social environment;
5. The prospects for relatively higher returns from making short-term portfolio investments—such as in stocks, bonds, foreign exchange, or derivative assets—as opposed to investing in the creation of new capital stock.

To our knowledge, there have been four recent statistical models exploring the determinants of investment in South Africa. These models are summarized in Appendix 2. In addition, Professor Léonce Ndikumana of our team has conducted new tests on the determinants of investment in South Africa over the 30-year period 1972–2001. Ndikumana's model is conducted with detailed data based on nine industries and 27 manufacturing sub-sectors within the South African economy.

In Ndikumana's most recent model, as well as the four previous ones, all of the above-cited factors do play a role in influencing investment. But for the purposes of our study, the primary question is not simply to know that these factors do influence investment, but rather 1) How much do they influence investment? and 2) What policy measures are available to the government to encourage the factors that could raise the rate of investment?

In considering the results from Ndikumana's model along with the four previous studies, we can reach the following conclusions about policies to promote investment.

1. *GDP growth and investment.* All studies find that increasing the rate of GDP growth will lead to an increase in investment. Ndikumana's model suggests that increasing GDP growth from, say, 3 percent on average to 4.5 percent on average will increase the investment/GDP ratio by about 1 percent.

   For policy purposes, government intervention can rapidly contribute to faster GDP growth by injecting more government spending into the economy—that is, by increasing the amount of money the government spends without increasing its tax revenues. This of course entails increasing the government fiscal deficit. Increasing the deficit can also have other consequences, as we will discuss below. But the point is that this is the most direct path through which the government can increase spending in the economy, which in turn will lead to more investment.

   Beyond this, to raise the rate of GDP growth as a means of stimulating investment presents a problem of time sequencing: more consumption spending, more net exports, and more investment itself will all contribute to GDP growth, and faster GDP growth in turn stimulates investment. But that still raises the question of how to raise consumption, net exports and investment spending prior to the injection of faster GDP growth. We return to this point below.

2. *Cost of capital—interest rates and taxes.* At one level, the five formal studies all reached an unsurprising conclusion: that if one lowers taxes on business or interest rates, this will have a positive effect on investment. However, these studies do vary considerably as to how strong they expect the effects will be of these measures to reduce the costs of capital. Most of the studies find that the effects are likely to be modest, perhaps not even detectable in a statistical sense. Ndikumana has separated out the effects of lowering the interest rates and corporate tax rates. He finds that reducing the real interest rate (i.e. the nominal rate minus the inflation rate) from, say, 10 percent to 8 percent will lead to an increase in the investment/GDP ratio of 1.3 percent. Ndikumana finds that lowering the tax rate on business will not have any noticeable effect on investment.

   However, even if we recognize that the effect of lowering the interest rate is likely to be modest, there is one important advantage to exploiting this effect for policy purposes. That is, we do have policy tools that can lower interest rates through a straightforward time-sequencing—i.e. we have the means to lower the interest rate and thereby encourage investment without having to wait for other changes in the economy to occur first. These policy tools are: 1) monetary policy to lower the general level of market interest rates; and 2) credit allocation policies to lower rates below market rates for firms that have been selected to received subsidies. We explore ways of effectively implementing these policies in Chapter 3.

3. *Profitability.* It should not be a surprise that most studies find that higher profitability will encourage investment. However, it is unclear what factors within the control of policymakers will be most effective at promoting profitability. For example, in Ndikumana's model, increased government expenditures on infrastructure will have a strong positive effect on investment. This is because improving, for example, the country's roads, ports, irrigation systems, and telecommunications systems will enable businesses to operate more efficiently. According to Ndikumana's study, increasing the share of public investment relative to GDP from 5 percent to 7 percent (the average for Sub-Saharan Africa) will lead to approximately 6.7 percent more private investment.

Put in other terms, public investment in South Africa (and elsewhere) "crowds in" private investment to a statistically and substantively robust extent. Thus, the more resources the government can commit to expanding public investment, the greater the likelihood that the economy can reach the stated ASGISA goal of a 25 percent investment/GDP ratio by 2014.

It is also true that there are other paths of raising profitability, for example lowering wages. Hirsh's comments suggest that relatively high wages—the "labor market regime"—do dampen investment. However, as we have discussed above, lowering unit labor costs through wage cutting is not a viable policy approach. Among other important considerations that we have discussed above, pushing down wages will create social discontent, which will also engender a less stable investment climate. Of course, wages cannot rise in excess of productivity growth without cutting into profits and/or encouraging accelerating inflation. This is precisely why, in Chapter 5, we discuss the establishment of so-called "incomes policies" as a means of establishing an institutional environment for sustainable wage growth.

4. *Instability.* As Hirsh's observations convey, we can distinguish two types of instability that will influence private investment. The first is economic instability, including exchange-rate volatility, rapid price changes in stock and bond markets, and rapid movements in the country's overall inflation rate. The second is social instability. This refers to factors such as the crime rate, labor market disruptions such as strikes, and the degree of credibility enjoyed by the major political institutions. Both the economic and social indicators of instability have been found to exert a significant influence on investment. It is clearly beneficial that exchange-rate fluctuations

and other financial market disruptions be maintained at a relatively low level.   The inflation rate should similarly be maintained at a relatively stable level. A political climate such as that which prevailed in the last decade of apartheid—with political repression, a high level of strike activity, and major uncertainty as to the stability of the political system—will certainly discourage private investment.

The issue here again is the policy implication of addressing these influences on investment. Monetary policy, exchange controls, and capital controls can work to stabilize the exchange rate and inflation rate, as we will discuss further below. Other measures can contribute here as well, including exchange and capital controls to stabilize the exchange rate and incomes policies to control inflation. In terms of social stability, the key considerations here are the very things which are the basic focus of this study—i.e. the creation of decent jobs and the reduction in poverty. And here again, a program of lowering unit labor costs through wage cutting would only work to reduce social stability.

5.   *Portfolio investments as an alternative to investing in capital stock.* Trading in stocks, bonds, foreign exchange, or financial derivatives offer investors the possibility of more rapid returns in the short term than would be possible through investing in capital stock, especially in situations when the economy is operating at a high level of uncertainty. In Ndikumana's model, the effects of portfolio investment on capital investment operate through the level of public debt outstanding in the economy. He finds that an increase in the level of public debt relative to GDP does dampen expenditures on plants and machinery, and that this effect is separate from the positive effects of an increase in public investment expenditures on efficiency. What appears to be happening here is that an increase in the supply of new government bonds provides an option for private investors which then reduces their willingness to spend on structures and machinery.

This effect of investors substituting portfolio investments like government bond purchases for real investments in machinery and buildings is consistent with the data that show an explosive rise in portfolio trading in South Africa. We can see this from Figure 4.2, which shows the trends in the secondary trading on South Africa's stock and bond markets. The general story from these figures is clear. On the lower scale of both panels, we see the trend of gross capital expenditures declining sharply as a share of GDP from the 1980s onward. But along with this well-known pattern, we also see a rise in secondary market trading in stocks and bonds as a share of GDP. Beginning in the mid 1990s, this increase in secondary market stock and bond trading relative to GDP explodes. This is most pronounced with respect to the bond market, with bond trading rising from an average of 0.9 percent of GDP over the 1970s to an average of 483 percent in the 1990s—

Figure 4.2 Stock Trading, Bond Trading and Capital Investment in South Africa, 1970–2004

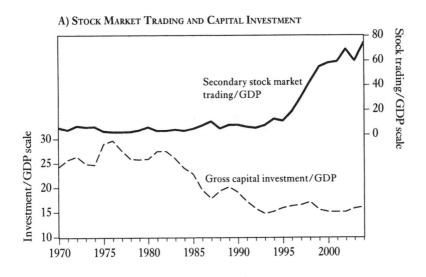

A) STOCK MARKET TRADING AND CAPITAL INVESTMENT

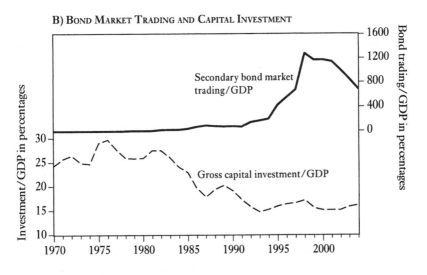

B) BOND MARKET TRADING AND CAPITAL INVESTMENT

Source: Reserve Bank of South Africa.

i.e. the value of bonds traded in the South African exchange was nearly 5 times in excess of the economy's GDP. The figure for 2004 was 685 per-cent—i.e. nearly 7 times GDP.

The rate of increase in stock market trading is well below that of the bond market. Still, considered on its own terms, stock trading rises five-fold from the 1970s to the 1990s relative to GDP, and, considering the figure for 2000, there was an 11-fold increase relative to the average for the 1970s.

The key point in all of this is that, despite the explosive growth in these secondary markets, this growth does not correlate with positive develop-ments in terms of either productive investment growth, GDP growth or the investment/GDP ratio. Of course, these figures do not, on their own, suggest anything about possible directions of causation between the explo-sion of trading on secondary financial markets and the decline of produc-tive investment growth. But one can at least observe that 1) the level of portfolio trading is growing exponentially in South Africa's financial mar-kets; while 2) real productive investment is, at best, stagnating. The policy implication of this pattern is that government should create incentives for investors to channel funds into productive investments as opposed to port-folio trading. We will discuss details as to how to accomplish this in our consideration of credit allocation policies.

Raising saving rates to promote investment
A widely held view is that high saving rates are the main factor that will encour-age higher investment, both for the South African economy today and more generally. Indeed, debates about the validity of this perspective have occupied economists for literally hundreds of years. This study certainly is not the place to review that debate, much less attempt to resolve it.[1] However, for our discus-sion here, there is a straightforward way of at least getting to the heart of the issue without having to plunge into long-standing controversies in economics. The point is that, even if we allow that high saving is a precondition for high investment, it is still the case that the channel through which saving influences investment is through interest rates. That is, high saving is said to produce high investment because high saving will lead to lower interest rates, and the lower interest rates, in turn, will encourage investment.

Once we recognize this *interest rate channel* through which high saving is supposed to produce high investment, it is then clear that the models by Ndikumana and the others that we have reviewed for South Africa do effectively measure the potential influence of the saving rate on investment. This is because these models do investigate the influence of interest rates on investment. It is true that the models do not take one step backward from examining the investment/interest rate nexus, to try to measure the extent to which the saving rate, relative to other potential factors, may influence movements in interest rates. But in fact, neither the theory nor the evidence is strong that low saving rates themselves produce high interest rates or vice versa. For example, there was a sharp increase in South Africa between 1980 – 2000 in the level of *lending and borrowing* in the domestic economy relative to a given rate of saving. Domestic lending equaled 38.3 percent of gross saving in 1980, but rose to 122.3 percent in 2000. It is this ratio of lending relative to saving, rather than the saving rate itself, that exerts direct influence on long-term interest rates.[2] But this, in any case, is a secondary issue for our purposes. The main issue is how interest rates affect investment, whatever may be the various factors that in turn affect interest rates.

Foreign direct investment for South Africa

The models that we have reviewed of the factors determining investment patterns in South Africa are meant to apply to both foreign and domestic investment. The underlying point is that the same factors that will encourage domestic firms to spend money on new structures and machinery—the overall level of demand; interest rates; profitability; uncertainty; and the alternative of buying stocks, bonds, and derivative financial assets as opposed to new structures and machinery—are likely to also be the major factors influencing the investment decisions of foreign businesses.

At the same time, South Africa, like many middle- and low-income countries in the current global economic policy environment, has had high expectations about prospects for attracting foreign direct investment (FDI), especially in response to the end of apartheid. Indeed, the GEAR program had predicted a sharp increase in FDI, and this increase in FDI, in turn, was anticipated to have been a major engine of growth for the economy. But this has not occurred. We can see this from the figures in Table 4.1, which, for the years 1996–2000, shows the GEAR program projections for FDI flows into South Africa and what the actual flows were in these years. As we can see from the table, the actual inflows of FDI were below the GEAR projections in each of the years other than 1997. However, even in 1997, the sharp increase in FDI was due to several mergers and acquisitions, as opposed to "greenfield" investments in new equipment and machinery.

The pattern shown in Table 4.1 is consistent with the broader pattern of evidence presented in Stephen Gelb and Anthony Black's survey of FDI in Africa, including South Africa. With respect to South Africa specifically, Gelb and Black conclude:

> The majority of new foreign investors entering South Africa during the 1990's established small or medium size affiliates with limited impact on employment creation or capital inflows. Nearly half the entries involved acquisitions of existing operations, rather than greenfields or joint ventures setting up new enterprises. Many investors mitigated risk by limiting the irreversibility of their investment, by outsourcing production and focusing on services (2004, pp. 210–11).

Table 4.1 Foreign Direct Investment into South Africa, 1996–2000:
GEAR Projections vs. Actual Investment Flows (figures are in millions of dollars)

	1996	1997	1998	1999	2000
GEAR	155	365	504	716	804
Actual[1]	8	3006	-249	691	77

Note: [1] Relative to 1994–95 average of FDI inflows of $810.5 million.
Sources: GEAR, p. 7; UNCTAD (2004), Table Annex: B.1.

Considering South Africa's recent experience with FDI in comparative terms, the evidence shows that South Africa receives fewer inward flows of FDI and more inward flows of portfolio investment—stocks, bonds, and derivative asset purchases—than comparable countries such as Egypt, Mexico, Thailand, and Uruguay (IMF 2003, 2004). South Africa also appears to be a larger source of FDI *outflows* than other countries at its level of development. This is certainly the case relative to other countries in Africa, where South Africa is the largest source country for FDI inflows (UNCTAD 2004).

There is no full consensus as to why FDI inflows into South Africa have been significantly lower than some observers had expected. The relevant econometric findings are broadly consistent with the evidence we have reviewed as to the factors influencing investment in general, i.e. both domestic and foreign investment. This evidence suggests that that faster economic growth, improvements in the public infrastructure, a more skilled work force, and a more stable rand would all encourage more FDI. However, the fact that South Africa has not been attracting FDI to the same extent as comparable countries suggests that, at least in the short-term, it may need to rely at this stage primarily on domestic investment to first raise the country's investment rate. The expectation would then be that foreign investors would respond favorably to a higher level of domestic investment and economic growth.

Overall policy conclusions for promoting investment
Five overall conclusions flow from the foregoing discussion that will be central for our focused discussions in the next section on policy approaches:

1. An increase in the overall rate of GDP growth will lead to more investment. This effect is likely to operate first on domestic investment, and only with a time lag on foreign investment. Government deficit spending can promote GDP growth to some extent, especially if the spending associated with the rise in government borrowing is targeted to increase public investment. However, excessive reliance on government borrowing

can be counterproductive, as we will discuss further in the discussion on fiscal policies.

2. Lowering interest rates will certainly stimulate productive investment. This interest rate effect may be modest, but there is still an important advantage of lowering interest rates as a policy intervention. It is that at least the direction of effect is certain and there is no difficulty in terms of establishing the time sequence between the policy intervention—i.e. monetary or credit allocation policies to lower interest rates—and the intended effect— i.e. making cheaper credit available to private investors.

3. Stabilizing exchange rates, the financial markets, and fluctuations in inflation can contribute to promoting both domestic and foreign private investment. The policy mechanisms to achieve these outcomes would involve monetary policy and incomes policies for the exchange rate and inflation rate, capital controls for the exchange rate and financial markets, and financial market regulations to promote stability.

4. Increased social stability should also promote both domestic and foreign investment. But improving social stability will itself come through a broader program of increasing employment opportunities and the social inclusion of the poor. Efforts to reduce unit labor costs through wage cutting will, by contrast, provoke social unrest and thereby discourage investment.

5. The opportunities to move funds into speculative portfolio trading do discourage investment in buildings and machinery. Policies to raise the costs of portfolio trading relative to productive investments—including measures that we discuss below to raise the costs of portfolio trading while concurrently providing subsidized credit to employment-expanding productive investments—should therefore contribute to promoting productive investment

Private Consumption

In 2003, household consumption spending constituted 64 percent of total domestic spending in the South African economy. Should it be a goal of policy to increase consumption spending as a means of promoting economic growth, as opposed to limiting consumption spending and thereby raising private saving?

As discussed earlier, this set of questions around saving, investment, and consumption is at the heart of long-standing controversies as to whether an increase in saving is the prior basis for an increase in investment. In our discussion above, we were able to avoid working through this entire debate by posing a more focused question: what are the direct factors influencing investment? Within the consideration of direct factors, it is clear that increasing overall demand in the economy—which includes consumption demand, as well as investment, net exports and government spending—will promote investment and economic growth. We can therefore assume that raising the overall level of consumption of domestically-produced goods in the economy will promote faster economic growth, assuming all other factors are otherwise equal. How then to raise the overall level of consumption?

Consumption and income

Consumption spending will generally vary closely with changes in income. Within our own model for South Africa developed by Professor James Heintz, we find that, within a longer-term framework (i.e. 3–6 years),[3] a 1 percent increase in household income will produce something close to a 1 percent increase in consumption.[4] This result is broadly consistent with the findings of previous models for South Africa and models for other countries. Professor Heintz explains his consumption model in Appendix 3.

Domestic versus imported goods

In 2000, South Africans spent an estimated 92 percent of their total consumption spending on domestically produced goods and 8 percent on imports.[5] Obviously, only the spending on domestic goods promotes economic growth in South Africa. Thus, policy measures to increase the proportion of spending on domestic goods will also promote economic growth in South Africa.

Consumption and interest rates

A fall in interest rates will induce an increase in consumption. According to Heintz's model, the effect of this will be weak in the short run, but will become more significant within a three–six-year time frame. Thus, if the interest rate on lending falls from say, 10 percent to 9 percent, this should lead to an increase in consumption of about 2 percent. That would mean that, at the 2004 household consumption level of R870 billion, lowering the average lending rate from 10 to 9 percent would bring R17.4 billion more spending into the South African economy. This result is also broadly consistent with findings of previous studies on South African consumption behavior.[6]

There are two distinct channels through which this interest rate effect will work in South Africa. One effect is that the lower interest rates will encourage consumers to borrow more, and thereby increase their purchases of homes, cars, and consumer durables. The other effect will be to lower the payments households have to make on their existing debts, since payments on most debts vary with changes in interest rates. Through this channel, even if consumers do not borrow more money due to the fall in interest rates, they will still have more income to spend, since it will require less money to pay off their existing debts.

Consumption and inflation

Another feature of Heintz's model is that increases in inflation will lead to a decline in consumption spending in the short run, i.e. within the first six months after an inflationary increase. However, these effects of a moderate rise in inflation will dissipate after roughly six months. Overall, therefore, the impact of moderate increases of inflation on consumption will be negligible as long as real disposable income remains unchanged. Inflation that results in a reduction in real household incomes would have a negative impact on consumption.

The three key policy considerations for promoting growth through consumption will therefore be: 1) raising incomes; 2) increasing the proportion of spending on domestically produced goods; and 3) lowering interest rates.

Among these three, we again need to consider the issue of time-sequencing of policies.

Time sequencing of policies

Income channel

Raising incomes will be an effect of economic growth. In particular, higher incomes will result from increasing the number of jobs and raising incomes for the poor. But we cannot expect to obtain much of a boost in consumption through this channel until there is a prior expansion in jobs and economic growth.

Domestic spending channel

Increasing the share of domestic goods in the overall consumption basket will result through a longer-term strategy of building up import-competitive industries in South Africa while maintaining a stable and competitive exchange rate. It will also occur as the income distribution becomes more equalized, since lower-income households will have a higher proportion of domestically produced goods in their consumption basket than more affluent households. Low-income households will spend most of their incomes on food, housing, and services such as transportation.

Interest rate channel

Here again, the policy of lowering interest rates will have the advantage of providing a clear short-term time-sequencing between the policy intervention and its intended effects. A fall in the interest rate will induce more spending, which in turn promotes economic growth and investment in a clear sequence of steps: i.e. 1) lower interest rates lead to 2) more consumption spending; which produces 3) an increase in overall spending; leading to 4) more investment.

Net Exports

An export-led growth strategy is of course a major feature of the neoliberal approach to promoting economic growth in developing countries. There is no question that developing countries in general, and South Africa in particular, can benefit through increasing their net exports. Among other things, for South Africa to maintain a healthy level of net exports relaxes the constraints on the country's balance of payments that might otherwise result from a rising rate of imports as economic growth accelerates.   However, the relevant question for South Africa is to determine realistically whether net exports can serve as the primary engine of economic growth and job creation at present or in the foreseeable future. Our view, as we discuss below, is that this is not likely, even while we also recognize clear benefits through promoting exports as one component of a broader growth strategy. As such we favor a balanced approach, in which exports are seen as one component, though not the primary engine, of an overall growth strategy. This approach seems fully consistent with the ASGISA framework, at least in its current preliminary form.

The benefits of a strong export sector are clear. First, successful exporting firms are a major source of decent jobs in high-productivity industries. These sectors can also generate important up- and downstream linkages to labor intensive industries, such as agriculture, that will primarily serve the domestic market. We therefore aim to propose a set of balanced export-promoting and sectoral policies as one feature of an overall program to accelerate economic growth, expand employment and reduce poverty. We do not expect that such policies will generate a surge in net exports or employment, since, among other things, the current South African economy is also still strongly dependent on imports in several key areas. Indeed, according to Ndikumana's investment model, investment growth responded positively to appreciations of the rand. This suggests that, at least for investors, they rely more heavily on obtaining imported inputs and capital goods at lower rand prices than they do on selling the products they produce on export markets.

Even while export promotion will not be the primary source of growth in the economy, it will still be important to sustain a successful export sector of the economy in order to allow the economy to grow at an accelerated rate without creating an excessive demand for imports relative to export capacity. It is with this policy concern also in mind that we review factors influencing both exports and imports in South Africa.

Trade, export growth, and employment

In the 1990s, South Africa continued a process of trade liberalization that began in the 1980s with an aim to integrate the country more fully into the global economy. Through this period, trade protections were reduced on average (Cassim et al. 2003, Department of Trade and Industry 2002, Edwards 2001a). Although the 1990s can be generally characterized as a period of liberalization, it is important to recognize that significant levels of protection remain in place (Cassim et al. 2003, Fedderke and Vaze 2001). Furthermore, the extent of liberalization varies from sector to sector and the level of enforce-

Figure 4.3 Exports as a Percentage of GDP in South Africa, 1960–2005

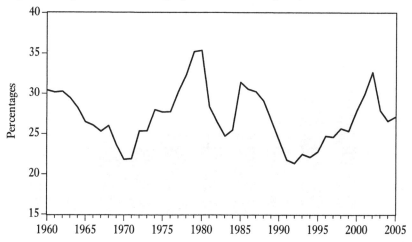

Source: Reserve Bank of South Africa.

ment remains uneven (van Seventer 2001, Cassim et al. 2003, Fedderke and Vaze 2001).

Trade liberalization in the post-apartheid era has been seen as an important component of a more general process of "transformation towards a competitive outward-oriented economy" (National Treasury 1996) articulated in the government's early macroeconomic growth strategy. Greater integration was to give South Africa access to new markets, expose industries to competitive pressures to erode apartheid-era inefficiencies, reduce the cost of imported industrial inputs, allow the country to take advantage of scale economies, and encourage the economy to move up the value chain in export-oriented industries. In this regard, trade liberalization was an important part of an overall strategy aimed at industrial diversification and restructuring.

As we see in Figure 4.3, exports as a percent of GDP have increased since 1994. This provides evidence of a growing outward-orientation of the South African economy. Exports as a share of GDP only reached similar magnitudes in the late 1970s and early 1980s during a speculative rise in the price of gold. However, the recent growth in exports cannot be explained simply as an outcome of increased openness. The fall in the value of the rand during much of this period contributed significantly to the expansion of exports.[7]

The majority of South Africa's exports are currently purchased by advanced industrial economies—approximately 66 percent in 2003. Figure 4.4 shows the share of exports by destination country or region. The United Kingdom, the United States, Japan, Germany, and other European Union countries are the main mar-

Figure 4.4 Share of South African Exports by Country/Region, 2005

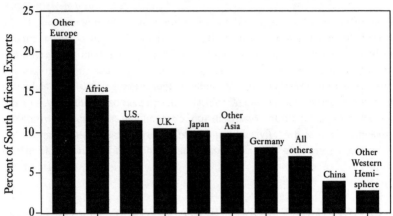

Source: IMF Direction of Trade Statistics (2006).

kets for South African exports. Improving access to these markets through bilateral and multilateral negotiations remains a priority for the country's trade policy. However, market access will also depend on the country's competitiveness relative to these importing economies and other developing country exporters.

The impact of trade liberalization on employment and earnings remains an area of controversy. On the one hand, critics of South Africa's current rate of liberalization argue that global integration has been a significant cause of the country's poor performance in job creation. On the other hand, proponents of liberalization counter that trade policy has had a net positive impact on employment, while other factors, such as technological change or excessive labor costs, are responsible for low rates of employment growth.

The expansion of exports has contributed to economic growth and has had an undeniably positive impact on employment, if considered in isolation (Edwards 2001a). However, an assessment of the impact of liberalization cannot be limited to an examination of export trends. There is general consensus that import penetration increased rapidly during the post-apartheid years (Edwards and Golub 2004, Cassim et al. 2003, Edwards 2001a and b, Bell and Cattaneo 1997). The net impact on employment depends on how the positive effects of export growth balance with the negative effects of greater import penetration.

Assessing the effect of liberalization on employment is made more complex by the differential impact of export growth and import penetration on the various sectors of the economy. In general, exports have expanded in relatively more capital-intensive sectors of the South African economy while import penetration has been concentrated in the most labour-intensive sectors (Edwards 2001a,

Bell and Cattaneo 1997). This dynamic is paradoxical: South Africa, with high rates of unemployment and a large labor surplus, is increasingly exporting capital, but importing labor. It raises serious concerns that trade liberalization will be job-destroying on average (Bell and Cattaneo 1997). This pattern is clearly consistent with the broader evidence we have reviewed on rising capital intensity over the aggregate South African economy.

Sectoral analysis of the manufacturing sector suggests that industrial composition in South Africa has not shifted dramatically during the post-apartheid period (Chabane et al. 2003, Edwards 2001a). Much of the increase in capital-intensity of the South African economy happened *within* sectors and was not a result of capital-intensive sectors increasing their share of total production in response to trade liberalization. Taking all these factors into account, research suggests that the net impact of trade on employment in recent years has been positive, but small (Edwards 2001a). However, the estimated impact of patterns of trade on employment cannot be ascribed to trade liberalization alone. As mentioned above, more competitive exchange rates during much of the post-apartheid era would have bolstered export performance and limited the harm caused by import penetration. If the exchange rate remained at its 1994 level throughout this period, the net impact of trade liberalization on employment could very likely have been negative.

The growing capital-intensity of exports reduces the direct employment-creating potential of expanding trade. However, growth in exports can have indirect effects on employment by raising national incomes, increasing demand for the products of upstream industries, and generating multiplier effects elsewhere in the economy. This is most likely to happen when the growth in exports is associated with movements up the global value chain so that South Africa captures an increasing share of global value added. However, export-driven increases in value added are not a foregone conclusion. For example, in many countries, increased product assembly and production of components for high value-added global industries (e.g. electronics and motor vehicles) has not raised the value added of manufactured exports (UNCTAD 2002). This occurs when intense competition in these segments of the global production networks and reliance on imported inputs limit the value added that these sectors capture.

In summary, trends in international trade have not had a sizeable positive impact on economic growth or employment in South Africa. The growth and employment gains associated with export growth have largely been offset by the negative impact of import penetration. The increasing capital-intensity of exports also raises doubts as to whether an export-led growth strategy will be able to meaningfully address the country's unemployment challenge. This is not to claim that export growth has not had positive impacts on employment in recent years, but rather to question whether the current magnitudes of the employment effects are sufficient to significantly contribute to reducing unemployment.

These observations lead to an overall policy approach: to continue to promote exports because it creates decent jobs and good opportunities for sectors of the economy to grow. In addition, exports will need to continue to grow to prevent a trade imbalance from emerging, assuming that imports will increase along with an accelerated rate of economic growth. At the same time, based on the evidence to date, one should not expect there to be a big boost to economic growth coming directly from net exports.

Government Spending

As mentioned above, increases in government spending financed by a fiscal deficit will provide a direct injection of spending into the domestic economy. This deficit-financed increase in government spending, in turn, will increase investment through the overall spending channel—i.e. investment increases in response to increases in overall spending in the economy.

At the same time, increasing the fiscal deficit raises other issues beyond simply the straightforward fact that it is a reliable means of injecting spending into the economy in the short run. As mentioned above, the deficit also sets off countervailing forces, such as the fact that the greater availability of government bonds for sale allows investors to purchase these bonds rather than spend their money on new productive investments in buildings and machinery.

Given this array of countervailing factors, it will be necessary to address the overall effects of deficit spending within a broader framework of the government's fiscal policy stance. This is an issue to which we return in Chapter 5 of this study.

INCREASING LABOR INTENSITY

We have seen earlier the evidence on South Africa's rapidly declining rate of labor intensity relative to the economy's total production of goods and services. We saw, for example, that just between 1994 and 2001, nearly two fewer workers were used in formal employment to produce R1 million in output. We also have seen from our simple hypothetical exercise projecting alternative economic growth and labor intensity projections into 2014, that, independent of changes in the economy's growth rate, around 2 million jobs will be lost if this pattern of declining labor intensity continues through the next decade.

The government has advanced a major initiative to promote labor intensive production methods. This is the so-called Expanded Public Works Program (EPWP), which is precisely a measure to promote labor intensive techniques in many of the governments' public works projects. However, the EPWP, at its current level of implementation, is not capable of generating a significant improvement in overall employment. Moreover, the information we have to date suggests that the government has no plans in place to significantly increase the EPWP program beyond the measures currently being pursued.

In this section, we begin by reviewing the basic problems with the EPWP at its current level of implementation. We then shift our focus to examine a second, related approach to reversing the trend toward declining labor intensity. This is to promote accelerated growth among South African firms that are capable of generating high "employment multpliers"—that is, firms that will produce a large number of jobs throughout the South African economy for a given amount of spending, utilizing their current production techniques. Identifying such firms will, in turn, serve as a basis for our later discussions in which we propose a program of credit subsidies to promote the growth of labor intensive business expansion.

Expanded Public Works Program

The most prominently discussed explicit initiative in the area of job creation is the Expanded Public Works Program (EPWP). To date, this has been developed as a five-year, R20 billion government program. As mentioned above, we are not aware of plans within the ASGISA initiative to expand the size of this program.

The program, to date, includes the following components:

1. *R15 billion for infrastructure investments*—increasing the labor-intensity of government-funded infrastructure projects, including building of roads, bridges, and irrigation systems;
2. *R4 billion for environmental investments*—creating work opportunities in public environmental improvement programs; and
3. *R600 million for social services*—creating work opportunities in public social programs, e.g. home-based care workers and early childhood development workers.

The aim of this program is to create one million "cumulative work opportunities" over five years. Included in the one million work opportunities are both part- and full-time jobs. According to the legislation which governs the EPWP, all jobs created under the program are to be limited to no more than two years in duration. This is true even while employment at least in the areas of environmental improvement and social services are not project-specific and, in principle, could be of longer duration. In practice, almost all the jobs created through the program are full-time. But all of them are temporary, with an average duration of four months. Moreover, only 200,000 people are employed in this program at any one time.

In what sense does such a program constitute an "expanded" public works program? In his September 2004 article (2004a) in *ASIST*, Sean Phillips, the director of the program within the Department of Public Works, focuses on three considerations (see also Phillips 2004b):

1. Public works programs are being expanded beyond the traditional focus on infrastructure into social, environmental, and economic work activities;
2. The EPWP does not involve the development of a new program—it involves the consolidation and expansion of existing best practices across government; and
3. The intention is to stimulate an increase in budgets for components of the program that prove to be successful.

In principle, the government's initiative to pursue an expanded public works program as a means of increasing employment is a major positive development. However, as it is being implemented, the program is not capable of significantly reducing unemployment or poverty. This is true despite reports in the press that may have created inflated expectations. For example, an article in the *Cape Times* under the heading "Massive Public Works Jobs Plan to Deal Blow to Poverty and Lift Economy to New Level" includes the following passage:

> The government is to unveil a 'massive' public works jobs plan to deal a blow to poverty and take the country to a new level of economic development. Speaking yesterday at the release of the Towards a Ten Year Review, government spokesman Joel Netshitenzhe said the plan would lead to the employment of hundreds of thousands of people at a time. "It will be quite massive. It might not require new resources but it will involve better utilisation of projects that exist already" (17/10/03).[8]

There are three basic problems with the EPWP as it has been implemented to date. The first is that it is simply too small to be expected to make a serious dent in the country's unemployment problem. Referring to the R3 billion/year for public infrastructure expenditures, McCord and van Seventer (2004) have generated a provisional estimate that this level of spending will produce a net increase in employment of about 80,000 jobs/year. The term "net" here refers to the fact that the program does not entail new government expenditures on infrastructure, but rather that more labor-intensive methods of production will be utilized with the projects that have already been budgeted. The net creation of jobs through this program therefore refers to the number of jobs created through utilizing labor-intensive production technologies as opposed to machine-intensive methods. McCord and van Seventer describe, for example, the pilot Gundo Lashu road-building project in Limpopo that utilized labor intensive methods. According to their preliminary estimate, the total employment from this project was four times greater than what would have occurred through utilizing machine-based techniques.

This increase in employment that results from utilizing the labor–intensive methods is certainly to be welcomed. However, given an official labor market of 15.8 million, with an official unemployment rate of 26.2 percent (4.1 million people), the generation of 80,000 net jobs from the EPWP would reduce the unemployment rate by one–half of a percentage point—i.e. unemployment would fall from 26.2 to 25.7 percent. This is less than the statistical margin of error in the estimation of the unemployment rate.

The second problem with the program is its stipulation that all employment opportunities created under the program are to be of limited duration—being employed, for example, on a single road–building project with the job ending once the road has been successfully completed. It is true that jobs involving the construction of infrastructure lend themselves naturally to a limited, project–specific time commitment. However, jobs in the areas of environmental maintenance and social services do not reach such natural completion points. There is nothing inherent in these types of jobs that would make them limited in duration.

The fact that the jobs are stipulated to be of limited duration is especially problematic because such jobs do not generally provide longer–term benefits to workers. Thus, in surveying workers who had been employed in public works projects in Limpopo and KwaZulu Natal, Anna McCord of the University of Cape Town (2004a) found that the stability of employment and income were the most important things workers were seeking through the employment opportunities generated by public works projects. These considerations were more important than the amount of money being earned during the time of employment. Moreover, McCord found that those who worked at temporary jobs in public works did not improve their prospects for permanent jobs. Indeed, in her survey of former workers on the Gundo Lashu program in Limpopo, McCord found that the unemployment rate among former public works project employees was 80 percent, compared with a mean rate of 60 percent among the rural Limpopo population. This finding contradicts the anticipation of proponents that one important benefit of even such temporary jobs is that they would provide valuable labor market experience to people who have been chronically underemployed. Even the brief job experience provided by the EPWP is supposed to increase the attachment of the chronically underemployed to the formal labor market. This appears not to be the case. And because these short–term public works jobs do not appear to provide longer–term labor market benefits to the workers employed by them, it is not surprising that, according to McCord, they also are not likely to provide longer–term benefits in terms of poverty reduction.

The third problem is with the basic idea of relying on increases in the labor intensity of existing infrastructure projects as a major source of job creation. Again, increasing labor intensity without significantly sacrificing efficiency is a desirable goal in its own right. However, it is not likely to yield significant benefits in employment growth even if we allowed that *all* infrastructure projects currently budgeted in South Africa—i.e. the roughly R30 billion/year in spending, rather than the R4 billion currently falling under the rubric of the EPWP—followed the principle of increasing labor intensity. We can see this through the following simple exercise.

1. As we saw in Table 2.4, the employment/output ratio for the entire economy, including both formal and informal types of jobs, in 2004 was 8.6 jobs/R1 million in output. Taking the inverse of this figure—an output/employment ratio—we obtain that every employed worker produces, on average, roughly R116,000 in output per year (i.e. R1 million/8.6 workers).
2. If we assume that this infrastructure is produced at roughly the average output/employment ratio for the economy overall, this means that the R30 billion expenditure on infrastructure projects would employ a little less than 260,000 people (i.e. R30 billion/116,000).
3. Assume that more labor-intensive production methods were utilized on all R30 billion in new infrastructure spending, such that the demand for labor doubled per unit of infrastructure provision. This is an implausibly large shift in relative labor intensity, but is nevertheless useful for illustration. Such a shift in labor intensity of infrastructure production would mean that the infrastructure expenditures would directly produce an additional 260,000 jobs relative to what would otherwise result through spending at the existing output/employment ratio. Note that there would be no large-scale multiplier effects from this shift to more labor intensive methods, since the program does not call for an increased level of overall spending by the government.

A net increase in employment of 260,000 jobs would certainly be welcome in South Africa. However, to put this gain in perspective, it would mean reducing the official level of unemployment from 4.1 to a bit less than 3.9 million people, which translates into a decline in the official unemployment rate from 26.2 to 24.6 percent. Note that this same basic conclusion would hold even if we assumed—still more implausibly—that the labor intensity on the R30 billion in infrastructure projects were to *triple* relative to current prevailing techniques. This would produce roughly 500,000 new jobs, which again would represent major progress. But it would still mean that 3.6 million as opposed to 4.1 million people would be jobless—an unemployment rate of 23.0 rather than 26.2 percent.

The overall conclusion from this exercise is that even if we greatly expand the concept of the EPWP to cover fully R30 billion/year in infrastructure projects, this still wouldn't make a serious dent in reducing unemployment, and thereby, in reducing poverty as well. This is because the concept of the EPWP is based on shifting existing levels of government expenditure commitments toward more labor intensive methods rather than promoting labor-intensive activities within an overall program of increased expenditures.

Put in other terms, there will not be a significant improvement in the jobs situation unless there are significant increases in spending from somewhere in the economy. Something like a large-scale EPWP can be a significant feature of a broader initiative to increase spending, growth, and employment. From the preliminary materials, it appears that the ASGISA program is aiming to commit significant new funds for infrastructure, but the spending components of the ASGISA remain unclear at the time of writing.[9] But for the EPWP to be most effective in meeting the aims of job creation and poverty reduction, the emphasis of the additional expenditures should be on: 1) creating permanent jobs as opposed to temporary work opportunities; and 2) giving significantly higher priority to spending on road maintenance as well as construction, environmental protection, and social services, where labor intensity will be most high, and where opportunities are greater for longer-term job security.

Targeting Activities with High Employment Impacts

It is clear that there will not be any significant increase of employment through increasing the labor intensity of public infrastructure projects alone, much less the subset of infrastructure projects targeted by the EPWP. The more effective approach would be to design policies with the greatest potential to generate jobs throughout the entire economy. How should this be accomplished?

It is important to recognize, first of all, that activities that will produce the biggest overall boost in jobs are not necessarily the activities that utilize the most labor-intensive production methods. This is because some activities may be relatively capital intensive in their production techniques, but they may purchase products from other sectors in the South African economy that are highly labor intensive.

The clearest example of this kind of linked relationship between capital- and labor-intensive industries within the South African economy is that between agriculture and agro-processing, which includes grain mills, meat, the production of dairy products, and the generation of biofuels. Agriculture is highly labor intensive in South Africa, while agro-processing is highly capital intensive. However, agro-processing firms in South Africa purchase their raw materials from farmers, South African farmers in particular for the most part. As such, domestic jobs in agriculture will expand as an outgrowth of expansion in agro-processing. This relationship between the domestic agricultural and agro-processing industries—where agro-processing purchases products from agriculture—is termed an "upstream linkage" in the professional literature. Correspondingly, a "downstream linkage" refers to a relationship in which, for example, agro-processing firms sell products to other South African firms, such as breweries.

In this section, we present evidence that distinguishes industries according to their total job-creating potential, including both direct job generation and their employment multipliers. The point of this exercise is to demonstrate some possibilities for job creation through encouraging strong job-creating activities to grow at a rate in excess of the economy's average growth path.

At the same time, as we have described earlier and will examine in detail in Chapter 5, our general policy approach is not to select any particular sectors or industries per se for subsidies to promote their accelerated growth. Our general policy approach, as described elsewhere in the study, is rather to allow producers in all industries to demonstrate their capacity to achieve high employment gains. We do make exceptions to this general approach, in particular, with small-scale agriculture. We do also support the promotion of small-scale business activities generally, both individually-owned SMMEs and cooperatives, though without specifying *sectors* among these small-scale and cooperative enterprises. But the point of our discussion here is to illustrate the types of activities that are capable of generating employment, then considering what the impact would be on the economy's overall employment path if such activities were encouraged to grow at an accelerated rate.

As such, our approach is less sharply targeted than the government's ASGISA initiative, which does identify specific sectors as priorities, including business process out-sourcing and tourism as "immediate priorities," and biofuels along with agriculture and agrarian reform as "top priority" sectors. At the same time, our more open-ended approach to subsidizing employment creation is not incompatible with the government's identification of priority sectors for growth. As we will see from our exercises in this section, many of the priority sectors selected by the government are ones whose firms are likely to be able to generate large positive employment gains.

Labor intensity and employment multipliers

To illustrate the crucial distinction between labor intensity and employment multipliers among industries within the South African economy, in Table 4.2 we rank 10 major industries of the South African economy according to these two criteria. Again, we are measuring labor intensity as the ratio of total employment in the industry per R1 million of the industry's output.

It is important to note that the employment multiplier for each industry is the total number of *formal jobs* generated in South Africa when the industry produces R1 million worth of goods or services. Using the available methodology and statistics on industrial employment linkages, we are not able to estimate linkages between formal industrial sectors of the economy and informal employment. However, it will be useful later to consider some assumptions about the formal/informal economy employment linkages. Doing so will enable us to provide a broader picture of the effects of our employment-targeted program.

Table 4.2 Employment Generation in South Africa on an Industry-by-Industry Basis

A) LABOR INTENSITY BY INDUSTRY:

Employment levels in industry per R1 million in output

Agriculture	18.6
Apparel and textiles	9.0
Social and community services	5.6
Mining	4.0
Wood, paper, and furniture	4.0
Capital goods	3.9
Motor vehicles	2.8
Accommodation and travel	2.2
Agro-processing	2.3
Chemicals	1.5

B) EMPLOYMENT MULTIPLIERS BY INDUSTRY:

Total employment created in South Africa per R1 million in industry sales

Agriculture	27.9
Apparel and textiles	18.2
Agro-processing	18.0
Wood, paper, and furniture	15.3
Social and community services	14.9
Mining	13.0
Accommodation and travel	11.7
Capital goods	11.3
Chemicals	9.5
Motor vehicles	8.6

C) EMPLOYMENT LINKAGES BY INDUSTRY:

Employment multiplier–industry labor intensity

Agro-processing	15.7
Wood, paper, and furniture	11.3
Mining	11.0
Accommodation and travel	9.5
Social and community services	9.3
Agriculture	9.2
Apparel and textiles	9.2
Chemicals	8.0
Capital goods	7.4
Motor vehicles	5.8

Source: See Appendix 3.

As we see in Panel A of Table 4.2, agriculture is, by a significant amount, the most labor intensive industry operating in South Africa, with 18.6 workers employed in the industry for every R1 million of output produced. The next most labor-intensive industry is apparel and textiles, which employs 9.0 workers per R1 million in output. By contrast, agro-processing is next to the last when ranked according to labor intensity, employing only 2.3 workers per R1 million of output.

However, we see in Panel B that the rankings change significantly by measuring the full employment multipliers of the various sectors. Agriculture does remain first in the rankings, generating a total of 27.9 jobs in South Africa for every additional R1 million of final demand for the industry's products.[10] Apparel also remains second on the list, with 18.2 domestic jobs created for every R1 million in final demand. However, we now see that agro-processing has risen to third on the list, creating 18.0 million domestic jobs per R1 million in final demand, i.e. virtually an identical amount of total employment creation as the apparel industry. The wood/paper/furniture industry also rises substantially when ranked in terms of total employment multipliers. It generates 15.3 domestic jobs for every R1 million in final demand, even though production within the industry itself utilizes only 4.0 workers per R1 million of output. At the other end, it is useful to note the two industries with the weakest employment multipliers—chemicals at 9.5 jobs, and motor vehicles at 8.6 jobs per R1 million of final demand.

Given these two sets of results, it is also useful to observe the industries with the largest upstream and downstream domestic employment linkages—that is, the largest difference between the employment multipliers of the industry and the level of job creation within the industry itself for every R1 million of final demand. We show these linkage rankings in Panel C of Table 4.2. As we see there, agro-processing has the largest employment linkages by a significant amount, generating 15.7 domestic jobs through these linkages. Wood, paper and furniture is ranked second in terms of employment linkages, generating 11.3 indirect jobs in South Africa per R1 million in final demand. The motor vehicle industry is least effective among those industries listed here, producing only 5.8 up- and downstream jobs in South Africa per R1 million in final demand.

Additional criteria in choosing activities for subsidies

In evaluating the types of activities to select for government promotion, other factors of course need to be considered beyond strictly their employment effects. We would suggest that three additional factors should be of central concern. These are 1) balance between expanding jobs and enhancing productivity; 2) balance of payments constraints; and 3) poverty reduction. We consider these in turn.

1.   *Balance between expanding jobs and promoting productivity.* South Africa faces a rather difficult challenge in that, while facing the need to greatly expand

employment opportunities within the country, it also justifiably seeks to promote productivity growth and the utilization of modern technologies. These two purposes can be in competition, given that, at a given level of output, the increasing utilization of machines in production will entail relatively less demand for workers. To balance these potentially competing purposes, it will be desirable to promote the growth of some capital-intensive industries. The optimal way to achieve this balance will be to target some industries for growth that are themselves capital intensive but that maintain strong upstream linkages with domestic labor-intensive industries. According to the evidence in Table 4.2, the most appropriate industry by this criterion is clearly agro-processing, including the ASGISA "top priority" sector of biofuels. Wood/paper/furniture is also an appropriate industry by this criterion.

Firms within the mining industry may seem to be an appropriate choice for subsidized growth. The mining industry has been a major employer in South Africa and maintains a high employment multiplier at present. But the rate of extraction from the mines has been heavy for decades. As a result, the quality of the remaining mineral deposits has been depleted and the costs of extraction have risen correspondingly. It therefore seems unlikely that firms within the mining industry would be likely candidates to target for subsidized growth. Finally, according to this criterion, firms within the motor vehicle industry would also likely be inappropriate targets for subsidized growth. As we see from the industry-wide data, motor vehicle producers, likely to be relatively capital-intensive firms, are also likely to operate with weak employment multipliers.

2. *Balance of payments constraints.* As we have discussed earlier, we do not expect South Africa to gain a significant boost in employment growth by increasing its volume of international trade. At the same time, the economy cannot sustain a growth path geared toward employment generation—or indeed, toward any other goal—if it is unable to at least maintain growth in exports comparable to its demand for imports.

There are two interrelated but distinct ways to consider the need to maintain balance in the economy's degree of integration with the global economy. The first way is straightforward: evaluating industries with respect to their capacity both to succeed as exporters and to compete with foreign firms seeking to supply imports to the South African market. The second consideration is the extent of linkages that exists between industries in South Africa, and among sectors within any given industry. Here we refer to an industry's downstream as well as its upstream linkages. Industries with strong up- and downstream linkages will promote growth in the domestic economy and thereby diminish demand for imports as growth proceeds. Industries with strong domestic economy linkages should therefore be promoted, while those with weak linkages should either be discouraged or restructured to strengthen these linkages.

We obtain a sense of the characteristics of the 10 industries we are considering by these two criteria in Table 4.3. Here we show the 10 industries in this section according to four criteria: 1) upstream linkages; 2) downstream linkages; 3) penetration into export markets; and 4) penetration into South African markets from imports. The table reports index numbers for each of these four categories. For each category, we show index numbers that can range from 0 to 10. The table also explains how we derived each of the index numbers. The 10 industries are listed in order of their employment multipliers, so that agriculture is listed first, apparel and textiles is listed second, and so on. Among these industries, agriculture scores relatively well in terms of both up- and downstream linkages. Its global orientation is modest both in terms of exports and imports. This means that South Africa's agricultural sector is in a position to grow without having to focus on maintaining its share of the domestic markets against import competition.

In contrast with agriculture, apparel and textiles ranks substantially lower in terms of both up- and downstream linkages. Moreover, the index number reflecting the extent of import penetration within apparel and textiles is roughly double the index number for export penetration. These figures reflect the fact that textiles and apparels produced elsewhere in Southern Africa—such as Mauritius and Madagascar—as well as from China have been successful in penetrating the South African market. Within the existing policy framework, it is not likely that the extent of this competition will diminish in the foreseeable future. As such, our reading of the evidence suggests that, within the existing policy framework, apparel and textiles would not generally include a large number of firms that would be capable of generating large employment multipliers. At the same time, we recognize that the ASGISA program has targeted apparel and textiles as one of its "medium-term priority sectors." If the ASGISA program did entail efforts to achieve competitiveness and promote local sourcing, clothing and textiles firms could certainly become effective recipients of support in terms of their capacity to promote employment.

Working down the list, agro-processing, wood/paper/furniture, and social/community services all perform well in terms of their global orientation, in that their export indexes are high relative to their import indexes. Thus, promoting accelerated growth among firms in these industries will not place a significant strain on the country's balance of payments. Of these industries, all but social/community services generate reasonably strong up- and downstream linkages. The weak linkages for social and community services is not particular to the structure of the South African economy, but is rather characteristic of the nature of this industry. That is, with services such as com-

Table 4.3 Balance of Payments Considerations for Selected South African Industries

	Domestic economy linkages		Global economy orientation	
	Upstream linkages	Downstream linkages	Penetration into export markets	Penetration into South African markets by imports
Agriculture	6.5	7.2	1.2	0.6
Apparel and textiles	4.5	3.8	1.0	1.9
Agro-processing	7.9	3.0	0.8	0.8
Wood, paper, and furniture	6.8	6.6	2.1	1.0
Social and community services	3.6	2.0	0.2	0.2
Mining	6.0	3.1	7.9	2.0
Accommodation and travel	6.4	4.8	2.0	1.8
Capital goods	5.1	5.3	1.5	4.4
Chemicals	6.8	6.2	1.6	2.0
Motor vehicles	3.7	3.7	1.6	3.0

Upstream Linkages: Domestic inputs as a percentage of production costs
Downstream Linkages: Domestic industrial demand as a percent of total industrial and final demand
Export Orientation: Exports as a percentage of total final demand
Import Penetration: Imports as a percentage of total supply
Note: Figures are index numbers. Definition of index numbers is presented above.
Source: See Appendix 3.

munity-level health care, social support, and retail services like personal care, the service being purchased is primarily the direct labor effort of the worker at the business location, i.e. the social worker, nurse, or barber.

Finally, the industries that rank relatively low according to their employment multipliers—i.e. capital goods, chemicals, and motor vehicles— all do poorly in terms of their global orientation, with relatively higher indexes for import penetration than export orientation. Thus, given their current structures, the growth in all these industries will tend to exert more pressure on South Africa's balance of payments. This does not mean that firms in these industries should not be promoted for accelerated growth under any circumstances. However, it does mean that if policymakers choose to promote firms in these industries, they should recognize the problems that exist in terms of both their job-creating potential and their balance of payments constraints. We will examine further the merits of pursuing restructuring within these industries later in this study. However, our present purpose is to identify industries that are most likely to be capable of promoting labor intensity over the next decade without exerting pressure on the balance of payments. The capital goods, chemicals, and motor vehicle industries do not rank high according to these present criteria.

3. *Poverty reduction.* As we will discuss in more detail below, it will not be possible to rely on employment generation alone as a means of improving the welfare of the poor in South Africa. Other measures in the area of social transfer programs will also be necessary here. At the same time, if one is targeting specific industries for accelerated growth, one important criterion for choosing industries is whether the activities that take place within any given industry—either in terms of employment possibilities or the goods and services the industry produces—will benefit the poor.

By this criterion, one clear priority sector is small-scale agriculture. This is first of all because small-scale agriculture remains the activity on which large numbers of low-income families rely as an important, if frequently supplemental, source of food. And while the proportion of low-income households engaged in agriculture as a primary source of income is small at present, this is in part due to the financial barriers to obtaining and maintaining a small holding—barriers that could be substantially relaxed through a large-scale credit subsidy program. [11] Another consideration is that when the domestic production of food expands, this should exert downward pressure on food prices. When food prices decline, the poor receive a relatively greater welfare gain than those at higher income levels, since food constitutes a relatively greater share of the total consumption basket of the poor. Of course, food prices won't decline to the extent that the agricultural sector is dominated by large-scale oligopolistic firms, who both have pricing power and are responding to global commodity price fluctuations. This then provides an additional reason for targeting agricultural smallholders for accelerated growth, as opposed to large-scale firms with oligopolistic pricing power. The other industry that should be a clear priority by this criterion is social and community services. This is first of all because, to a significant extent, the services provided by this industry will directly benefit the poor. Community health clinics promoting AIDS prevention and treatment are an obvious case in point. In addition, small-scale businesses can grow relatively easily in areas such as personal services, thus offering opportunities for the poor to establish their own small-scale businesses.

An illustrative exercise in promoting employment growth

Considering the evidence we have reviewed on labor intensity and employment multipliers for the formal economy, as well as the additional considerations for targeting industries—i.e. combining capital and labor intensity, balance of payments and social inclusion of the poor—it will be useful to consider the benefits of promoting for accelerated growth firms that operate in industries that score well by these criteria. Thus, for the purpose of this exercise, we consider that firms in five industries are targeted for accelerated growth. These industries are agriculture, agro-processing, wood/furniture/paper, social/community services, and accommodation/travel. We are focusing on industry-level targeting for the purpose of this exercise because the available data on labor intensity and employment multipliers are at the industry level. But again, as we will discuss more in Chapter 5, our proposal is to offer credit subsidies to firms in all industries that can demonstrate their ability to generate large employment multiplers.

Of these five industries, all but wood/furniture/paper have been identified in some way by the ASGISA as a priority. Tourism is included as an "immediate priority sector," and biofuels—a form of agro-processing—and agriculture itself are the two "top priority sectors." Social and community services as such are not included as among the private sector priorities. However, in the area of "second economy initiatives," areas such as early childhood development, among the EPWP priorities, and SMMEs are identified as priorities.

The ASGISA does also include other sectors as priorities, including business processing outsourcing as an "immediate priority," and chemicals, creative industries, clothing and textiles and downstream minerals beneficiation as "medium-term" priorities. We are not suggesting that firms in these industries should not receive priority support. But we are concerned that, if firms in these areas are to be supported, there is clarity as to their capacity to generate strong positive employment effects.

By the same token, with the industries that we have prioritized in our illustrative exercise, we don't assume that all firms in these industries will be effective in generating domestic employment. That is why, outside of small-scale agriculture, SMMEs, and cooperatives, we argue that firms would need to apply on an individual basis for subsidized credit, the principle means of subsidized support we are proposing in this study.

In Table 4.4, we review data showing the relative size of our five selected industries in the overall South African economy. As Table 4.4 shows, these five industries in combination account for a major share of the overall South African economy, 22.1 percent in terms of total output, and 34.8 percent in terms of overall employment. Hence these industries are large enough as a share of the overall economy that their growth at an accelerated rate would have a major impact on the overall economy. At the same time, these industries in aggregate are not so large that policy interventions to target them would have to be cast too widely to be effective. As we will discuss below, we do think that South African policymakers can establish effective interventions to promote accelerated growth in business activities—in these industries or other industries as well—that would constitute roughly 25–30 percent of GDP. This is roughly the size of these industries considered in aggregate. This is another reason why it is useful to consider these five industries in our illustrative exercise.

Table 4.4 High Employment Growth Industries as Share of South Africa's Output and Employment

	Industry output as share of total output (percentages)	Employment as industry share of total employment(percentages)
Agriculture	3.3	17.1
Agro-processing	4.2	2.7
Wood, paper, and furniture	2.6	2.9
Accommodation/transportation	7.1	4.4
Social/community services	4.9	7.7
TOTALS	22.1	34.8

Source: See Appendix 3.

It is, finally, useful here to also note the disparity between the share of output and share of employment when adding the relative size of these five industries. The disparity is due almost entirely to agriculture. As we see in Table 4.4, agriculture employs 17.1 percent of all formal workers in South Africa but produces only 3.3 percent of all output. These figures clearly suggest the substantial gains that could accrue to South Africa through enhancing agricultural productivity—via measures such as the public works programs targeted at rural infrastructure. It is precisely through raising agricultural productivity, in combination with expanding job opportunities in agriculture, that this gap could diminish between levels of agricultural output and employment.

Employment effects of increased growth with rising labor intensity
In Tables 4.5A–C (see pages 72 and 73), we now consider the combined effects on formal employment of accelerating growth with raising labor intensity via subsidizing firms in these industries for accelerated growth. We illustrate these growth and labor intensity effects in a manner similar to our more simplified hypothetical exercise in Chapter 2.

Thus, in Table 4.5.A, we again show actual economic conditions that prevail in South Africa today in terms of economic growth, employment, and the employment/output ratio. In Table 4.5.B, we then examine the effects on employment over the decade 2005–2014 under three alternative sets of assumptions.

The first set of assumptions is that the South African economy proceeds over the next decade at roughly the same pattern of activity as it had over the decade 1995–2004. That is, we assume that the economy grows at an average annual rate of 3 percent per year, and that the employment/output ratio within each industry of the economy declines at an average rate of 1 percent per year. Under this scenario, as we see, total employment in South Africa in 2014 will be

9.8 million people, and total job creation over the decade will have been roughly 900,000 jobs.

The second set of assumptions is that the average growth rate of the economy accelerates to 4.5 percent, as a result of macroeconomic policy interventions that succeed in promoting growth. However, under this second scenario, there are still no policy interventions to reverse the trend of declining labor intensity. We therefore again assume that the employment/output ratio by industry continues to fall at an average annual rate of 1 percent. Under this scenario, we see that total employment in South Africa will be 10.8 million. The expansion of employment over the 2005–2014 decade will be 1.9 million jobs.

In the third set of assumptions, we allow both for aggregate expansionary policies as well as measures aimed specifically at promoting labor intensity. Specifically, in this illustrative exercise, we assume that the non-subsidized segments of the economy—accounting for, as we saw above, roughly 80 percent of the economy's total output—will receive a stimulus equivalent to that needed to support average economy-wide growth at 4.5 percent per year. However, we now also assume that the subsidized activities, accounting for roughly 20 percent of total output, will receive a proportionately larger growth stimulus of 8 percent.[12] Moreover, because of the efforts to raise labor intensity through rapidly expanding the subsidized activities, we now also assume that the employment/output ratio by industry remains constant over the decade. Under this set of assumptions, we see in Table 4.5.B that overall employment in 2014 will be 12.4 million people. The expansion in employment over the 2005–2014 decade will now total 3.5 million jobs.

In Table 4.5.C, we compare the effects on employment of these three scenarios relative to one another. Thus, the table first shows the difference between the 3 percent growth versus 4.5 percent growth scenarios, with declining labor intensity under both cases. As we see, raising the average annual growth rate to 4.5 percent will yield an additional 1 million jobs by the end of the decade.

Next, we compare the 4.5 percent growth scenario with the scenario in which we promote both the 4.5 percent growth rate for non-subsidized activities and an 8 percent growth stimulus for subsidized activities, yielding an overall growth rate of 5.3 percent plus no decline in the employment/output ratio. As we see, the difference between these two scenarios as of 2014 will be 1.6 million net jobs.

Finally, we compare the effects of allowing the South African economy to proceed along its current path of 3 percent growth with declining labor intensity with the growth path that combines accelerated overall growth and an 8 percent growth stimulus for subsidized activities. Here, of course, we observe the most extreme difference in the two outcomes: the program to raise both overall growth and increased labor intensity will produce 2.6 million more jobs than allowing the South African economy to proceed along its current growth path.

Table 4.5 Employment Effects of Combining Accelerated Economic Growth with Increased Labor Intensity

A) ACTUAL LEVELS OF ECONOMIC ACTIVITY IN 2004

Average GDP growth rate 1994–2004	3.1%
Total employment 2004	11.6 million
Employment/output ratio 2003	8.6 (jobs/R1 million in output)

Source: See Appendix 3.

B) EMPLOYMENT IN 2014 UNDER ALTERNATIVE ASSUMPTIONS

	Employment in 2014	Employment creation, 2005–2014
Scenario 1:		
Steady state from current economic trends	9.8 million	0.9 million
1) 3% annual growth rate		
2) 1% annual decline in employment/output		
Scenario 2:		
Accelerated growth with no credit subsidies	10.8 million	1.9 million
to promote labor intensive growth		
1) 4.5% average annual growth rate		
2) 1% annual decline in employment/output		
Scenario 3:		
Accelerated growth with credit subsidies	12.4 million	3.5 million
to promote labor intensive growth		
1) 4.5% growth for non-subsidized activities		
2) 8% growth for subsidized activities		
3) 5.3% combined average growth for subsidized and non-subsidized activities		
4) Employment/output constant		

Source: See Appendix 3.

Table 4.5 (cont.) *Employment Effects of Combining Accelerated Economic Growth with Increased Labor Intensity*

C) Differences in Employment Creation Scenarios

3% growth with declining employment/output; no labor intensity targeting vs. 4.5% growth with declining employment/output; no labor intensity targeting	1.0 million jobs
4.5% growth with declining employment/output; no labor intensity targeting vs. 5.3% growth with constant employment/output and labor intensity promotion	1.6 million jobs
3% growth with declining employment/output; no labor intensity targeting vs. 5.3% growth with constant employment/output and labor intensity promotion	2.6 million jobs

Overall effects on level of employment and unemployment rate

How do these alternative scenarios for employment growth translate into changes in the economy's overall level of employment, including informal employment? How much is the unemployment rate likely to change? To attempt a rough answer to these questions, we have to make some assumptions about two considerations over the next decade: 1) the growth rate of the labor force; and 2) the growth rate of informal employment as a proportion of the total labor force, what we will term the "informalizaton rate."

We think it is most sensible to work with the simplest possible reasonable assumptions about both of these factors. Given the range of influences that might affect both of them, we are unlikely to achieve more in the way of accuracy by constructing relatively complicated prospective scenarios.

Thus, the first assumption we work with is that South Africa's labor force growth rate will be equal to the 1.9 percent annual projected rate of population growth over the next decade. This assumption simply assumes that the same proportion of the country's total population will be entering the work force over the next decade as does so currently. The second assumption is that the proportion of informal employment in the South African economy—the informalization rate—will remain constant, which is at 27 percent of total employment. In previous research on the relationship between economic growth and informalization in developing countries, Heintz and Pollin (2006) found that average growth rates in the range of 5 percent or more can produce a decline in the proportion of informal employment as a share of total employment. However, more moderate growth rates did not prevent informalization from spreading, though again, on average, the rate of informalization did fall in countries where economic growth was faster. Given that we are projecting an economic growth rate for South Africa roughly in the range of 3–5 percent, it is likely that the rate of informalization will rise above 27 percent in the next decade. If growth gets to the upper limit of this range, of around 5 percent, perhaps the rate will remain at around 27 percent. In any case, by assuming a constant informalization rate of 27 percent, we are making conservative assumptions about the overall growth in employment that will accompany the alternative scenarios we have developed for both economic growth and labor intensity.

In Table 4.6, we present projections for overall employment and unemployment in 2014 under two of the scenarios we have considered in Table 4.5 above. The first is Scenario 1, which is the steady-state scenario of 3 percent average growth and a 1 percent average decline in labor intensity. We then return to Scenario 3, in which we assume a growth rate of 4.5 percent for non-subsidized activities and an 8 percent growth stimulus for the subsidized activities—in this illustrative exercise, the firms that operate in agriculture, agro-processing, wood/paper/furniture, accommodation/transportation, and social/community services. We also assume that the overall labor intensity remains constant. Working with these two additional assumptions about the growth in the labor force and the ratio of informal/total employment, we are now able to see the effects of the two scenarios in terms of overall employment and unemployment.

In particular, under Scenario 1, we see that a total of 13.0 million people will be employed in South Africa in 2014 and 6.5 million will be unemployed. The unemployment rate will be 33.3 percent. Under Scenario 3, a total of 16.5 million people will be employed and 3.0 million will be unemployed. The unemployment rate will be 15.4 percent.

These findings bring us to three major, and interrelated, conclusions about possibilities for significantly improving the employment situation for South Africans over the next decade.

1. It is a matter of great importance whether the economy continues along a path of growth and labor intensity similar to that which occurred between 1994–2004, or whether it succeeds in both accelerating growth generally, and especially promoting rapid growth in the activities within the economy that are either labor intensive or generate high employment multipliers.
2. If the economy continues along the path it experienced between 1994–2004, there is no chance that the government will succeed in meeting its goal of reducing unemployment by half. Quite the contrary, assuming the ratio of informal employment to total employment is unchanged, to continue along the path of the previous decade will only produce a significant increase in the unemployment rate, to something on the order of 33 percent.

Table 4.6 Total Employment and Unemployment Rate in 2014 under Alternative Scenarios for Economic Growth and Labor Intensity

	(1) Labor force	(2) Formal employ-ment	(3) Informal employ-ment	(4) Total employ-ment	(5) Total unemploy-ment	(6) Unemploy-ment rate (= columns 5/1)
Scenario 1: Steady state from current economic trends *1) 3% annual growth rate 2) 1% annual decline in employment/output*	19.5 million	9.8 million	3.2 million	13.0 million	6.5 million	33.3%
Scenario 3: Accelerated growth credit subsidies to promote labor intensity *1) 4.5% growth for non-subsidized activities 2) 8% growth for subsidized activities 3) 5.3% combined average growth for subsidized and non-subsidized activities 4) Employment/output constant*	19.5 million	12.4 million	4.1 million	16.5 million	3.0 million	15.4%

Additional assumptions:
1. Labor force growth is 1.9 percent per year.
2. Informal employment/total employment = 27 percent.

Source: Calculations based on data in Table 4.5.

3. Even if economic growth does accelerate to something like 4.5 percent in non-subsidized areas and 8 percent in subsidized activities, it will still be the case that by 2014 the unemployment rate will be around 15 percent— i.e. even under our favorable Scenario 3, the unemployment rate will not quite fall to half of its current rate of roughly 26 percent as of 2014.

The overall point then is this: only through an aggressive, though still realistic, program of employment targeting will there be any possibility for the South African economy to come close to meeting the government's goal of halving the country's unemployment rate by 2014. At the same time, in the absence of an aggressive program targeted at employment expansion, the like-lihood is very high that opportunities for jobs will worsen, not improve, over the next decade.

Poverty Reduction

Our projections for employment and the unemployment rate over the next decade make clear that, even under an aggressive program of employment targeting over the next decade, it will still be the case that unemployment is likely to be as high as around 15–16 percent in 2014. This means that a very high proportion of South Africans will not themselves benefit from an employment-targeted program over the next decade, even assuming the program is highly successful in meeting its targets for economic growth and labor intensity. This finding only underscores the need for additional policy measures to reduce poverty in South Africa.

We have reviewed a range of proposals by South African policy analysts for expanding poverty reduction programs. To the best of our knowledge, these include:

1.   The Basic Income Grant (BIG).
2.   Expansion of the Expanded Public Works Program, especially in the area of social service delivery. Included here would be, for example, measures to address the HIV/AIDS crisis, such as neighborhood or individual home-care paramedical support.
3.   Expansion of existing pension and income transfer programs covering children, the elderly, and the disabled.
4.   Expansion of government spending on basic health delivery and primary education.

We will not attempt here to explore the specifics or relative merits of these and related proposals. However, in our discussion below on fiscal policy, we will consider the issue of the government's capacity to finance a significant expansion in direct spending on poverty reduction, regardless of the specific breakdown as to how such funds might be allocated. For our purposes, the overriding issue is the clear need to finance an expansion of such activities, given the fact that, even under the most favorable scenario of employment growth, there will still be more than 15 percent unemployment as of 2014.

NOTES

1.   See Pollin (1997) for some detailed perspectives from within the academic literature. Pollin (2003) presents a brief overview of this literature.
2.   Data on the lending/saving ratio for South Africa are from the South Africa Reserve Bank and the International Monetary Fund, *International Financial Statistics.*
3.   After three years, approximately 75 percent of the impact of a change in household disposable income would be realized; after five years, around 90 percent of the impact would be evident.

4. The short-run marginal propensity to consume is estimated to be 0.91. In the long-run, we expect incomes and consumption to increase proportionately. This expectation of an income elasticity of one is consistent with the estimates for South Africa.

5. Calculated from the 2000 Supply and Use Tables, Statistics South Africa. Estimates do not include the value of imported inputs for domestically produced goods.

6. These studies include Fielding (1996), Aron and Muellbauer (2000), and Selvanathan and Selvanathan (2003).

7. The drop off in exports seen in 2003 is partially the result of an appreciation in the value of the rand at that time.

8. This quotation is taken from McCord (2004b), a paper which also includes several other examples of press reports regarding the EPWP.

9. Thus, Davies and van Seventer write in April 2006, "It is difficult to pin down with any great accuracy what the Accelerated & Shared Growth Initiative for South Africa means in terms of fiscal expenditures," (2006, p. 3).

10. By "final demand" we refer to the sale of a good or service to its final user, as opposed to an "intermediate" sale to a business firm that will utilize the good or service to produce some other product.

11. According to the September 2004 Labor Force Survey, approximately 16 percent of poor households have a member of the family engaged in agricultural activities. Of those households that do have members engaged in agriculture, 80 percent do so to provide an extra source of food. Thus, agriculture is not a primary source of either employment, food or income for the poor. We are grateful to Professor Charles Meth for pointing out these illuminating figures.

12. When we use the term "growth stimulus" for an industry, we are referring to a particular magnitude of an initial stimulus that will have multiplier effects on employment and output throughout the entire economy. Therefore, the overall impact on economic growth will be many times larger than the initial stimulus. We use the impact on the overall growth rate to refer to the relative size of the initial stimulus. For example, a "4.5 percent growth stimulus" refers to the size of the stimulus given to a particular industry. If all industries in the economy were given a 4.5 growth stimulus, the economy as a whole would grow at 4.5 percent, taking into account all linkages, leakages, and multiplier effects. In cases where industries are targeted, the relative magnitudes of the stimulus will differ between targeted and non-targeted industries. For a given industry, an 8 percent growth stimulus would be 75 percent larger than a 4.5 percent growth stimulus, because a growth rate of 8 percent is 75 percent larger than a growth rate of 4.5 percent.

5. Policy Interventions for an Employment-Targeted Program

FISCAL POLICIES

There are three basic ways that shifts in the government's fiscal stance might make a significant contribution to employment generation and poverty reduction. They are:

1. *Shifts in the composition of government spending.* Raising the proportion of government spending on employing workers, and correspondingly lowering the proportion of spending on machines and buildings, is the idea behind the Expanded Public Works Program. This is a straightforward method of increasing the amount of employment generated by a given level of spending. In Chapter 4, we have shown how, at current levels of spending, this initiative will make a positive, but only modest, contribution toward employment expansion.

2. *Increases in the tax-financed level of government spending.* Here we refer to increasing the government's level of spending through tax increases, and utilizing the additional government funds for measures that promote employment growth or poverty reduction. The fiscal deficit does not change in this approach. However, aggregate demand could still increase if the tax increases are progressive. Under this scenario, the redistribution of income downward could contribute to an expansion of aggregate demand, since the marginal propensity to consume is higher among lower-income people. The constraint on tax increases is the effect that the higher tax burden would have on investors and consumers, with a significant effect leading to a slowdown in private investment and consumption.

3. *Increasing the fiscal deficit.* This would immediately increase aggregate demand, which in turn could promote employment, regardless of how the additional government funds were spent. But of course, if the funds were also spent on measures that explicitly targeted employment generation or poverty reduction, this would provide for an even larger increase in employment relative to a given increment of fiscal deficit. The constraint on deficit spending as an expansionary tool is "crowding out" of three distinct

types. The first type of crowding out refers to the rise in interest payments as a share of the total government budget. The second type of crowding out refers to the rise in interest rates generated by the increase in government borrowing, with this rise in rates in turn discouraging private sector borrowing and spending. The third type of crowding out is the situation we have considered earlier, where investors channel their funds to the purchase of government bonds—where they earn a safe return—as opposed to utilizing their financial resources for productive investments, i.e. purchasing machines and building structures.

We now consider increased fiscal deficits and tax increases in terms of how they might contribute toward increasing employment and reducing poverty.

Increasing the Fiscal Deficit

As we have discussed earlier, the government committed to a program of budget deficit reductions soon after taking office. We can observe the effects of this commitment in Figure 5.1, which shows the actual and predicted fiscal deficits for the South African central government between 1997/98 and 2008/2009. As the figure shows, the deficit fell sharply from 3.8 percent of GDP in 1997/98 to 1.5 percent in 2004/2005. At the current level of GDP, a reduction from a deficit of 3.8 to 1.5 percent of GDP represents a withdrawal of government spending on the order of R18 billion, or nearly 5 percent of the government's budget.

As we also see from the figure, the Treasury is estimating, as of its October 2005 Medium-Term Budget Policy Statement, a fall in the deficit for 2005-2006 to 1 percent of GDP, before rising to around 2 percent through 2008-2009. In short, through the medium-term, the Treasury is now expecting to maintain a tight fiscal stance.

However, it is notable that these estimates differ significantly from those made by the Treasury the previous year, in its 2004 Medium-Term Budget Policy Statement. In the previous year's document, the Treasury projected a moderate loosening of its fiscal stance, with deficits in the range of 3 percent of GDP through 2006-2007. This roughly one percentage point of GDP difference in the two deficit projections is quite significant in terms of the government's capacity to spend, representing about R14 billion in available funds. This is an amount which, by itself, is more than three times the size of the annual expenditures projected to date on the Expanded Public Works Program, of R4 billion/year (for five years).

It is therefore worth examining the case for the moderately more relaxed fiscal stance the Treasury was projecting in 2004 versus its more stringent estimates as of 2005. To begin with, a fiscal deficit either at 2 or 3 percent of GDP

Figure 5.1 South Africa Fiscal Deficit/GDP Ratio

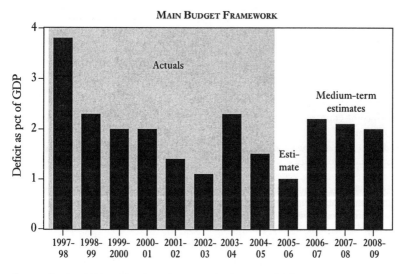

Source: October 2005 Medium Term Budget Policy Statement SA Treasury.

is well within the range of other countries in the current period. We can see this from Table 5.1 below.

As we see in the table, all groupings of countries have experienced a decline in their deficit/GDP ratios in the 1990s, through 2001. For the lower middle income countries, which include South Africa, the deficit/GDP ratio rose from the 1970s to the 1980s from 4.2 to 5.2 percent, before falling in the 1990s to 2.5 percent. With other country groupings, we see the same general pattern, though the size of the fluctuations differs in the different groupings. This overall pattern is clearly consistent with the worldwide macro policy agenda supportive of fiscal stringency. Nevertheless, against this background of increased fiscal tightness both in South Africa and elsewhere, the Treasury's projections as of 2004 to relax this stance a bit was a move in the other direction, if certainly a modest one. The more relaxed stance would provide the government significantly more flexibility to pursue key policy aims, such as the EPWP, without moving the deficit into a range that, by historical standards and global comparative standards today, could be construed as dangerous.

At the same time, we would not favor significant increases in the deficit beyond the 3 percent of GDP range that the Treasury had projected in 2004, even as a source of funds to support employment expansion or poverty reduction. This is especially the case since the deficit figures we are discussing are long-term structural deficits. The overall deficit—including the cyclical as well

Table 5.1 Overall Government Budget Balance, including Grants, 1970–2001 (budget balance as percentage of GDP)

Country groups	1970–1979	1980–1989	1990–2001
Low income countries	-4.9	-6.0	-3.6
Lower middle income countries including South Africa	-4.2	-5.2	-2.6
Upper middle income countries	-3.2	-3.3	-2.1
Middle income countries	-3.8	-4.4	-2.5
OECD countries	-2.8	-4.2	-2.8
Non-OECD high income countries	-0.5	-0.3	-0.5
Former socialist countries		-1.4	-2.8

Note: Overall budget balance is current and capital revenue and official grants received, less total expenditure and lending minus repayments. Data are shown for central government only. Former socialist countries are excluded from all other groups.
Source: World Bank, WDI-CD, 2003.

as the structural deficit—will necessarily increase beyond these projections during a recession. As such, any significant new government spending initiatives beyond what is already budgeted will need to be financed through some combination of either 1) more rapid GDP growth; or 2) higher tax rates.

Tax Financing of New Spending Initiatives

We believe that the government should pursue three major spending initiatives to promote employment growth and poverty reduction. These are:

1. Public investment/infrastructure;
2. Income transfers and social support; and
3. Credit/employment subsidies to businesses to promote accelerated employment growth.

We have discussed each of these program areas already, and will consider the credit/employment subsidy program in depth below. The first two areas of expenditure have also been identified as priorities within the ASGISA program, according to the preliminary information we have reviewed. For our discussion here, we are primarily concerned to provide a rough sense of the additional government spending that might be channeled into these areas to increase their effectiveness by a substantial amount. Based on our review of the ASGISA material on increased public investment, on proposals, such as the Basic Income Grant, to increase spending on poverty reduction, and finally, on our discussion

Table 5.2 Consolidated Government Revenue as a Share of GDP

Country	Per capita GDP ($US, 2002 PPP)	Revenue/GDP (in percentages, 2000–2003 averages)
Greece	$18,700	45.1
Poland	$10,560	41.8
Singapore	$24,000	29.0
Korea	$16,950	28.4
Uzbekistan	$1,670	28.0
South Africa	$10,100	24.1
Malaysia	$9,100	22.2
Indonesia	$3,200	18.9
Thailand	$7,010	15.8
Philippines	$4,200	14.7

Sources: OECD countries' revenue data are from OECD website (source OECD.org), Economic Outlook No 75: Annual and quarterly data, as the entry of "Total Receipts Government, % GDP." Asian countries' revenue data are from the Asian Development Bank (http://www.adb.org/Documents/Books/Key_Indicators/2004/default.asp), Key Indicators 2004: Poverty in Asia: Measurement, Estimates, and Prospects Per capita GDP at PPP from World Development Indicators 2004, World Bank.

below on credit subsidies, we would suggest that government spending should increase by an annual amount of about R20–30 billion at 2004 prices beyond what is currently being budgeted. The breakdown in increased expenditures would be roughly along these lines:

1.   Public investment/infrastructure: R5–7.5 billion;
2.   Income transfers and social support: R10–20 billion; and
3.   Credit subsidies to businesses to promote accelerated employment growth: R5–7.5 billion.

For the purposes of our current discussion of aggregate fiscal expenditures, let us assume a high-end spending increase in the range of R30 billion per year that would be financed both through an increase in the deficit from 2 to 3 percent of GDP, and through increased tax revenues. Because the deficit increase would mean an additional R14 billion in funds available for spending, that would mean that the additional R16 billion would have to come through either tax increases or from the revenue dividends of a higher economic growth rate.

Let us assume now that the government would need to raise fully R16 billion in new tax revenues. At current prices and GDP level, this would entail raising the revenue/GDP ratio by a bit more than one percentage point, from its 2004 rate of 24.7 percent to roughly 25.8 percent. As we see in Table 5.2, which shows average revenue/GDP ratios for 2000–2003 for a range of countries, this kind of increase in the revenue/GDP ratio would continue to place South Africa well below the revenue/GDP ratio for the lower-income OECD countries, including Greece (45.1 percent) and Poland (41.8). It would put South Africa roughly in line with a group of rapidly growing Asian economies, including Singapore (29.0 percent), Korea (28.4 percent), and Malaysia (22.2 percent). South Africa also would be significantly higher than some other Asian countries, including Indonesia (18.9 percent), China (17.4 percent), Thailand (15.8 percent), and the Philippines (14.7 percent).

It is not clear whether any of these countries provides a particularly appropriate comparison for South Africa. The key point is that neither the roughly 25 percent ratio at which South Africa currently operates, nor an increase to 26 percent, would establish South Africa as a significant outlier either among the OECD or the Asian comparison groups.

In terms of how to raise funds, it is useful to first recognize the primary sources of revenue at present. As we see in Table 5.3, as of 2004/2005, nearly 80 percent of all government revenue derives from three sources: personal income tax (31.3 percent), corporate income tax (19.9 percent), and the value added tax (27.7 percent). We believe that it will be necessary to increase revenue from these three primary revenue sources to partially cover the additional R16 billion that would pay for the priority areas we have identified, i.e. public investment, social transfers, and credit/employment subsidies. At the same time, rate increases on these taxes should not have to generate more than roughly one-third the total amount of revenues needed to finance these three programs. The remaining roughly R10 billion can be generated effectively through three new revenue sources: 1) extending the Uncertified Securities Tax that currently applies only to the secondary trading of stocks to cover bond trading as well; 2) enacting the Mineral and Petroleum Royalty Bill, recently introduced by the National Treasury; and 3) the increasing incomes and decline in poverty that would result through the employment-targeted growth program itself. We consider these in turn.

Extending the uncertified securities tax to bond trading
At present, this tax is applied to secondary market trading of stocks at a rate of 0.25 percent of the value of trades.[1] We propose that the tax be extended to apply also to secondary market bond trading. A wide range of countries do apply similar such taxes on bonds as well as stocks, or have done so in the recent past. We can see this from the table we present in Appendix 5, Table A5.1 (see page 167), which collects information on 39 countries that either were operating a tax on stocks as of 2002 or had done so in the recent past. As Table A5.1 shows, of these 39 countries, 26 also were operating a tax on corporate bonds as of 2002 or had done so in the recent past. Twelve countries had extended the tax to

Table 5.3 Primary Tax Revenue Sources for South African National Treasury, 2004–2005

	Tax revenues raised (billions of rand)	Share of total revenues
Personal income tax	111.0	31.3%
Corporate profit tax	70.8	19.9%
Other domestic taxes on goods and services	32.3	9.1%
Value added/sales tax	98.2	27.7%
TOTAL	247.6	88.0%

Source: National Treasury of South Africa, Medium Term Budget Policy Statement, 2005.

government bonds as well. Some relevant comparison countries that now have, or have recently had, a securities tax on both stocks and bonds includes Argentina, Brazil, Chile, Colombia, Greece, India, Indonesia, Malaysia, Morocco, Pakistan, South Korea, and Taiwan. As Table A5.1 also shows, most of these comparison countries have operated the tax on bonds at rates equal to the rates on stocks. If South Africa were to follow this pattern, that would mean 0.25 tax rate on the value of secondary trades of bonds.

As we have shown earlier, secondary market bond trading in South Africa has grown exponentially since the early 1980s. As of 2004, total trading amounted to R9.5 trillion, which equals 685 percent of GDP for that year. If a tax of 0.25 percent had been operating on this trading in 2004, that would have generated, by itself, R23.8 billion in government tax revenues. In other words, if the government extended the securities tax to the bond market at 0.25 percent, and assuming that the level of securities trading remained at its 2004 level, the revenue generated from the tax would, by itself, more than cover even a R20 billion expansion of income transfers and social support programs for fighting poverty. A revenue influx of this magnitude would pay, almost five times over, an expansion of credit and employment subsidies along the lines that we have discussed (and will consider more below).

Of course, it is unrealistic to expect that bond trading would continue at the same level once the tax is established, since this will mean an increase in the transaction costs of conducting bond trades. However, even if we allowed that trading would fall by 50 percent relative to its 2004 level, that would still imply that the tax would generate roughly R12 billion per year in revenue. Following this same logic further, one might also assume a tax rate at, say, 0.125 percent, i.e. one-half of the rate on stocks. Even with this tax rate, and still also assuming a decline in trading by one-half, revenues would still amount to roughly R6 billion, still again, an amount greater than what we have proposed for expansion of credit/employment subsidies.

In addition to this revenue potential, there are three additional reasons for extending the securities tax to cover bond trading. The first is that the tax is already in operation with respect to stock trading. Extending the same tax-collecting mechanisms to another market would not entail major administrative adjustments. Nor would we expect the degree of resistance to the tax by South African bond traders to be significantly different than what opponents of the stock trading tax have already expressed. In addition, this is a highly progressive tax, falling almost entirely on people who trade actively on bond markets. That is, it will fall almost entirely on wealthy individuals, and among those people, almost entirely among the subset of the wealthy who choose to trade their assets actively.[2] People who purchase financial assets and hold them will face infrequent tax obligations. Finally, as we have already reviewed, there is no evidence that the extremely high levels of secondary market bond trading that have prevailed in South Africa since the early 1980s have provided any benefit in terms of promoting productive investments. Rather, as we have seen, the exponential growth in bond trading in South Africa has coincided with a sharp decline in the ratio of real investment—in buildings and machinery—relative to GDP.[3]

Enacting the Mineral and Petroleum Royalty Bill

In 2003, the Treasury drafted a bill which would entail royalty payments made by holders of the rights for the extraction and sale of South Africa's valuable non-renewable mineral resources. The draft bill proposes quarterly royalty payments on the gross sales value of the minerals extracted. The proposed royalty rates would differ across the different types of minerals, precious metals, and energy products. The logic behind the royalty payments is straightforward. A portion of the revenues generated by the extraction of non-renewable resources represent 'scarcity rents'—payments made on the basis of the rarity of the commodity in question and not directly related to the costs of extracting, processing, and distributing mineral resources. Because the benefits from these scarcity rents do not result from anyone's efforts as laborers, managers, or firm owners, it is reasonable to provide that these benefits be shared broadly, to finance, for example, a portion of larger social service expenditures, the Expanded Public Works Program, or a program of credit and employment subsidies. In addition, since the revenues generated derive from the exploitation of natural resources that are not mobile, if the administration of the royalty system is handled with care, there is virtually no risk that mining operations would relocate out of South Africa to avoid paying the royalty.

Under the Treasury proposal, the royalty rates will be 1 percent of sales for most minerals, rising to 2–3 percent in some cases, to 4 percent for platinum, and a high of 8 percent for diamonds. Under this rate structure, we estimate that for 2003, the Treasury would have raised approximately R2.5 billion. Thus, at the proposed rate structure, the royalty potential is not nearly as large as with extending the securities tax to bonds. Nevertheless, R2.5 billion, by itself, would finance more than half of the Extended Public Works Program annual budget at its current level of operations.[4]

Income growth and declines in poverty

Assuming the trend rate of economic growth remained at the roughly 3 percent average that prevailed from 1994–2004, and that the existing levels of taxation remained unchanged, an additional R8.4 billion in government revenues would result simply due to economic growth. It follows that if the South African economy's long-term growth rate were to rise to something like the 5.3 percent we have projected for our employment-targeted program—i.e. 4.5 percent growth for non-subsidized activities and 8 percent for subsidized activities—this would also generate a further rise in the government's tax revenues. For example, for 2004, the difference in government revenue that would result from a 5.3 percent growth rate over 2003 versus a 3 percent growth rate would be R6.4 billion. In addition, precisely because the growth program we have outlined is targeted at generating rapid employment growth, this should also mean that the number of people who would be requiring social assistance programs should diminish.

However, the Treasury has already projected a significant growth dividend into their budgetary planning. For example, the 2005 MTBPS allows for a roughly 10 percent average annual increase in nominal revenues from 2006–2007 to 2008–2009. Thus, while it is important to recognize the benefits that would flow for the government from higher economic growth and faster poverty reduction, for the purposes of financing new programs beyond what the government has already budgeted, we have to assume that the additional funds would need to come from either increased taxes or government borrowing.

Thus, considered as a whole, if we conservatively allow that a securities tax on bonds generates R6 billion in revenue—i.e. roughly a quarter of what would have been generated if the tax were operating at the 2004 level of government bond trading—and that that the mineral royalty generates R2.5 billion, this amounts to a total of roughly R8.5 billion in increased revenue, separate from any revenue increase or cost reductions due to a growth dividend.

Overall then, it is reasonable to expect that about 60 percent of the revenue needs we have outlined could be covered through measures other than raising personal income taxes, profit taxes, and the VAT. The remaining roughly R6 billion in revenue needed from these traditional sources will therefore represent a modest increase of about 2.4 percent over what is already being generated through these sources.

MONETARY POLICY AND INTEREST RATES

Inflation Targeting

The government's commitment to inflation targeting exerts a major influence on the overall operations of the economy and, in particular, the realistic possibilities for significantly increasing employment prospects in South Africa. The South Africa Reserve Bank (SARB) established an explicit policy of inflation targeting as the primary focus of monetary policy in February 2000. This was after it had adopted a less explicit commitment to inflation targeting in March 1998. When taking this first step in March 1998 toward an inflation targeting regime, the Reserve Bank expressed its aim as being able to reduce inflation to levels comparable to those in the country's major trading partners, meaning especially the U.S., Britain, and other OECD countries. Since adopting an explicit inflation targeting policy in 2000, the targeted range for inflation has been between 3 and 6 percent.[5] According to T.T. Mboweni (2002), the Governor of the Reserve Bank, inflation targeting is a fundamental policy principle for South Africa because it "helps to anchor the public's inflation expectations, thereby improving planning for the economy, as well as providing an anchor for expectations of future inflation to influence price and wage setting."[6] Some observers suggest that since 2003, the Reserve Bank has adopted a somewhat more flexible approach to inflation targeting (Aron and Muellbauer, 2005). Nevertheless, to date, the target remains at between 3–6 percent, and maintaining this target intact is included in the preliminary presentations of the new ASGISA program.

Inflation targeting has been broadly successful at meeting its most direct goal, i.e. to lower the country's inflation rate. We can see this in Figure 5.2 below. As we see, inflation did fall from 1997–99, from 8.3 to 5.1 percent. It did then rise, though only modestly in 2000 and 2001. There was a sharp increase in 2002, to 8.7 percent. This inflation spike resulted from a run on the rand, causing the exchange rate to fall from 6.9 rand to the dollar in 2000 to 10.5 rand/dollar in 2002, a change of over 50 percent. The fall in the rand then pushed up consumer prices, in particular food prices.[7] However, once this episode subsided, the inflation rate for 2003 was back within the target, at 5.7 percent. The figure for 2004 was 4.3 percent. As of November 2005, inflation was down to 3.7 percent. In short, with the exception of the spike in 2002, inflation has remained within the target range from 1998–2004, and into 2005.

The primary means through which the Reserve Bank controls inflation is through adjustments in interest rates. Raising interest rates lowers the rate of borrowing and expenditure and thereby dampens the economy's level of aggregate demand. The Reserve Bank exercises direct control over the rate on government bond repurchase agreements—the so-called "repo rate"—and this rate

Figure 5.2 Annual Inflation Rate in South Africa, 1994–2004 (CPIX Rate)

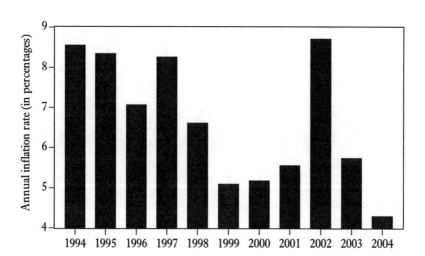

Source: Reserve Bank of South Africa.

operates directly on the short-end of financial markets and indirectly on longer-term rates.

Figure 5.3 tracks the movements of nominal and real interest rates in South Africa since 1994, distinguishing in the figure both the first and second phases during which inflation-targeting policies have been operating. This provides us with an initial picture of the effect of inflation-targeting policies on interest rates. The two interest rates we are tracking are the long-term government bond rate and the composite private lending rate reported in the IMF's International Financial Statistics publication. In the first panel of Figure 5.3, we observe the movements of the nominal long-term rates, and in the lower panel, we observe ex post real rates, i.e. the nominal rates minus the contemporaneous CPIX inflation rate.

First, we see that the inflation-targeting policies were initially implemented at a time of extraordinarily high interest rates. In the third quarter of 1998, the nominal government bond rate was 17.1 percent and the lending rate was 25 percent. The nominal rates fell sharply subsequent to that, during the period in which inflation targeting was in operation. The only exception was during 2002, when inflation surged.

In terms of real rates, we also see that both the government bond and lending rates were falling sharply during most of the period under both inflation targeting phases. This means that the downward movement of nominal rates

Figure 5.3 Nominal and Real Interest Rates in South Africa

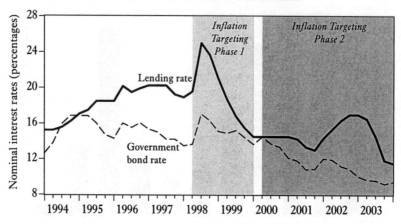

NOMINAL GOVERNMENT BOND AND PRIVATE LENDING RATE

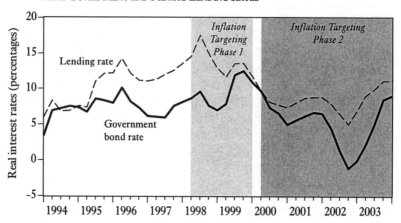

REAL GOVERNMENT AND PRIVATE LENDING RATES

Source: Reserve Bank of South Africa.

was more rapid than the decline in inflation. This should be recognized as a positive outcome associated with—though not necessarily caused by—inflation-targeting policies. It suggests that inflationary expectations were dampened after inflation-targeting policies were put in place.

However, the surge in inflation in 2002 seems to have brought a significant change in the behavior of interest rates. When inflation rose back up in 2002 to

Figure 5.4 Long-Term Government Bond Rate Differential between South Africa and the United States, 1994.1–2005.4

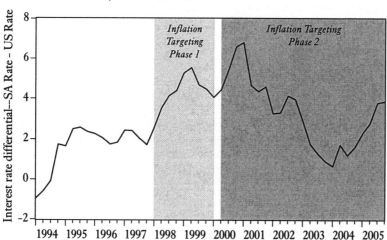

Sources: U.S. Federal Reserve; Reserve Bank of South Africa.
Notes: U. S. rate is for 10-year constant maturity bond; South Africa rate is 10-year maturity or higher. Inflation rates for both countries are 12-month percentage change in CPI.

8.7 percent, real interest rates also fell sharply, with the government bond rate reaching a negative level and the real lending rate falling to 5.0 percent in the fourth quarter of 2004 (2004.4). Then, when inflation declined in 2003 and 2004, both real interest rates then rose back up sharply, with the real lending rate reaching 11.1 percent in the first quarter of 2004, and averaging 8.0 percent for the full year.

The overall picture is that inflation-targeting policies did succeed for a time in lowering real interest rates. However, this decline was from an extraordinarily high level that prevailed in 1998, so that even while declining, the real rates remained, for the most part, in the range of 8 percent through 2001. Subsequent to 2002, maintaining the inflation target has been associated with increasing rates. If this pattern holds, it means that keeping the inflation rate within the 3–6 percent target range will be associated with the maintenance of high real lending rates, i.e. somewhere in the range of 8–10 percent.

This high level of interest rates since 2002 can also be observed when considered in comparison with the rates prevailing in the United States. In Figure 5.4, we show the differential in the real long-term bond rate between South Africa and that of the United States. Apart from a large increase in 2000 and then a large drop in 2003, the differential has fluctuated but not declined since 1994. This lack of decline in international interest differentials, despite the implementation of inflation targeting, has been seen as a puzzle by supporters of the inflation targeting regime (see, for example, Aron and Muellbauer, 2005). To us it suggests that the targeting regime has been able to lower nominal interest rates to some extent because of the interest rate declines in international financial markets more generally. However, beyond this, there has been little progress toward establishing a lower real interest rate environment.

From this reading of the evidence, we can conclude that the problem with inflation targeting is not that it has caused high interest rates by itself. A high interest rate regime preceded the implementation of inflation targeting. The point about inflation targeting is that it does not appear capable of bringing real rates down to a significant degree. This is not surprising, since this is not the purpose of inflation targeting. Rather, precisely because high interest rates are the instrument of inflation control, inflation targeting has meant that a high interest rate regime has continued throughout the 1990s and through 2004.

Interest Rates, Growth, and Inflation

What are the costs and benefits of maintaining the country's high interest rate regime? We have gathered some perspective on this question through our earlier consideration of the relationships between investment and interest rates as well as that between consumption and interest rates. The next step in the analysis is to combine the investment and consumption effects, and thereby observe the effects of lowering interest rates on overall South African GDP growth. In conjunction with measuring the effects on GDP growth, we would then also want to examine the effects of lowering interest rates on inflation itself.

To pursue these questions, Professor Epstein developed a simple econometric model of the South African macroeconomy, using the Vector Autoregression (VAR) framework. This model enables us to estimate the following:

1. How changes in interest rates affect GDP growth, after accounting for the effects of inflation and exchange rate fluctuations on GDP growth;
2. How changes in interest rates affect inflation, after accounting for the effects of GDP growth and exchange rate fluctuations on inflation; and
3. How changes in interest rates affect the exchange rate, after accounting for the effects of GDP growth and inflation on the exchange rate.

Specifically, we use this basic model to perform policy "experiments" to estimate the impacts on economic growth, exchange rates and inflation of a more expansionary monetary policy by the South African Reserve Bank. We also have used a similar model to estimate the impacts of increases in credit growth on economic growth and inflation. Appendix 6 presents a much fuller technical discussion of the model, methods and results. Here we present a basic summary of our findings.

At the outset, it is important to note that these estimates are based on highly simplified models of the economy that can only take into account a relatively limited number of possibly important variables. As such, they should be approached with caution. Still, it is likely that the suggested impacts generated by our model are broadly indicative of how the South African economy responds to changes in macroeconomic policies.

1. *Interest rates and economic growth.* The model estimates that if the central bank lowers the prime lending rate by 1 percentage point, and maintains the 1 percentage point lower rate for a five-year period, this will increase real GDP growth by 0.15 percent per year. For example, starting from a GDP growth rate of 3.0 percent and a nominal prime rate of 11 percent (corresponding roughly to the actual average figures for 1994–2004), if the prime rate fell to 10 percent and were held at 10 percent for five years, the average rate of real GDP growth over the five-year period would rise to 3.15 percent.

2. *Interest rates and inflation.* The same 1 percentage point decline in the prime lending rate will lead to a moderate increase in inflation. Our model estimates that over the course of five years, a sustained one percentage point decline in the prime rate would generate an increase in the average inflation rate on the order of 0.2 percent. For example, if the economy is experiencing a 5 percent inflation rate before the decline in interest rates, then during the five years of a lower interest rate regime, the inflation rate would average 5.2 percent.

3. *Interest rates and exchange rate.* The same one percentage point fall in the nominal prime lending rate will produce a depreciation in the value of the rand relative to the dollar by 0.6 percentage points, as an average over the five-year period. Note that over some of this five-year period, the model predicts that the rand would actually appreciate relative to the dollar to some extent. Overall, according to our model, the fluctuations in the rand that would follow from the lower interest rate policy would not be especially large by historical standards. For example, since 1994, the nominal exchange rate has varied from 3.4 rand to the dollar to 11.5, and the average annual rate of depreciation was 6.1 percentage points.

Monetary policy tools and the prime rate
Monetary policy interventions in South Africa now take place through the Reserve Bank's interventions in the market for repurchase agreements—i.e. the so-called "repo rate." The Reserve Bank does not exert direct influence over the prime rate. It is therefore necessary to consider the relationship between move-

Figure 5.5 Average Repo and Prime Overdraft Rates in South Africa, 1999–2005

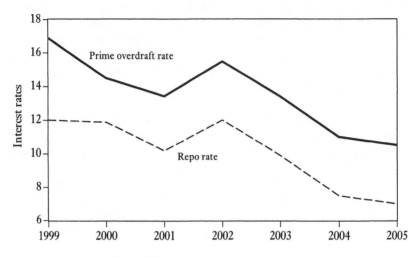

Source: Reserve Bank of South Africa.

ments in the repo and bond rates to determine how effectively the Reserve Bank could in fact influence the prime lending rate. To obtain some rough sense of this in Figure 5.5, we plot the movements of both the repo rate and prime rate between 1999–2004. As we see, these two rates do in fact move together in close correspondence over these years. This suggests that, if the Reserve Bank did want to reduce the prime rate to promote accelerated economic growth, they do have the tools at hand to do so.

How much growth from lowering rates?

In our discussion above on growth, labor intensity and employment, we estimated the employment effects of raising the growth rate of unsubsidized business activity in South Africa from 3 percent to 4.5 percent. We can now consider how much we can use a decline in interest rates to move the unsubsidized activity in the direction of 4.5 percent growth. In Table 5.4 below, we summarize the estimated effects of lowering the prime lending rate by 4 percentage points and maintaining it at that lower level—in our example from 11 to 7 percent—for five years. As we see, the impact will be to raise GDP growth from 3 percent to, on average, 3.6 percent; raise inflation from 5 to 6 percent on average; and to cause an acceleration of the average rate of depreciation of the rand/dollar exchange rate. The maximum annual rate of depreciation over the five-year period would rise by 12 percent. At that maximum rate of depreciation the rand/dollar ex-

Table 5.4 Estimating Impact of Interest Rate Decline on GDP Growth, Inflation and Exchange Rate Changes

	Figure before interest rate decline		Figure after interest rate decline		
GDP growth (average annual impact)	3.0%		3.6		
Inflation (average annual impact)	5.0		6.0		
	Rand/ dollar level	Average annual depreciation rate	Rand/ dollar level after five years	Average annual depreciation rate	Cumulative change over five years
Exchange rate change (Rand/dollar)	6.3	1.07%	7.1	2.2%	12%

Notes: Illustrative model based on approximate 2004 data and VAR estimates:
effect of lowering nominal prime lending rate from 11% to 7% for five years
Source: See discussion in text and Appendix 4.

change rate could go, for example, from 6.3 rands/per dollar to 7.1 rands/dollar, i.e., well within the historical range for this relationship. Over the entire five-year period, the exchange rate impacts are, on average, expected to be more modest. As the appendix shows, the model predicts that the overall average depreciation of the exchange rate over the five-year period would be around 2 percent per year. Compounding this over the five-year period would also result in a 12 percent depreciation, leading to a depreciation in the exchange rate from 6.3 rand per dollars in the first quarter of 2000 to 7.1 by the end of 2004 in the absence of any other changes in the exchange rate.[8]

In short, the benefits of the interest rate decline would be substantial, but they would only bring the economy less than half way toward the growth rate of 4.5 percent for the unsubsidized activities in the economy. However, there are other policy options available for closing this gap. First, the Reserve Bank could lower interest rates by *more* than 4 percentage points. As we have seen, our model suggests that the inflationary effects of these reductions are likely to be relatively modest. At the same time, exchange rate volatility does increase with further decreases in interest rates. As a result, alternative measures—including capital management techniques—should be considered as complementary policies.

In addition, if the Treasury were to move back toward the somewhat more relaxed fiscal stance that it was projecting in its 2004 MTBPS—i.e. a fiscal deficit in the range of 3 percent of GDP as opposed to 2 percent of GDP—this will also contribute to accelerating the trend growth rate of unsubsidized activities toward the range of 4.5 percent. Thus, in combining this more relaxed fiscal stance with lower unsubsidized interest rates and the growth in private credit associated with credit subsidies, it is reasonable to anticipate, within the framework of this VAR exercise, an average growth trend in the range of 5.3 percent.

As we also see from the discussion above, the reduced interest rates should raise the inflation rate modestly and might also contribute to more exchange rate volatility. Such changes should be readily manageable. It is also true that expansionary fiscal policy could also exert concurrent upward pressure on inflation and downward pressure on the rand. But these issues take us to a broader set of policy concerns regarding controlling inflation and the exchange rate. These are questions we will consider later.

PUBLIC CREDIT ALLOCATION
AND DEVELOPMENT BANKING

Public credit allocation policies in South Africa could play a crucial role in advancing a serious program to expand employment and reduce poverty. This fact has clearly been recognized through the country's "financial charter." The charter is premised on the idea that the country's financial institutions should be engaged in advancing social development. This proposal offers measures to further mobilize the country's public and private financial institutions in behalf of promoting accelerated economic growth, employment expansion and poverty reduction.

What are credit allocation policies? These are the set of policies through which credit is supplied on concessionary terms to private firms, with concessions provided on the basis of a country's developmental goals. Credit allocation policies are often conducted through development banks that are either publicly owned or semi-public entities. However, credit allocation policies need not operate only through development banks. Indeed, because South Africa currently operates with such an extensive, well-developed private financial system, it follows that this private system should be mobilized, along with the public development banks, to address the country's program of employment creation.

Our proposal is actually a hybrid policy intervention, in that it is simultaneously providing firms with both an employment and a credit subsidy. As such, the proposal has a benefit relative to a more traditional general employment subsidy in that the government will not have to devote enormous resources to provide subsidies to all firms based on their number of employees. The government also would not have to carefully monitor firms to accurately measure their marginal increase in hires, as would be the case with a marginal employment subsidy program. This is true even while, as we discuss below, the proposal does entail significant amounts of monitoring, to ensure that funds are utilized toward their primary intended aim of employment creation. Finally, the hybrid approach also avoids the problem with a traditional credit subsidy, which is that it is providing incentives for firms to borrow in order to purchase capital equipment—i.e to subsidize capital over labor expenditures. Under this sort of measure, there could still be employment benefits due to the increase in overall expenditures and output by firms because of the availability of cheap credit. But this employment gain could be counterbalanced to the extent that the credit subsidies encourage further increases in the use of more capital intensive production methods.

Of course, the issue in seeking to mobilize both the public development banks and the private financial system toward addressing the country's employment problem is how to design policies in which incentives for both borrowers and lenders are clear and strong. We propose that South Africa utilize three main policy tools to attract private lenders and borrowers into financing activities that will substantially boost employment.

The three policy tools that we propose are:

1. *A substantial expansion in both the level and scope of activities of the country's existing public development banks.*
2. *An extensive system of loan guarantees.* South Africa does currently guarantee loans, but, as we will see, the system is far too modest at present to exert a significant impact on the country's development path; and
3. *A system of asset-based reserve requirements.* This refers to requirements that financial institutions hold a given percentage of their loan portfolio in social priority areas, such as small-scale agriculture or biofuels. To the extent that they do not include these activities in their portfolio, they must hold cash as a substitute. The South African financial system operated between 1956–89—i.e. through most of the apartheid era—under a system of so-called "prescribed assets." We are certainly not proposing a return to that previous system. At the same time, allowing for an entirely distinct historical situation in democratic South Africa, our proposal will include features that resemble the previous system. Significantly, as we will discuss, such measures can be designed with far more flexibility than was the case with the previous system. In addition, of course, this set of policy interventions needs to also be directed toward the purpose of fighting unemployment as opposed to upholding the apartheid economy.

We describe the main features of these three proposals in some detail below. But it is first important to emphasize that such a broader approach to credit allocation and development banking—i.e. one involving the private financial system as well as public development banks—is consistent with the experiences of many relatively successful developing countries. This point becomes clear in the illuminating discussion of development banking by Alice Amsden in *The Rise of "The Rest"* (2001). Amsden begins her discussion of this topic with the general observation that:

> The state's agent for financing investment was the development bank. From the viewpoint of long-term capital supply for public *and private* investment, development banks throughout "the rest" were of overwhelming importance (p. 127, emphasis in original).

Amsden goes on to document this in the cases of Mexico, Chile, Korea, Brazil, and Indonesia. But she also points out that "the government's role in long-run credit allocation was substantial even in parts of 'the rest' where development banks were of relatively minor importance," (p. 129). These cases include Malaysia, Thailand, Taiwan, and Turkey. She writes of these cases, "when necessary, the whole banking sector in these countries was mobilized to steer long-term credit to targeted industries, acting as a surrogate development bank."[9]

The general point here is that development banks can play a central role in financing a major employment-generating program in South Africa. But we need not assume that using credit allocation policies to promote employment should be limited to the possibilities that exist through using the existing development banking apparatus.

The Current State of Credit Allocation Policies in South Africa

As mentioned above, South Africa does already operate with an extensive system of development banks as well as a modest loan guarantee program. It is not currently making use of the system of prescribed assets that operated between 1956–89. We review here the current status of the credit allocation programs in the country before outlining our proposals for a more ambitious set of policies aimed at employment creation and economic growth.

Development banks

To our knowledge, South Africa does now have in place eight national institutions that operate, through various types of lending and other activities, as public development banks. These eight institutions are:

- The Industrial Development Corporation of South Africa (IDC);
- The Development Bank of Southern Africa (DBSA);
- The Land Bank of South Africa;
- The National Housing Finance Corporation;
- The Rural Housing Loan Fund;
- The Postbank;

- Khula Enterprise Finance; and
- The National Empowerment Fund.

There are regional development corporations in addition to these, such as Ithala Development Finance Corporation, which is 100 percent owned by the Kwa-Zulu Natal government; and the Eastern Cape Development Corporation.

In terms of lending activity, the largest development bank in South Africa at present is the Industrial Development Corporation (IDC). According to the IDC's 2005 Annual Report, in 2004–2005 the bank approved R3.8 billion in new loans. This is 1.6 percent of South Africa's gross capital formation for 2004. The IDC also "anticipated" creating 16,700 jobs through its 2004–2005 activities. This is equal to slightly more than 0.1 percent of the official South Africa workforce for 2004 and 0.4 percent of the number of officially unemployed as of that year. In short, from this most current evidence, the IDC is playing a very modest role in addressing the country's needs in terms of financing capital formation and creating employment. The other two large public development banks in South Africa are the Development Bank of Southern Africa (DBSA) and the Land Bank. [10] For the current discussion, we focus on the activities of the IDC, the country's largest development bank.

The IDC's 2003 Annual Report explains its overall goals and performance standards in more detail than the more recent 2004 and 2005 Reports. It is useful to review some of the points presented in the 2003 document. In particular, the 2003 Report states that the IDC's corporate performance should be measured according to six parameters, which are assigned relative weights in the degree of their importance. The relative weights for the different criteria are as follows:

1. Financial returns—40%;
2. Role in economy—20%;
3. Developmental Role—15%;
4. Strategic Imperative—Human Resources—7%;
5. Strategic Imperative—Implementation of New IT System—5%; and
6. Strategic Imperative—Key Initiatives—5%.

Of course, the distinctions between some of these categories are artificial, e.g. between "role in economy" and "developmental role." Nevertheless, this categorization is indicative of how the IDC operates. Let us consider these in a bit of detail.

Financial returns
According to its established criteria, the single most important purpose of the IDC, by a significant margin, is to make profits. This becomes clear by examining their summary performance statistics further. In terms of their "average in-

terest rate differential"—their first indicator of "financial returns"—the IDC had set a goal in 2002–2003 of earning a 1 percent differential between their portfolio rate and their average borrowing costs. However, the IDC exceeded this goal by quite a bit: its actual interest rate differential was 3 percent. In short, the IDC appears to be operating according to standards of profitability comparable to what would be true for a private bank. This is fully consistent with what officials of the IDC had told us when we visited their offices in August 2004. This approach would also be consistent with the fact that IDC is a self-financing entity.

Role in economy

The IDC's total loan approvals in 2003–2004, at 3.2 percent of gross capital formation, were somewhat below the stated goal of financing between 3.4–4.2 percent of gross investment. Nevertheless, the more important point is that the range they are setting for themselves is very modest. Consider again Amsden's discussion of the experiences in other countries:

> Mexico's Nacional Financiera accounted for about twice the value of long-term loans of all private credit institutions in 1961 ... It also accounted for over 60 percent of the total of stocks held by private credit institutions. Nor was [Mexico's] position atypical. In India, it was estimated by the late 1960s that more than one-fifth of total private investment in industry was financed through development banks and 'the share of development banks in medium- and long-term loans would, of course be much higher...' In Chile, between 1961 and 1970, the fixed investment of targeted projects by CORFO was scheduled at 55 percent of all fixed investment in industry, including artisan industry. CORFO is estimated to have controlled over 30 percent of investment in machinery and equipment, more than one-fourth of public investment, and close to 20 percent of gross domestic investment (pp. 127–29).

The proportions that Amsden reports for development banks as a share of investment were maintained at roughly these levels through the 1980s and even the 1990s, though the figures do decline somewhat with time. As such, we can conclude that relative to other developing country experiences, the role of the IDC in the South African economy is very small. This point remains true if we include the lending activity of the DBSA, the Land Bank, and all other development banks in South Africa.

Developmental role

The IDC defines its "developmental role" in terms of the total number of jobs that will be created through its lending activity. As we have already seen for 2004–2005, that contribution has been only modest.

In short, to date, the IDC—and by extension South Africa's development banks as a whole—are making very limited contributions in terms of their impact on the overall economy as opposed to the benefits they are providing to individual businesses and projects.

Table 5.5 South African Government Loan Guarantee Program:
Contingent Liabilities and Accruals

	Stock of outstanding contingent liabilities	Estimated flow of accruals on contingent liabilities[a]	Estimated accruals as a proportion of contingent liabilities	Estimated accruals as proportion of total government expenditure
1999/2000	R79 billion	R22.6 million	0.03%	0.01%
2000/2001	R73.2 billion	R19.2 million	0.03%	0.01%
2001/2002	R84.2 billion	R274 million	0.32%	0.1%
2002/2003	R70.7 billion	R10 million	0.01%	0.003%

Source: Medium Term Budget Policy Statement, 10/26/04 Statistical Annexure B, Tables 4 and 8.
Notes: [a] Accruals are estimated on the basis of data in Table 4 (p. 202) of the Statistical Annexure B. The relevant data series in the table is "standing appropriations." According to Kuben Naidoo of the National Treasury, this category includes approximately R20 million/year for subscription fees to the UN, IMF and other organizations. The remainder of the category consists of accruals on contingent liabilities. Contingent liabilities are from Table 8 (p. 214), the bottom "total" line of the table.

At the same time, it is important to recognize that, at the time of writing, the IDC has undertaken a major new initiative to refocus their resources in behalf of promoting employment expansion. This new IDC initiative is described in depth in an April 2006 paper, "Targeted Employment Programs: The Case of the Industrial Development Corporation" by the IDC's Chief Economist Lumkile Mondi. To the extent that the IDC succeeds in implementing this new initiative, it will have moved strongly in the direction that we are advocating here.

Loan guarantee program
The government does already operate a loan guarantee program. We obtain a sense of the size of the program through the figures in Table 5.5. As we see, the total stock of contingent liabilities ranged from 1999/2000 to 2002/2003 between R84 billion and R70.7 billion. Of this total, nearly 90 percent are loans for public enterprises, with the largest recipient of guarantees being Transnet (R18 billion in 2002/2003—25% of total contingent liabilities), followed by the Trans-Caledon Tunnel Authority (R15.2—22%), and the Development Bank of Southern Africa (R11.3—16%). Thus, these three recipients absorb 55 percent of the loan guarantee program, as reported in the 2004 Medium-Term Budget Policy Statement.

We can also see from the table that accruals on the contingent liabilities— the amounts the government actually pay out when loans default—are a trivial proportion of government expenditures—at 1/100th of 1 percent or less in three of the four years, and only 0.3 percent in 2001/2002 when the Treasury paid out lenders following a major bank failure.[11] These ratios indicate the very low level of risk the government has been willing to assume with its loan guarantee program. Of course, the priority of assuming little risk establishes virtually no flexibility for the loan guarantees to promote an ambitious program of employment targeting.

Asset reserve requirements and prescribed asset policies

During the apartheid era, South Africa's financial system did operate under a system of so-called "prescribed assets." However, our proposal varies sharply in several important respects from the previous prescribed asset system.

The prescribed asset system was introduced in the Pensions Fund Act of 1956. It was compulsory for every fund to invest at least 10 percent of its total assets in government stock and another 40 percent in prescribed stock (which also included government stock). These figures peaked at 22.5 and 55 percent respectively at the height of apartheid. Prescribed assets included investments in National Defense Bonds, Iscor, Sasol, various water services, economic development, and homeland development corporations. When the system was abolished in 1989, the prescribed asset level was at 53 percent of total pension fund assets. At the same time, many funds voluntarily held an even higher proportion of their total funds in the prescribed assets.

Though no new system of prescribed assets has been implemented in the democratic era, several proposals have been advanced along these lines. In particular, at the 2003 Growth and Development Summit, President Mbeki emphasized as one of the three "key agreements" of the summit a proposal that would

> Develop suitable instruments to direct 5% of investible income of a wide range of public and private organizations, including the pension funds and insurance companies, towards job creating and poverty alleviating projects, (p. 4 of *Department of Labour for South Africa 2003*).

Mbeki emphasized the importance of the point in also stating that:

> We should be certain of when the investment mechanism for the employment of the 5% of investible income from retirement income and other businesses, would be set up and start operating.

President Mbeki's point coming out of the Growth and Development Summit is also reiterated by presidential economic advisor Alan Hirsch in his 2004 paper, "South Africa's Development Path and the Government's Programme of Action." Under the heading "Growth of the First Economy," Hirsch lists a series of interventions that could contribute toward raising the country's investment rate. The first item that he lists is as follows:

The completion of the Growth and Development Summit discussion on the meaning of the commitment for 5% of institutional funds to be committed to infrastructure and productive investments, (p. 7).

More than two years after the Growth and Development Summit proposals, however, no serious progress had been made in establishing a workable plan for committing financial resources for job creation and poverty reduction. Indeed, a news story of July 19, 2004, in *This Day* reported that "President Thabo Mbeki publicly expressed his annoyance with the poor progress on the commitments by the growth and development partners at the national Economic Development and Labour Council in April last year." In short, the development of an effective system of credit allocation consistent with the country's employment needs and other social goals remains to be done.

Credit Allocation Proposals

Size of program
The credit allocation program should be a key instrument for promoting employment growth. This would suggest a level of subsidized lending that is roughly R40 billion per year (in 2004 prices). This would mean underwriting loans equal to about 25 percent of the country's private fixed capital formation as of 2004.

Borrowers: who should receive subsidized credit?
The fundamental purpose of the expanded credit allocation policies, of course, will be to underwrite a program of rapid employment growth. Subsidized credit should be directed towards businesses and projects that are viable as business activities but that will also make significant contributions to employment growth.

As an initial organizing principle, we propose that businesses can become eligible for subsidized credit based on two main sets of criteria. The first is what we will term "social priority lending" for small-scale activities. We identity three areas for social priority lending:

1. *Land reform and rural development.* The most serious problems of poverty and unemployment in South Africa are in the rural areas. Even if it were feasible, it is obviously not desirable to promote policies that would encourage more people to move into the cities to find decent work. Therefore, we need to advance policies that create jobs in rural areas. Credit allocation, as well as infrastructure spending, can be a primary tool for achieving this.
2. *Promotion of small and medium-sized enterprises.* This is a stated government priority. It is also clear that there is considerable opportunity for increasing the representation of small- and medium-sized enterprises in townships and other historically oppressed areas. This need also coincides exactly

with the additional government priority of "black economic empowerment" in the area of business opportunities.

3. *Promotion of collectives and other alternative ownership forms.* Promoting collective private enterprises is a priority for the South African government. As MP Jeremy Cronin pointed out forcefully in our August 2004 interview with him, collective enterprises capture much of the spirit of solidarity that was nurtured in the country's long freedom struggle. In this spirit, it is only logical that, just as there should be special financial opportunities for private SMMEs, there should be comparable opportunities for small- and medium-sized cooperatives to develop. Indeed, financial cooperatives are one potentially very important organizational form that should be supported.

By their nature, cooperatives will tend to operate with relatively labor-intensive production processes. Therefore, providing subsidized loans to these activities will also promote rapid employment expansion.

The second criterion is straightforward: any firm that does not fall within the "social priority" criterion will be eligible for concessionary loans if it can demonstrate that its projects will produce large positive employment effects. Thus, in applying for loans, a firm will have to provide an Employment Impact Statement (EIS) demonstrating the overall number of jobs that its investment will create. The Employment Impact Statement should include both the direct and indirect job effects—i.e. both the number of hires that the firm itself will make and the up- and downstream impact when the firm receiving the loan purchases inputs from other South African firms.

Under this criterion, firms will not be obligated to provide a formal employment multiplier analysis comparable to that which we presented earlier. But even if they do not provide such a formal analysis, the firms should have to produce compelling evidence demonstrating clearly the overall employment benefit of their projects, both directly through their own hiring increases as well as through their domestic upstream linkages.

Under this criterion, the types of activities that are well known to be able to generate large employment multipliers—such as bio-fuels and other forms of agro-processing—will have an easier time producing a credible Employment Impact Statement, even while other types of firms and activities will be equally eligible to try to meet the established employment criteria.

Of course, the requirement of producing an EIS will itself create barriers to entry for firms seeking subsidized credit. To produce the EIS will entail significant time and costs, and some degree of expertise in producing documents of this nature. Projects that will be capable of carrying out the necessary steps to apply for loans by this criterion are therefore likely to be large-scale. As such, both small and medium, as well as large-scale firms will be eligible for subsidized credit. But each firm type will become eligible for subsidized credit through a different set of procedures.

Lenders: utilizing both public and private banking systems

Taken as a whole, our credit allocation proposals would entail a coordinated effort between the public and private financial sectors, and between the three types of proposed measures—i.e. expanding the role of the public development banks as well as mobilizing the private financial system through loan guarantees and asset reserve requirement policies.

Returning to the performance standards stated in the IDC's 2003 Annual Report, the key idea for expanding the role of the country's development banks is to substantially increase the relative importance of what the IDC terms its "development goal" of job creation, as well as its "role in the economy" of financing capital formation, while, concurrently, allowing the standard of "financial returns" to be relaxed for the IDC as well as the other development banks.

We have stated above that total subsidized credit in the economy would need to amount to roughly 25 percent of private investment in order to promote employment growth adequately. There is no need to assert a hard-and-fast rule as to what proportion of this roughly R40 billion in annual lending (in 2004 prices) should be provided by public versus private financial institutions. But we can use the IDC's high-end lending target for 2003–2004 of 4.2 percent of all investment an initial point of departure. This standard for the IDC is already established for 2003–2004 lending, and it suggests that all the country's eight national development banks (as well as, perhaps, its regional banks) could combine to provide loans on the order of roughly 8 percent of all investment— or roughly double the amount pledged by the IDC alone in 2003—without having to dramatically reorganize the existing organizational structures of the development banks. At 2004 levels of investment, that would mean about R13 billion in loans from development banks. As we discuss below, it should not be difficult for the private financial system to supply the remaining R27 billion in loans for this program (assuming the 2004 level of investment).

Encouraging small-scale banking to serve this market segment
At present, South Africa's financial institutions are not especially well designed to make loans to small-scale borrowers in the social priority sectors. It is therefore important to develop a new sector of the banking industry capable of making these loans effectively. Thus, one feature of the expansion of lending activities to SMMEs, coops, and smallholding farmers—the social priority areas—will necessarily entail encouraging the formation of financial institutions capable of operating at this level.

One way this could work effectively would be through the existing development banks. That is, in increasing the capitalization of the development banks, part of their expanded responsibilities would include promoting the formation of small-scale financial institutions capable of operating a system of lending and loan guarantees such as we have described here. Large-scale private banks could then form partnerships with the newly created small-scale institutions serving the social priority markets. As we discuss further below, this would also facilitate the process through which the large-scale banks can fulfill their asset reserve requirements.

Sources of New Loan Funds
The subsidized credit program we have outlined does not necessarily entail increasing the overall amount of lending and borrowing in the South African economy. The source of funds for the increase in subsidized credit could conceivably be a pure reallocation of a given amount of overall credit, with non-priority areas obtaining less credit by exactly the amount that priority areas receive subsidized loans. However, it is likely that the subsidized credit program will generate some net increase in lending in the South Africa economy. As discussed in the previous section, we have factored an expansion of private credit into our VAR modeling exercise.

What will be the sources of this net increase in loan funds? Over time, the increased level of output and income generated from the expanded activities in priority areas will generate, through the expenditure multiplier, a corresponding increase in domestic saving. But in the initial phase of this program, before net saving rises, the increased loan funds could still be made available as needed at appropriate interest rates. This could be done through conventional expansionary monetary policy interventions—that is, a Central Bank intervention to increase reserve funds of private banks through open-market operations. Such interventions would be consistent with the low interest rate policy we have described above.

Note that these allocation measures would make it unnecessary for the economy to increase its domestic saving rate, expand the growth of monetary reserves or the velocity of circulation, or attract foreign savings. Of course, if the economy were to maintain its current level of non-productive credit allocation, it would be necessary to generate more reserves through some combination of the expansionary measures mentioned above.

Costs of program
How much would such an expanded program likely cost the Treasury in terms of accruals on contingent liabilities? The following exercise provides a sense of the relevant proportions. We assume, as above, that we would want about R40 billion in concessionary loans per year being granted (that is, as a share of GDP equal to its 2004 level). In pursuing such an aggressive government-sponsored credit program, we would also have to assume that the default rate on the subsi-

dized loans would rise sharply relative to the ratio of accruals/contingent liabilities within the current government budget. Let us therefore make three basic assumptions about a renewed government loan guarantee program:

1. The government program underwrites R40 billion in loans per year;
2. The default rate on the loans is 15 percent; and
3. The guarantee on these loans covers 75 percent of principal.

Under these three assumptions, it follows that the accruals to the government would amount to R4.5 billion/year (i.e. R40 x .15 x .75). This figure would of course represent a significant commitment by the government. Still, with the government's budget at nearly R370 billion for 2005–2006, a commitment of R4.5 amounts to 1.2 percent of total government spending. One could obviously also alter the assumptions in the exercise—e.g. assume a 10 or 20 percent default rate as opposed to 15 percent; or a coverage guarantee of 50 percent as opposed to 75 percent. Changing these assumptions will then alter the figure for government accruals. Nevertheless, under any broadly similar set of assumptions, a crucial result nevertheless emerges: the government has the capacity to underwrite a major loan guarantee program, equivalent to roughly 25 percent of all private investment in 2004, with a budgetary commitment of no more than 1–2 percent of total government spending.

Extent of Credit Subsidy
The terms of the subsidy must meet four criteria:

1. Subsidies must be large enough for the program to succeed in stimulating borrowing for productive purposes and, in particular, employment generation;
2. The program must still be seen as providing potential profit opportunities for lenders;
3. The loan terms must be broadly consistent with the structure of interest rates, rewards, and risks within the South African financial market as it currently operates; and
4. The terms must be easily understood by participants in the financial system.

A logical starting point for establishing an appropriate interest rate on subsidized loans is the government bond rate. Government bonds have the lowest default risk of all bonds within the South African financial system. At the same time, the South African government bond rate reflects everything about the general level of risk in South Africa, including both inflation risk and country risk.

A subsidized loan to a private borrower would also incorporate general levels of country risk and inflation risk. The default risk on a subsidized loan would then depend on 1) the credit profile of the individual borrower; and 2) the extent of the loan guarantee. Based on this, the rate on concessionary loans should be set as an increment above the government bond rate. How large an increment above the government bond rate should then depend on the borrower's profile and on the extent of the government guarantee on loans.

To make this clearer, we can stipulate that a government bond issue in rand faces virtually zero default risk. Thus, the interest rate on a private loan with a 100 percent guarantee should be set at exactly the government bond rate. By contrast, the appropriate rate on a loan with no guarantee is, by definition, the market interest rate on that loan. As such, the government bond rate and the market interest rate define the range within which concessionary rates should be set.

The appropriate concessionary rate can therefore be derived simply as follows:

$$I^{lg} = i^m - LC, \text{ where}$$
$$LC = C(i^m - i^b),$$

and I^{lg} is the rate on loan guarantees, i^m is the market interest rate for a loan of a given risk class and maturity, C is the percentage of a loan that the government is guaranteeing, and i^b is the government bond rate for a given maturity.

To illustrate this calculation with an example, consider a case, which closely approximates actual South African financial market conditions in November 2005, in which the government bond rate is 7 percent and the so-called "marginal lending rate" is 12 percent. In such a case, and assuming a 75 percent loan guarantee program, the concessionary loan rate I^{lg} would be 8.25 percent.

Of course, the concessionary loan rate would rise if the government guarantee were less. Thus, if we assume that the loan guarantee is 50 percent rather than 75 percent, the concessionary loan rate rises to 9.50 percent.

Would this Program be Profitable to Private Lenders?
If the South African financial market is accurately assessing the risk differential between different types of loans, then it follows that lending under the loan guarantee program at concessionary rates should be profitable to lenders. This is especially the case since the loan guarantees would not be extended on the basis of funding more risky activities per se, but rather activities that are capable of generating rapid increases in employment. It is likely that projects with large employment effects will tend to be more risky than other projects, if for no other reason than the aim of the program will be to bring in new borrowers— SMMEs, small landholders, and coops—under the "social priority" lending category. However, the larger-scale projects that will require an Employment Impact Assessment need not be especially high-risk ventures.

Table 5.6 Losses to Lenders from Loan Defaults with Non-Guaranteed and Guaranteed Loan Portfolios (assuming R1 million in gross revenue for no-default case)

	Non-guaranteed loan portfolio	Guaranteed loan portfolio
Default rate on R1 million contracted interest and principal	5 percent	15 percent
Losses to lender from defaults	R50,000	R150,000
Lenders' share of losses from defaults	R50,000	R37,500

However, to illustrate the issue of profitability for lenders, consider a simple example, which we present in Table 5.6, where we assume that the default rate is indeed substantially higher for a portfolio of guaranteed loans. Following the earlier discussion, we still assume that the default rate on guaranteed loans is 15 percent. This means that the default rate on non-guaranteed loans is 5 percent. Now let us compare two loan portfolios, one of guaranteed loans and the other of non-guaranteed loans. Assume the gross cash revenue on both portfolios is R1 million if there are no defaults on either loan. In Table 5.6, we see the net losses for lenders at these default rates. As we see there, losses for private borrowers with non-guaranteed loans are R50,000, but are R37,500 under the portfolio of guaranteed loans.

This simple example doesn't take into account all of the factors that might affect the profitability of the portfolio of loan guarantees. First, we need to allow that, for lenders, making guaranteed loans would entail extra administrative burdens. This would reduce the relative profitability of making guaranteed loans.

On the other hand, for lenders seeking a low-risk portfolio, there is likely to be a scarcity of government bonds and low-risk private borrowers available for their portfolio. The loan guarantee program would effectively expand the pool of low-risk lending opportunities by a substantial amount. It should therefore also tend to reduce the rates on all loans in the low-risk class.

In addition, if the government also implemented a system of asset reserve requirements, financial institutions would face costs of holding sterile cash reserves if they did not make employment-targeted loans. Through combining the loan guarantees with the asset reserve requirements, financial institutions would benefit both from holding a low-risk loan portfolio and from avoiding having to hold a portfolio of cash reserves rather than employment-targeted loans.

Incentive Structure and Monitoring of Borrowers
Under the East Asian model, the incentive structures, performance standards,

and accountability requirements were straightforward. The fundamental performance standard was export success. Firms that received loans but then failed to succeed as exporters were no longer eligible for subsidized loans. More generally, operating with clear performance standards, as well as with penalties for failing to meet the standards, was the key to the success of credit allocation programs in South Korea and other economies described by Amsden (2001).

The situation in the current South African case is not as straightforward. For one thing, measuring success at employment generation is likely to be more difficult than measuring export success. In addition, and more important, opportunities to receive subsidized credit should be open to a wide range of firms. The social priority category especially should clearly be open to firms that cannot provide significant collateral or do not have a substantial prior record of business success.

At the same time, while the aim of the credit allocation program is to be as open and inclusive as possible in terms of providing opportunities to receive subsidized credit, it will also be crucial that the program operate with effective incentive and monitoring structures in place, including significant penalties for failure as well as rewards for success. In the absence of effective incentive and monitoring structures, the probability is high that the program will not achieve its goals of generating a major expansion of employment opportunities.

In short, the incentive and monitoring systems should at once be consistent across firm types, while also recognizing the different requirements and needs of small firms, coops, and farmers, as opposed to large-scale operations.

Proposals for Incentive and Monitoring Structures
Of course, all firms will first be evaluated by the most basic criterion of whether they are meeting the schedules for repaying interest and principle on the loan. Moreover, where appropriate, businesses will also be obligated to pledge collateral to receive credit. However, as mentioned above, there will be some cases where businesses will not be able to produce adequate collateral but should still be eligible to receive loans. At the same time, given that government funds will be pledged in these loans, normal collateral requirements are not likely to be adequate as a disincentive to default. Thus the need for both greater flexibility and more stringent safeguards in the subsidized credit program.

Design of escrow accounts. The creation of escrow accounts can serve as a flexible tool with both small- and large-scale loan contracts. With small-scale loans, the escrow account can be used in cases where potential borrowers do not have adequate collateral to pledge. With large-scale borrowers operating under the terms of their Employment Impact Statements, the escrow account can serve as an incentive for borrowers to meet their employment commitments and to penalize firms failing to do so.

Table 5.7 Creation of Escrow Account for Social Priority Lending (R10,000 Loan at 10 percent simple interest)

	Contributions to escrow account
1) Borrower contribution to qualify for loan	R500
2) Lender contribution at loan approval	R1,500
3) Funding of escrow account at loan disbursal (= lines 1 + 2)	R2,000
3) Borrower annual contributions as share of interest payments	R100/year
4) Accumulated value of account at time of loan maturity	R3,000

Social priority lending. As noted above, SMMEs, small-scale farmers, and coops should all be eligible for social priority loans. In some cases, significant levels of collateral can be included as a component of a loan agreement. This would clearly be the case when land or structures are owned by the borrower and can be pledged. However, many potential borrowers that would be eligible for social priority loans will not own assets. In addition, the government will not necessarily wish to have large amounts of land and buildings reverting to them in the case of loan defaults. Thus, there is a need to create an escrow system that both opens wide opportunities for small-scale and first-time borrowers, while concurrently establishing firm incentives for them to repay their debts.

A system of escrow accounts could be designed to reflect this set of considerations. To be eligible for loans, borrowers at all levels would have to make some cash contribution to an escrow fund. The level could be adjusted according to how expansive the government would choose to be in offering opportunities for small businesses and asset-poor people. At the same time, some portion of the total loan amount would also be committed to the escrow account rather than being immediately available to the borrower. In addition, some portion of the borrowers' repayments would also be deposited in the escrow account rather than received by the lender. The full amount of the escrow account would then be released to the borrower at the time the loan had been repaid. If the borrower defaults on the loan, the escrow funds would revert to the government. The lender, of course, would receive the government-guaranteed funds.

Let's illustrate this with a simple example, presented in Table 5.7. Assume a small business firm receives a loan for R10,000, with a simple interest rate on the loan of 10 percent, to be repaid with interest over 10 years. To be eligible to receive the loan, the borrower would have to pledge, say, R500 to the escrow account. As such, those unable to raise the R500 would not be eligible for a loan of this amount. The lender would then place, say, R1,500 in the escrow account. So the initial amount received by the borrower would be R8,500. The escrow account would then be funded initially at R2,000. In addition, when the borrower pays R1,000/year in simple interest, R100 is also deposited directly into the escrow account. Thus, by the end of the 10-year loan period, the escrow account is now worth R3,000. The borrower receives this R3,000 if the loan is repaid, but the funds revert to the government if the loan is in default. An escrow account figure at roughly this level—i.e. at roughly 30 percent of the value of the initial loan—should, in most cases, provide a significant incentive for borrowers to pay off their loan as contracted. At the same time, only modest demands on borrowers resources—i.e. R500—would be needed for borrowers to be eligible for this social priority lending program.

Of course, this type of incentive system assumes that the borrowers wouldn't be aiming to simply pocket the R8,500 loan disbursement then default on their obligation. Yet it is safe to assume that some borrowers will be planning to default after receiving their disbursement. The way to protect the integrity of the lending system in this case would be to only offer much shorter-term loan disbursements—say, a 2-year maximum loan period rather than a 10-year time to maturity. But the 2-year loan would also include provisions to provide further credit once an initial disbursement has been repaid.

Beyond some variation on this escrow account system, firms that receive social priority loans should only face the normal monitoring that occurs between borrowers and lenders.

Large-scale employment impact loans. Firms that produce Employment Impact Statements will need to be monitored so that they demonstrate that they are fulfilling their pledges in terms of employment generation. In the United States, for example, there has been considerable experience with state and municipal governments providing incentives for businesses in exchange for these firms' pledges to create large amounts of new employment. But for the most part, businesses receiving such subsidies face little monitoring to determine whether they are fulfilling their employment pledges, much less facing penalties for failure to achieve those pledges (see Pollin and Luce 2000, Chapter 3). Obviously, this would not be a desirable approach to employment policy in South Africa.

To the contrary, as a component of the overall employment expansion initiative, firms would have to face some significant penalties for not fulfilling their employment targets. Without this feature of the program, there will not be incentives for firms to meet the terms on which they were awarded loans.

We propose three types of penalties:

1. *Standard credit evaluations.* Borrowers who fail to achieve their employment targets will not be eligible for additional subsidized credit; while at the same time, borrowers that do meet these terms will be viewed favorably for further loans.

2. *Reductions in loan guarantees for lenders.* Lenders to firms that fail to meet employment targets will have to forfeit a share of their loan guarantee at stipulated points as the loan moves toward maturity. Consider, for example, a 10-year loan with a 75 percent government guarantee. The firm and lender will have to provide evidence on employment impacts every three years, for example. If the firm fails to fulfill its employment target over the first three years, then the loan guarantee falls to 50 percent. If the business then succeeds in meeting its target by the sixth year, the guarantee returns to 75 percent. Note that this stipulation would put a burden of monitoring employment effects on the lenders as well as the borrowers. It follows that the lenders should assume this burden if they are also going to be eligible for such substantial guarantees.

3. *Use of an escrow account.* The use of escrow accounts here would be similar to our proposal for social priority lending. Loans that are subsidized will require the establishment of an escrow account into which borrowers and lenders would both contribute. For example, on an R1000 loan, the borrower will need to contribute, say, R50 into the account, while the lender will contribute R100. The borrower will therefore receive R900 as the principal distribution from the loan. In addition, say R25 in annual interest payments are also deposited in the escrow account as loan payments are made. If the employment target has been reached by the end of the loan payment, then the escrow funds are released to the borrower. If the borrower fails to reach the employment target, then the escrow funds revert to the government. Since both the borrower and lender would lose money through the failure to meet the employment target, that would create an incentive on both sides to meet the targets.

Creating Disincentives to Defraud the System. The obvious way to defraud the system of loan guarantees is for borrowers and lenders to collude in obtaining guaranteed loans from the government, then deliberately default on these loans to collect the government guarantee. As colluders in such an enterprise, the borrower and lender would then share the government guarantee payment.

As a simple example, consider a case in which a bank makes a R10,000 social priority loan purportedly to a farmer. But in fact, the loan is actually made to a person colluding with the banker to collect funds from the default—both borrower and lender have entered into the loan contract only to have the loan recorded as a default as quickly as possible. Once the default is accepted as legitimate by the government, the government is then obligated to pay the lender R7,500, assuming a 75 percent guarantee on the loan. The borrower and lender can then split these funds. Of course, they would have also earlier worked out an arrangement for sharing the R10,000 in fraudulent "loan funds."

A loan guarantee system can be designed to minimize the opportunities for such fraud. The first type of disincentive would be to set the guarantee and the initial escrow contributions such that the incentives for fraud are minimized. In addition, this set of incentives can be combined with strict penalties for fraud as well as rewards for people who discover and report on such schemes. We now illustrate these considerations in Table 5.8, building from our previous numerical examples.

As Table 5.8 shows, the main parameters of this case are as follows:

1. Amount of Loan: R1000
2. Terms of Loan: 10 years at 5 percent annual simple interest
3. Government Guarantee: 75 percent of principal on loan
4. Escrow Account: Borrower contributes R100; Lender contributes R200
5. Amount of Funds for Borrower Expenditure: R800

No Default Case. With this loan, if there is no default, the borrower pays R50 per year in interest plus repaying principal. At the end of 10 years, the borrower also receives the R300 (plus accrued interest) on the escrow account.

Default Case. Borrower is out R100 of own money, plus opportunity to receive the R200 additional money in the escrow funds. The lender is out R250, receiving R750 in government guarantee.

Incentive to defraud the system. Assume the borrower and lender are in a conspiracy to defraud the government of the R750 of the loan guarantee. Their arrangement is that each will receive half of the money coming from the government guarantee, i.e. each receives R375 from loan guarantee.

The net outcomes are as follows:

Borrower: Nets R275 (= R375 from guarantee—R100 contribution to escrow)
Lender: Nets R175 (=R375 from guarantee—R200 to escrow).

This incentive to defraud the system could be large enough to encourage this type of operation. If so, the way to weaken such incentives would, straightforwardly, entail some combination of either 1) reducing the level of the guarantee; or 2) increasing the escrow fund obligations for both the borrower and lender.

If we assume that the guarantee is only 50 percent of the loan, but the escrow commitment remains the same, the incentives reduce to the following:

Borrower: Nets R150 (= R250 from guarantee—R100 contribution to escrow)
Lender: Nets R50 (= R250 from guarantee—R200 contribution to escrow)

Table 5.8 Numerical Example on Collateral and Escrow Fund

	Case 1	Case 2
Guarantee	R750	R500
Escrow		
Total escrow	R300	R300
Borrower contribution	R100	R100
Lender contribution	R200	R200
If default, govt. pays	R750	R500
Net gains from fraud		
Borrower gain	R275 (=R375 - R100)	R150 (=250-100)
Lender gain	R175 (=375 – 200)	R50 (=250-200)

Notes: Loan terms: R1000, 10 years at 5 percent
Government guarantee: varies, 75 percent versus 50 percent
Escrow contributions: constant at 10 percent borrower; 20 percent lender

We go through these two examples in Table 5.8.

From these examples, we can see that reducing the size of the guarantees and increasing the amount of the escrow commitments reduce incentives for fraud. But by pursuing such measures, one also obviously weakens the benefits to be accrued from the loan guarantee program, and thereby the prospect that the program could be used as a major financing tool contributing to employment expansion.

Incentive-based monitoring. The way to sustain a more expansionary loan guarantee program—including higher guarantee ratios and lower escrow contribution ratios—is to also create severe penalties for fraud along with strong incentives for "whistleblowers" to report abuses of the system. This means mobilizing incentives to monitor the system rather than relying primarily on government investigators to prevent fraud. This approach to monitoring financial market regulations was developed by Dean Baker (2003) with respect to the so-called Tobin Tax—a tax on speculative transactions in global currency markets. A variation on Baker's idea could be applicable here. For example, in the case of a R1000 loan with a 75 percent guarantee:

1. Penalty to lender for gaming the system: "treble damages"—i.e. R2250
2. Reward for whistleblowing: full amount of guarantee—i.e. R750

Through combining the escrow system with the incentive-based monitoring approach, it should be possible to establish a workable set of incentives to operate a loan guarantee program for both small-scale social priority projects and large-scale employment impact loans.

Asset reserve requirements

South Africa has had considerable experience with its previously operating system of prescribed assets for pension funds. The system that we propose incorporates features similar to those of the earlier program. However, it departs from the earlier approach in several significant ways:

1. The proposed system is more extensive, in that it would apply to all private banks, not only to pension fund holdings.
2. The costs of participating in the system are balanced by benefits. Banks would fulfill their asset reserve requirement through their loans to the priority projects, i.e. through providing the subsidized loans that will be guaranteed by the government.
3. The system can be designed to be far more flexible for any single financial institution than was the case with the prescribed asset framework. As we describe below, no single institution will itself be required to hold any set proportion of assets in its loan portfolio.

The system we are outlining draws from experiences in the United States, Western Europe, and many developing economies (see Pollin 1993, 1995). Table 5.9 illustrates the basic principle of how the policy works. It would require financial institutions to hold a designated proportion of their assets in loans to priority areas or else hold the same proportion of their total assets in a sterile cash reserve account. The cost that the financial institutions would face, of course, would be the loss of interest income from holding the sterile cash asset rather than loans to firms in the targeted industries. The example in the table stipulates that institutions hold 20 percent of their loans in the priority areas. If they hold less than 20 percent, they need to cover this gap by holding cash. By holding less than 20 percent in priority loan areas, of course, the bank would also be losing out on its opportunity to include government-guaranteed loans in its portfolio.

Beyond this most simple example, there are some ways to significantly increase the flexibility of this system while maintaining its overall purpose. First of all, it would not be necessary for every financial institution to carry a loan portfolio that included all targeted industries. Banks could distribute their lending to targeted industries according to their own priorities. Second, not every financial institution would need to make direct loans of any kind to businesses in targeted industries. What could rather evolve is a system of market niches and specializations—for example, Khula Enterprise Finance would be focused on making loans to small-scale businesses, while the Rand Merchant Bank, in turn, would make loans to Khula. More generally, as we mentioned above, the public development banks could encourage the formation of small-scale banking operations that could serve the market for social priority lending. As this small-scale banking sector expands through serving the social priority sectors, the

Table 5.9 Applying a Simple Asset Reserve Requirement Formula to South African Financial Institutions

BANK 1: MEETS RESERVE REQUIREMENT

Assets		Liabilities
Loans		
For stock and bond purchases—	800	Time deposits— R1000
For targeted industries —	R200	
Reserves	0	

BANK 2: DOES NOT MEET RESERVE REQUIREMENT

Assets		Liabilities
Loans		
For stock and bond purchases—	R800	Time deposits— R1000
For targeted industries—	0	
Reserves	R200	

Note: Asset reserve requirement: 20% of loans allocated to targeted industries

larger private banks could enter into partnerships with these banks as a way of meeting their reserve requirements.

The asset requirement system could become more flexible still if the requirements were implemented as proposed by former U.S. Federal Reserve Governor Sherman Maisel (1973), as a system of market auctions rather than quotas. Through an auction system, institutions would not be required to carry the specified proportion (say, 20 percent, following the example in Table 5.9) in loans to priority areas. Financial institutions that exceed the limit would obtain a permit that they could then sell to institutions whose loans to targeted industries are below the minimum. Individual institutions could therefore choose to maintain particular market niches. At the same time, the system would ensure that some market niches carried an extra burden of either higher reserves or purchases of "preferred asset permits."

Overall then, a system of asset reserve requirements would serve as an effective complement to the loan guarantee program. The key feature of both programs combined is that they will enable the financial system to be mobilized on behalf of an employment-targeted economic program while still allowing considerable decision-making freedom both for financial institutions and non-financial businesses. The financial institutions, for example, would still be responsible for establishing the creditworthiness of businesses and the viability of their projects. The businesses would still be responsible for the design and implementation of their investments. Indeed, businesses would still be free to pursue nonpreferred projects and banks could still finance them. It would simply be the case that financing costs for non-preferred projects would be higher, and this difference in costs would need to be high enough so that the aims of the employment-targeted program would become a priority throughout the financial system.

CONTROLS ON EXCHANGE RATES AND CAPITAL FLOWS

Exchange rate variability can create significant problems for monetary policy. Excessive depreciations can raise inflation rates, while excessive appreciations can generate loss of output, profits, and employment in some industries. Variability itself can be harmful by generating more uncertainty and thereby possibly discouraging private investors.

All of these issues will become central if South Africa commits itself to a more expansionary set of fiscal, monetary, and credit allocation policies—i.e. to a set of measures that we believe will be the foundation of an employment-targeted program. Policymakers have to take seriously the possibility that financial market investors might have a negative reaction to such a program, and this could lead to a sell-off of the rand. Such a reaction by the financial markets could happen entirely as a result of a shift in investor perceptions, regardless of whether the fundamental indicators of economic stability—such as fiscal deficits and the inflation rate—may have only changed by the relatively modest amounts we are proposing. If there were to be a significant shift in investor attitudes causing significant downward pressure on the rand, this in turn could lead to undesired movements in interest rates, thereby making it difficult for policymakers to lower interest rates as a means of promoting faster growth of GDP and jobs. Of course, this scenario would not necessarily occur, but it is nevertheless important to acknowledge that the possibility exists and to examine options for responding effectively.

The problem we are describing here is an instance of the famous policy "trilemma" governments face in conducting macroeconomic policy within the framework of highly integrated global capital markets. With highly integrated capital markets, it becomes impossible for a country such as South Africa to pursue these three goals at once: 1) to conduct an autonomous monetary policy, in behalf of an inflation target, employment target or any other target; 2) to maintain fixed exchange rates; and 3) to allow free capital flows into and out of the country. Thus, if South Africa is committed to an autonomous monetary policy and to liberalized capital markets, then, according to this view, it must be willing to allow unrestrained fluctuations in the value of the rand. However, letting the rand fluctuate at will can, in turn, undermine the country's capacity to advance an effective program of accelerated GDP growth and employment expansion.

Capital controls, exchange controls, and more generally, capital management techniques—encompassing a variety of policy interventions to manage a country's capital inflows and outflows—have been proposed as mechanisms for reducing the sensitivity of domestic financial markets, including exchange rates, to macroeconomic policy. For South Africa, such measures could potentially serve to at least partially insulate the economy against any excessive negative overreactions by financial markets to an employment-targeted economic program such as we are proposing. The key question for South Africa then is: to what extent and under what conditions can capital management policies enhance the autonomy of macroeconomic policy, including helping to manage exchange rates? Unfortunately, as we will see, there aren't simple answers to this question. At the same time, the evidence we have surveyed leads us to conclude that, at the least, such measures would support efforts by the Reserve Bank to lower nominal interest rates within the range of about 4 percentage points that we are proposing. In addition, severe bouts of exchange rate volatility will be less likely when capital management policies are deployed to prevent such episodes. The fact that South Africa has a long history of utilizing capital management techniques, including exchange and capital controls, enhances the prospect that such measures could be used effectively at present to at least provide support for a more expansionary set of fiscal, monetary, and credit allocation policies.

Background on Exchange Controls in South Africa

South Africa has used exchange controls and other capital management techniques since at least 1939. The application of these techniques has ebbed and flowed over the years. The current governing legislation was set out in 1961.

A.M. Bruce-Brand of the Reserve Bank has written a useful history and overview of how South Africa has used exchange controls (2002). According to Bruce-Brand's official account, the purposes of exchange controls have been the following:

1. To ensure the repatriation within the South African banking system of all currency acquired by residents of South Africa;
2. To prevent the loss of foreign currency resources through the transfer abroad of real or financial capital assets held in South Africa; and
3. To effectively control the movement into and out of South Africa of financial and real assets while at the same time not interfering with the efficient operation of the country's commercial, industrial, and financial systems.

In sum, according to Bruce-Brand, the main goals of the exchange controls have been the preservation of savings and the management of inflows and outflows.

Prior to 1979, the rand was pegged to either the U.S. dollar or the pound sterling. Exchange controls restricted residents' capital flows. Moreover, proceeds from the sale of assets by non-residents were placed in blocked rand accounts, which made the repatriation of capital difficult (Aron, et al. 2004). The dual currency exchange rate established in 1979 introduced greater flexibility in the use of controls. A commercial exchange rate was announced on a daily basis in line with market forces. A financial exchange rate applied to most non-resident transactions, with all other transactions channeled through the commercial rand market. As described by Aron et al., the intended impact of the dual system was to break the direct link between domestic and foreign interest rates, as well as to insulate the capital account from certain categories of capital flows. In 1983 the commercial rate was set free to be determined in the market, subject to direct intervention by the Reserve Bank, and the dual rates were unified. At that time, controls on non-resident capital movements were removed. Those on residents remained but were treated more leniently.

The unified currency remained stable for a few months, but began a sharp descent in 1983, in correspondence with the gold price decline at that time. In 1985, following a prolonged period of political crisis, and more immediately, after then-President Botha's Rubicon speech and the declaration of the state of emergency, U.S. banks recalled their loans, precipitating a debt crisis. This was followed by a debt standstill, and subsequently a series of debt rescheduling agreements. The unified rand fell even further, and eventually the financial rand was reintroduced and capital controls on residents were tightened in 1985. The dual-currency system remained in existence until its unification a decade later, in March 1995, under a managed float (Aron et al. 2004).

With the reintegration of South Africa into the world following the end of the apartheid regime in 1994, the government decided to progressively liberalize the capital and exchange controls. According to Bruce-Brand's study for the Reserve Bank (2002), the government followed this sequence:

1. Abolish exchange controls on all current account transactions;
2. Abolish exchange controls on non-residents;
3. Gradually become more lenient in approving applications for outward FDI;
4. Allow institutional investors to acquire more foreign assets to diversify their portfolios;
5. Progressively relax all other controls on resident individuals; and
6. Release emigrants' blocked funds.

According to official statements, the government authorities "gradually became much more lenient in the exercise of discretion in the administration of exchange controls." In short, since 1994, the government has progressively relaxed both the rules and the level of enforcement of these rules.

Table 5.10 Capital Controls in South Africa in 2002 and 2004

	2002	2004
Resident individuals	Outflows limited; must surrender foreign exchange receipts; emigrant outflows very limited	No major changes
Resident corporations	Can apply to transfer up to R750 million in Africa; R500 elsewhere; all loans from outside the Common Monetary Area require approval	Up to R2 billion in Africa; 1 billion elsewhere (per year); more ability to use offshore loans to finance FDI abroad
Resident institutional investors	On application, may acquire foreign portfolio assets up to 15%–20% of the total portfolio	No major changes
Resident authorized dealers	Export receipts must be sold to authorized dealer; foreign currency may be sold to non-residents *only* if they have underlying assets in South Africa; may be sold to residents only if they have a proven foreign exchange commitment with a non-resident	No major changes
For non-residents		
Outflows	Not restricted or controlled	No major changes
Use of domestic funds	Highly restricted	No major changes
FDI inflows	Controlled	More ability to use offshore and onshore loans to finance inward FDI

Sources: Bruce-Brand (2002); National Treasury (2004).

In practice, this gradual relaxation has been uneven. More specifically, during the 2002 currency crisis, the Reserve Bank strengthened the enforcement of the rules. Since that time, as capital inflows have increased and the Reserve Bank has closed out its financial debt (its so-called "open book"), it has further relaxed both the controls' enforcement and the explicit controls themselves (National Treasury, Budget Circular, 2004).

Table 5.10 above shows the controls in place as of 2002 and then the changes that occurred in 2004. The primary controls had been applied to residents, and these were relaxed in 2004, especially for corporations. The pattern between these two years is consistent with a more general pattern of fluctuations in the degree to which controls have been applied. This longer-term pattern is portrayed in Figure 5.6, which presents an index on the degree of openness of the South African financial markets between 1966–95. As the figure shows, the degree of financial openness began increasing before the transition to democracy in 1994. Though the index number doesn't continue past 1995, the general pattern would be toward continued openness, with a temporary tightening of controls in 2002.

Impacts of Capital Management Techniques

Brief general review of studies
There is a large literature that attempts to assess the effectiveness of capital controls (see Dooley 1995; Epstein and Schor 1992; and Epstein, Grabel and Jomo, K.S. 2005 as three surveys in a large literature). Effectiveness is examined in such studies along two primary dimensions: 1) their ability to maintain a "wedge" between domestic interest rates and foreign rates; and 2) their ability to help prevent currency crises, i.e., either large-scale changes in exchange rates or the forcing of countries off of a peg through reserve loss. More recent research has also looked at the ability of controls (especially on capital inflows) to prevent over-valued currencies and currency instability and the ability of controls to provide autonomy for central bank expansion.

No clear-cut consensus exists on these issues. However, Michael Dooley's survey for the National Bureau of Economic Research suggests at least one large area of agreement with respect to the effectiveness of controls on insulating interest rates and exchange rates from international pressures. Dooley concludes that

> Capital controls do seem to be effective in insulating domestic interest rates and exchange rates from international factors, but usually only to a moderate degree, especially if the time period is a long one; and only if the overall set of macroeconomic policies are internally consistent (1995, p. 29).

Beyond this, more recent studies provide stronger evidence that capital controls can help prevent serious bouts of financial instability or crisis (Epstein, Grabel, and Jomo 2005). During the 1997–98 Asian financial crisis, for example, countries that used controls on outflows and/or inflows were more likely to be able to avoid the contagion effects flowing out of the crisis. In addition, the evidence suggests that Chile was able to avoid an overvalued exchange rate and tilt toward a longer-maturity structure of borrowing. In the case of Malaysia, Kaplan and Rodrik (2001) have found that controls on outflows temporarily allowed policymakers to pursue a more expansionary macroeconomic policy.

Overall then, a careful reading of the evidence would suggest that, when implemented with reasonable care, controls can be effective in reducing finan-

Figure 5.6 Financial Integration Index for South Africa, 1966–1995

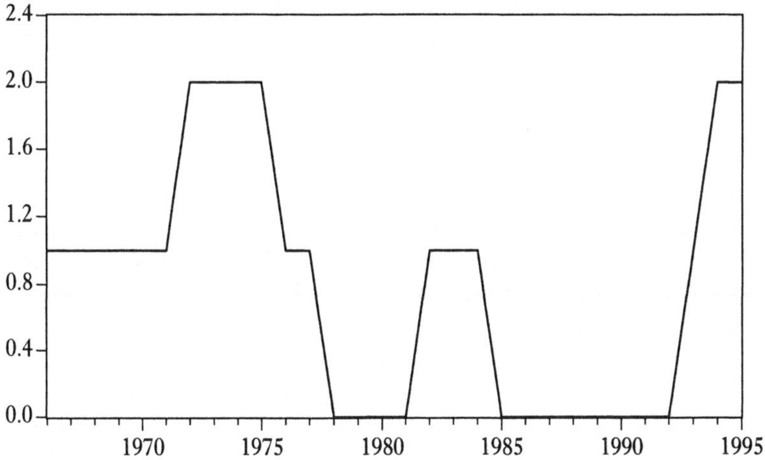

Notes: Index range is 0–4, with 0 representing completely controlled markets and 4 representing completely open markets.
Source: Milesi-Ferretti (1998).

cial instability, and can also make at least a modest contribution toward enhancing the autonomy of policymakers vis-à-vis global financial forces.

Effectiveness of controls in South Africa

There have been surprisingly few studies of the effectiveness of capital controls in South Africa. The most rigorous and important is a 2001 paper by G.N. Farrell of the Reserve Bank (2001). Farrell studied the effectiveness of the period of dual exchange rates and tighter controls on residents of South Africa. The goal of the dual exchange rate system was to insulate the market for current account transactions from the more volatile financial market transactions, i.e. according to Farrell, "to separate the foreign exchange transactions of non-resident portfolio investors on the capital account from all other foreign exchange transactions," (Farrell 2001, p. 1). Farrell studied the period February 1983 to August 1995 in which a dual exchange rate system was operating. He then compared this period with an earlier period and later period—February 1983–August 1985; and March 1995–October 1998, during which a unified exchange rate system was in place. Using formal statistical techniques, Farrell found that the volatility of the rand was lower during the dual exchange rate period than during the two periods of unified exchange rates.

Farrell's findings suggest that policymakers may want to consider reinstating something like the dual exchange rate system that prevailed from 1983–95.

At the same time, something like this dual exchange rate system would not by itself address all the potential financial market forces that could contribute to financial instability within the context of a more expansionary macroeconomic policy. More specifically, a dual exchange rate system could almost certainly reduce the impact of lower interest rates on inflation by reducing the link between lower interest rates and the fluctuations of the *commercial rand* exchange rate (the one used for current account transactions). However, unstable inflows and outflows of capital might still affect interest rates in financial markets to the extent that they are tied to the *financial rand* as opposed to the commercial rand exchange rate. This suggests that some other configuration of controls—one that can influence both commercial and financial flows of capital—might be more effective as a policy tool.

Beyond the Farrell comparative study on the dual exchange rate system, research is limited on the effectiveness of controls in South Africa. It may nevertheless be helpful to review some basic data comparing the changes in controls with fluctuations in both the levels of interest rates in South Africa and the differentials in interest rates between South Africa and the United States. Figure 5.7 presents a basic descriptive picture here. It shows the movements between 1973–95 in the financial integration index that we initially presented in Figure 5.6, along with patterns over this time period for both the real prime rate in South Africa and the interest rate differential between South Africa and the United States.

We can see in the figure, to begin with, that our real interest rate data series and the interest rate differential series move fairly closely together. Beyond this, the graph offers some suggestive evidence on the effectiveness of capital controls, as measured by the financial integration index. Thus, we see that the main periods of decline in both the real prime rate and the interest rate differential are periods when capital controls were relatively tight—1978–81 and 1985–90. We also observe the inverse: the periods of most rapid increase in both the interest rate and the rate differential were periods when controls were being loosened. This pattern is broadly consistent with the evidence reviewed above that capital controls can allow some reduction in interest differentials, at least over a limited time period.

The information in Figure 5.7 also suggests that the degree of these controls varies over time in South Africa. So, by itself, these data cannot provide information on the ability of controls to maintain a "wedge" between domestic and world interest rates for an indefinite period. Indeed, if anything, the information in Figure 5.7 suggests that the effectiveness of the controls for maintaining lower interest rates and differentials might be on the order of one or two years. As the figure shows, when the financial liberalization index falls to 0 (controls are tightened), the interest rate and differential first fall, and begin to rise again after a few years or so.

Figure 5.7 Capital Controls, Interest Rates and Interest Rate Differentials, 1973–95

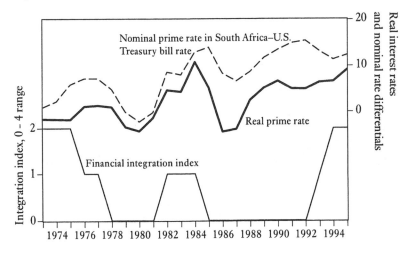

Sources: Milesi-Ferretti (1998); Reserve Bank of South Africa, IMF *International Financial Statistics.*

In Figure 5.8, we again utilize the financial integration index to examine the relationship between capital controls and exchange rates. It plots the integration index against the movements of the change in the nominal exchange rate. These relative movements suggest that there may be some impact of capital controls on exchange rate changes. When capital controls are tightened, exchange rate fluctuations diminish. When they are relaxed, exchange rate changes increase. This is consistent with Farrell's (2001) finding that the dual exchange rate system did reduce exchange rate variability.

Overall perspective on exchange and capital controls

South Africa has had a long history with exchange and capital controls. The government has an experienced enforcement apparatus in place, and the private financial institutions are accustomed to dealing with such regulations. In addition, global financial markets are accustomed to South Africa periodically adjusting the extent of its controls, depending on the broader goals of economic policy at any given time. Beyond this, the general professional opinion among academic economists and policymakers has become increasingly favorable toward controls, especially since the Asian financial debacle. In short, from a range of perspectives, there is a strong case for South Africa to move toward using its system of controls more actively as one component of a broad employment-targeted economic program. In this context, it should be clear that operating with a relatively modest set of controls would not mean that South Africa

Figure 5.8 Capital Controls and Exchange Rate Changes in South Africa, 1973–95

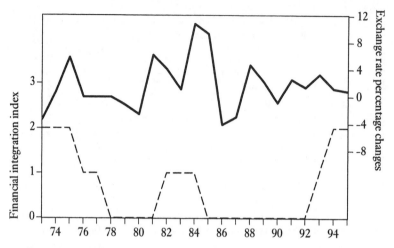

Sources: Milesi-Ferretti (1998); Reserve Bank of South Africa, IMF *International Financial Statistics.*

is moving toward a closed economy. It would rather mean that South Africa is committed to using all practical tools at hand to advance an ambitious program of employment creation, even while recognizing the constraints under which such a program would need to operate in order to succeed.

Despite the evidence we have reviewed as well as the shift in professional opinion in favor of controls, South Africa has been facing growing pressure from domestic and global financial institutions to eliminate its controls. For example, Goldman Sachs recently published a *Global Economics Paper* entitled "South Africa: Capital Controls Constraining Growth," in which they errone-ously claim that there is a negative relationship between capital controls and economic growth. However, the IMF itself has not been among those opposing controls for South Africa, at least in terms of short-run measures. Thus, in its 2003 Staff Report on South Africa, the Fund economists expressed opposition to relaxing controls until the country's ratio of foreign reserves to short-term debt improves. The IMF position was that (1) exchange rate volatility is costly for South Africa; (2) a higher ratio of foreign reserves to short-term debt dampens volatility; (3) exchange controls can also reduce volatility (this is implied); and therefore (4), exchange controls can be an effective substitute in the short-run for a less-than-optimal foreign exchange position.

Similarly, IMF economists present indirect supporting arguments for capital management in a recent analysis on the determinants of interest costs in South Africa (Arora 2004; see also Ahmed 2004). This IMF research studies the determinants of interest costs in South Africa relative to costs abroad, in particu-lar, "sovereign interest rate spreads" in South Africa relative to those abroad. They find that among the important causes of increases in these spreads—and therefore in interest costs in South Africa—are net open foreign exchange posi-tions taken by investors in South Africa and offshore. Capital management tech-niques, such as those used in Singapore, that can reduce these positions can therefore reduce interest costs in South Africa (Epstein, Grabel and Jomo 2005), which in turn would contribute to faster economic growth and employment creation. According to this IMF research, a type of "virtuous cycle" can also result: faster economic growth can also lead to lower sovereign spreads and there-fore lower interest costs for the South African economy, leading, again, to still more rapid economic growth.

Our view, in any case, is that maintaining a regime without at least latent capital controls would be a serious mistake. Now is in fact an appropriate time to strengthen the controls again, even before the government might undertake a broader expansionary program. This is because the currency is almost certainly overly strong, which has led to a significant inflow of portfolio investments into South African financial markets. Moreover, if the government is going to com-mit to an ambitious program to promote employment growth, it would be ben-eficial to have in place a tighter system of controls than is operating at present. Finally, the available evidence suggests that it is difficult to reinstate a system of controls once they have been completely eliminated and the apparatus of con-trol closed down (Epstein, Grabel and Jomo 2005).

The issue of exactly what type of controls to implement at present is a highly detailed and technical one, and beyond the scope of our discussion here. But for South Africa, a system of "trip wires" and "speed bumps," as suggested by the research of Ilene Grabel, would be a good start (see Grabel 2004). Under Grabel's proposal, the Reserve Bank and other financial authorities would de-vise a set of indicators that could act as early warning signals for foreign ex-change, exchange rate, or other financial sector problems. Then a system of speed bumps could be in place to slow down the destabilizing market activity. Recent research suggests that dynamic and flexible controls that can be strength-ened or weakened as conditions warrant are, for a relatively liberalized economy such as South Africa, the most effective capital management techniques to use.

In conclusion however, we need to recognize the limitations of such mea-sures, at least as they might reasonably be implemented in the current political climate. Such policies can certainly help reduce the overreaction of financial market traders to any change in macroeconomic policies such as we are propos-ing in this study, at least within a period of two to five years. Over a period of, say, five years, the controls will also be able to maintain interest rates at a level one to two percentage points below those that have prevailed in recent years. By that time, however, the benefits of faster economic growth would likely convince foreign investors that South Africa is a desirable place to invest. The country's so-called "risk premium" would then likely decline, facilitating a decline in South African interest rates relative to foreign rates.

INFLATION CONTROL AND ECONOMIC GROWTH

The government of South Africa has made clear that it is committed to attacking the country's severe problems of poverty and unemployment. At the same time, since the adoption of the GEAR program of macroeconomic policy measures, and even more explicitly, since the establishment of the inflation-targeting regime, the government has been committed to maintaining a low-inflation environment. The government clearly holds to the idea that maintaining a low-inflation environment is a necessary foundation for attacking poverty and unemployment in a sustainable way.

We certainly do not advocate a high inflation rate, or a relaxation of the inflation-targeting regime as an end in itself. However, the primary tool the government utilizes to control inflation is to maintain high interest rates. As part of our own set of proposals for attacking poverty and unemployment, we have advanced measures to lower interest rates—both across the board, and also by providing a large-scale subsidized credit program. If the government seeks a lower interest-rate environment as an intermediate tool for stimulating employment growth, it is likely that inflationary pressures will rise beyond where they have been recently under the inflation-targeting regime.

The question we must therefore examine is this: how high would the costs be to the South African economy of allowing the inflation rate to rise above its current target range of between 3–6 percent? This is obviously a major matter of concern. We will first review some relevant literature on the relationship between inflation and growth. We then report results from our own econometric examination of the relationship between inflation and growth. We finally discuss alternatives to high interest rates as an approach to inflation control, focusing primarily on incomes policies.

What is the Relationship between Inflation and Growth?

Answers to this question vary widely in the professional literature. Some of the most influential recent studies were those produced by the late Michael Bruno, along with his colleague William Easterly. Bruno was Chief Economist at the World Bank at the time he conducted his studies.

In his 1995 research, Bruno studied the relationship between inflation and economic growth for 127 countries between 1960 and 1992. Bruno found that the average growth rates fell only slightly as inflation rates moved up to 20–25 percent. Of particular importance for our concerns here with South Africa, Bruno found that during 1960–72, economic growth on average increased as inflation rose, from negative or low rates to the 15–20 percent range. This is because, as Bruno explained, "in the 1950s and 1960s, low-to-moderate inflation went hand in hand with very rapid growth because of investment demand pressures in an expanding economy," (1995, p. 35). Thus, inflation that results directly from economic expansion does not, according to Bruno's findings, create any significant barriers to expansion.

Bruno's 1995 findings were challenged by other researchers, who did indeed find that inflation leads to lower economic growth. However, in responding to these critics, Bruno and Easterly (1998) found that the clear negative relationship between inflation and growth operates only at very high inflation rates—what they define as in the range of 40 percent and above. Once these experiences of very high inflation are considered separately from those of moderate inflation, Bruno and Easterly again find that, for the moderate inflation cases, no clear relationship exists between inflation and economic growth.

Still again, other researchers have produced findings contradictory to Bruno and Easterly, even after separating out the experiences of high (i.e. 40 percent or more) inflation from moderate inflation. For example, IMF economists Ghosh and Phillips (1998), drawing from a data sample of IMF member countries over 1960–96, found evidence of a negative inflation/growth threshold at 2.5 percent. But they also acknowledge that thresholds of 5 to 10 percent generate statistical results very similar to their 2.5 percent threshold.

Their particular conclusions aside, the work of Ghosh and Phillips is within a widely accepted current stream of research that distinguishes the relationship to growth of different levels of inflation—observing how the effects of inflation on growth will vary at, say, 5, 10, 20 and 30 percent inflation rates. These researchers rely on nonlinear econometric estimating techniques to distinguish the growth/inflation effects at these alternative threshold levels. What is also especially relevant for the South Africa case, this most recent stream of researchers now also consistently finds that the growth/inflation relationship is different for industrialized countries and developing countries.

For example, a 2001 study by another team of IMF economists, Moshin Khan and Abdelhak Senhadji, identified the threshold point for industrial countries at which inflation reduces economic growth at a very low 1–3 percent. But their threshold point for developing countries was between 11–12 percent. This distinction in threshold points was also found in a 2004 study by Burdekin, Denzau, Keil, Sitthiyot, and Willett. They also utilized non-linear estimating techniques. However, they reached conclusions nearly opposite to Khan and Senhadji: that the negative inflation/growth threshold was higher for industrial countries, at 8 percent, than the threshold for developing countries, which was 3 percent.

Robert Pollin and Andong Zhu (2006) have recently developed another model that estimates the effects of inflation on economic growth. This model includes inflation as one potential factor influencing economic growth, after controlling for a range of other potential influences.[12] The growth/inflation estimates are based on data from 80 countries between 1961–2000. As with the more recent literature generally, the Pollin–Zhu model includes a non-linear component to capture the differential effects of relatively low versus relatively high levels of inflation. In addition, the models follow Bruno and Easterly (1998) in excluding inflation episodes in excess of 40 percent. Finally, this model examines the inflation/growth relationship for the full set of countries in different ways. It provides separate sets of results for OECD countries, middle-income countries, and low-income countries. It also considers the full sample of countries within four separate decades between 1961–2000. This study then utilizes four different estimating techniques with each of the various country- and time-period groupings to test for the robustness of findings using any given technique.

The main results of these exercises can be summarized quickly. Considering our full data set, they consistently find that higher inflation is associated with moderate gains in GDP growth up to a roughly 15–18 percent inflation threshold. But their results do diverge when they divide their full data set according to income levels. With the OECD countries, no clear pattern emerges in terms of identifying a negative inflation/growth threshold. With the middle-income countries, including South Africa, they then return to a consistently positive relationship between inflation and growth up to a 14–16 percent threshold, though the results are not statistically significant. The positive inflation/growth relationship holds more strongly and consistently with the low-income countries. With the groupings by decades, the results indicate that inflation and growth will be more positively correlated to the degree that macroeconomic policy is focused on stimulating demand. This finding is consistent with Bruno's observation that growth and inflation were more positively correlated over 1960–72, when active demand management policies were being widely practiced in support of maintaining high employment.

In short, the results from Pollin and Zhu's model are broadly consistent with Bruno's earlier studies, despite substantial differences between their methodological approaches. That is, the Pollin–Zhu model generates no statistically robust evidence suggesting that moderate inflation, in the range of less than 20 percent, will have a negative influence on economic growth. There was rather some evidence to support the view that such moderate inflation is positively correlated with growth.

Considering the findings from all the studies in addition to our own, nothing close to a consensus has been reached on this question, even while increasingly sophisticated estimating techniques have been deployed to control for various non-linearities in the inflation/economic growth relationship. At the same time, a few basic conclusions from these various studies that are relevant for the South African case do seem warranted.[13] A first basic conclusion is that regardless of whether researchers observe a negative growth/inflation relationship emerging in the low or high double-digit inflation range for developing countries, only one study found a clear negative relationship between growth and *single-digit* inflation specifically for the developing countries. This suggests that for South Africa, setting an inflation target at between 3 and 6 percent is not likely to offer benefits in terms of the economy's growth performance. If South Africa chooses to follow the low-end finding within the professional literature on the inflation/growth trade-off, that would still suggest an inflation target in the range of 8–9 percent.

A second basic conclusion is that, despite the wide range of techniques now being used to estimate the growth/inflation trade-off, no researcher has challenged one important point emphasized by Bruno in his initial 1995 work—namely, that the relationship between inflation and growth will be different depending on *what is causing* the economy's inflationary pressures. As Bruno found, demand-pull inflation, resulting from a process of economic expansion, will be positively associated with growth as long as the inflation rate remains moderate. Thus, if South Africa pursues an aggressive jobs program, one would expect that the inflationary pressures that may then emerge would not be harmful to growth, as long as, again, the inflation remains moderate.

By contrast, following the logic of Bruno's findings, inflation that results from excessive price mark-ups over costs by businesses, supply shocks, or exchange rate volatility will be associated with negative growth effects. But these negative growth effects will not be due to the inflation per se, bur rather stem from the monopolistic pricing power of businesses or from the economy's attempt at adjusting to the effects of supply shocks or to volatile movements of the rand.

Does Inflation Targeting Change the Growth/Inflation Relationship?

Proponents of inflation targeting within international academic and policymaking circles have argued that operating monetary policy under this type of arrangement changes the basic dynamic between growth and inflation. Specifically, the claim is that inflation targeting will both reduce the rate of inflation and enhance the credibility of policy. By enhancing credibility, inflation targeting will then reduce the so-called "sacrifice ratio"—that is, it will support a move to lower inflation with fewer costs in terms of lost output or increased unemployment.

In recent years, a number of studies have assessed the validity of these claims, including studies by the IMF and the U.S. Federal Reserve. Nearly all of these studies find that there is nothing to be gained in terms of a reduced sacrifice ratio through pursuing inflation targeting policies. We mention briefly here some of the main research findings in this area.[14]

Lawrence Ball and Niamh Sheridan wrote a 2003 IMF Working Paper on this issue titled, "Does Inflation Targeting Matter?" Their answer was unequivocal: they found *no evidence* that inflation targeting improves economic performance, either in terms of inflation, interest rates, the variance of inflation, output, interest rates, or the persistence of shocks. They write, "There is no evidence whatsoever that inflation targeting reduces inflation variability ... Our robust finding is that inflation targeting has no beneficial effects."

On the basis of the empirical work on the consequences of inflation targeting in Australia, New Zealand, and Canada, Alan Blinder, a former Vice Chairman of the Federal Reserve states, "nor does the recent experience of OECD countries suggest that central banks that posted inflation targets were able to disinflate at lower cost than central banks without such targets," (Blinder 1998, p. 63).

A 1999 study by Ben Bernanke, the present Chair of the U.S. Federal Reserve Board of Governors, along with Thomas Laubach, Adam Posen, and Frederic Miskin, reaches the same conclusion. Bernanke and colleagues write that:

> Inflation targeting is no panacea ... it does not enable countries to wring inflation out of their economies without incurring costs in lost output and employment; nor is credibility for the central bank achieved immediately on adoption of an inflation target. Indeed, evidence suggests that the only way for central banks to earn credibility is the hard way: by demonstrating that they have the means and the will to reduce inflation and to keep it low for a period of time (Bernanke, et al. 1999, p. 308).

One exception to this evidence is a 2001 paper written for the Central Bank of Chile by Vittorio Corbo, Oscar Landerretche, and Klaus Schmidt-Hebbel. They find that the sacrifice ratios have declined in emerging markets after adopting inflation targeting. They also find that output volatility has fallen in both emerging and idustrialized economies after adopting inflation targets at levels similar to (and sometimes lower than) those observed in industrial countries that do not target inflation.

Despite the Corbo et al. study, the overall weight of evidence still supports the view that inflation targeting has no special benefits. Of course, this does not mean that policymakers should necessarily change their commitments to controlling inflation. It rather means that, in formulating inflation control policies, they should 1) recognize the costs that are incurred—the sacrifice ratio—when they push to keep inflation at a very low level; and 2) consider alternative approaches to inflation control that may be more successful at reducing the sacrifice ratio.

Policy Implications and Proposals

The weight of the professional literature to date suggests that, as South Africa pursues an aggressive program of employment expansion, it should not weaken the program as long as inflation remains moderate, i.e. basically within a single-digit range. But what happens if inflation accumulates momentum, such that a rise to a 10 percent inflation rate leads to still greater inflationary pressures? Should South Africa then revert to raising interest rates, its standard policy tool at present for controlling inflation? In fact, two other policy tools are available, through which South Africa could contain inflation within a moderate range, without having to rely on high interest rates as its control mechanism.

The first tool is to pursue policies that weaken the monopolistic pricing power that exists now in some sectors of the economy. We raise this issue in our discussion on sectoral policies, and simply refer to it again in this somewhat distinct context.

The second tool is to pursue so-called "incomes policies." Incomes policies have been developed in various specific ways, but the basic idea is straightforward: that wage and price increases are negotiated economy-wide between the organized sectors of labor and business. The purpose of such economy-wide negotiations is precisely to sustain a process of economic growth without allowing accelerating inflation to undermine such growth opportunities. As we have discussed in Chaper 3, incomes policies can provide an institutional basis through which the South African economy can combine employment growth and wage restraint, without having to resort to wage cutting in its attempt to generate employment growth.

Incomes policies have been widely used as an inflation control tool in a variety of contexts. One common situation has been in bringing down inflation after it has risen to a range above 40 percent. For example, in their paper "Moderate Inflation" (1991) the late Rudiger Dornbusch and Stanley Fischer, the former Director of Research at the IMF and currently Governor of the Bank of Israel, describe how Mexico in the 1980s drew upon experiences in Argentina, Brazil, Peru, and Israel in developing a strategy to bring inflation down from the 100 percent range to something closer to 20 percent. Dornbusch and Fischer reported that the Mexicans learned two lessons from these experiences: 1) "that disinflation without fiscal discipline was unsustainable;" but that 2) "disinflation without an incomes policy, relying solely on tight money and tight budgets, would be unnecessarily expensive," (p. 31). In analyzing the Israeli experience with disinflation over the 1980s, Michael Bruno—who served as Governor of the Bank of Israel during the 1980s before becoming Chief Economist at the World Bank—documents in detail the major contributions of incomes policies to the success of the effort (1993, Chapter 5).

With respect to the current situation in South Africa, perhaps the more directly relevant experiences with incomes policies are those of the Nordic countries. This is because, in these countries, incomes policies have been used successfully as a tool for maintaining relatively low inflation over long periods of time rather than as primarily an instrument of disinflation, as was true with Mexico and Israel. Sweden, for example, succeeded in maintaining unemployment at an average rate below 2 percent between 1951–2000 while holding inflation at a 4.4 percent average rate. The application of incomes policies in Sweden, moreover, primarily took the form of centralized bargaining between unions and business, through which the aim of inflation control was recognized in the bargaining process. As such, the government did not have to rely on setting mandates for acceptable wage and price increases. The government did also utilize fiscal and monetary policies as tools for controlling inflation. But it did not have to apply these tools stringently, precisely because it could rely on its well-developed incomes policies as a complement to monetary and fiscal policies.[15]

The most basic critique of incomes policies is that, in order for the approach to have any chance of success, it is necessary that a country operate with a high level of organization among workers, and that there be some reasonable degree of common ground between workers and business. Otherwise, there will be no realistic prospect for economy-wide bargaining to yield results that will be honored widely. In the case of South Africa, there does already exist a high degree of organization both among sectors of the working class and among business. The relationship between unions and business is highly contentious. But this could possibly diminish to the extent that both sides saw the benefits of a program of accelerated economic growth and employment expansion.

Professor Stephen Gelb has developed preliminary sketches of how incomes policies could operate in South Africa (1996). Gelb argues for a system of voluntary wage and price constraints negotiated by a tripartite commission of labor, business, and government. As Gelb writes:

> Voluntary restraint implies the negotiation of a social compact, of which the limits on wage and price increases, as outlined above, form the core. All parties, including government, would agree to the ceilings on increases. In addition, other issues should be placed on the negotiating agenda for the compact, as identified in an earlier document, including monetary and interest rate policy, and the investment regime (p. 10).

The success of such voluntary restraints depends, of course, on their being understood as basic features of a broader program of economic growth, employment expansion, and poverty reduction. In other words, incomes policies should be seen as one major element of an alternative to high interest rates and slow economic growth as the mechanism of inflation control. Indeed, through the institution of NEDLAC—the National Economic Development and Labor Council, which operates precisely to promote economy-wide negotiations among business, labor, government and civil society representatives—South Africa already has in place the basic institutional structures for developing an incomes policy approach as an effective means of inflation control.

PRODUCTIVE SECTOR POLICIES

We have already examined the South African economy on a sectoral basis through our earlier sector-by-sector analysis of relative labor intensities and employment multipliers. This analysis, of course, was linked in turn to our proposal for stimulating employment growth through credit subsidies for activities with large capacities for rapid employment expansion. These ideas certainly form part of the foundation of our proposed program for employment targeting in South Africa.

At the same time, we do not wish to suggest that these are the only matters of concern with respect to sectoral policy. Nor do we believe that credit allocation policies are the only effective instrument for promoting targeted industries and sectors. In fact, the Department of Trade and Industry (DTI) uses an array of policy instruments to address the needs of specific industrial sectors, including differential trade policies, export incentives, import duty and tax credits, regional coordination and market development, infrastructure provision, and managed competition and pricing policies.

In this section, we examine two additional issues that fall within the broad framework of sectoral policy. The first is price setting and market power. The second is the importance of incorporating measures other than employment impacts as criteria for promoting specific sectors or activities. As we try to show, there are legitimate reasons for promoting some sectors within the auto industry and capital goods industry, even though these industries score poorly with respect to their overall employment multipliers. Such considerations are within the spirit of the preliminary work on the ASGISA program, which, at least in this preliminary state, has identified "medium-term" priority sectors such as chemicals on grounds other than employment expansion. We consider our two sets of issues in turn.

Getting Prices Wrong

The rapid industrialization of many countries in East Asia is frequently cited as an example of industrial policy being used effectively to solve coordination problems between industrial sectors, take advantage of long-run dynamic efficiencies, and address costly market failures (Amsden 2001, Chang 1994). Alice Amsden (2001) argues that rapid industrialization in these countries occurred because governments made a deliberate effort to "get the prices wrong" (p. 10). In other words, state-led interventions were able to achieve allocative and dynamic efficiencies that would not have been realized if unfettered markets were allowed to coordinate economic activities through unregulated price determination.

In South Africa, prices often differ significantly from what would prevail on an idealized competitive market. However, the situation is dramatically different from what occurred in the case of the East Asian miracle economies. Price setting often inhibits the realization of dynamic efficiencies and inter-sectoral coordination that could drive industrial development. These distortions raise the costs associated with upstream and downstream linkages and limit the benefits of multiplier effects in expanding output throughout the economy in response to an economic stimulus. Moreover, price determinations are frequently inconsistent with the objectives of industrial and social policies.

The administered prices of the parastatals—the publicly-owned utilities and economic services industries—are a case in point. Enterprises such as Eskom (electricity), Transnet (transportation), and Telkom (telecommunications) provide essential inputs and services to sectors throughout the South African economy. However, prices are poorly regulated and are not effectively coordinated with national policy objectives (Storer and Teljeur 2003). Prices are often the outcome of a process of negotiation rather than an integrated regulatory framework. For example, large industrial users of electricity are able to negotiate more favourable rates than are smaller commercial enterprises (Storer and Teljeur 2003). This effectively subsidizes the costs of production for larger firms at the expense of smaller-scale users, giving the former a competitive advantage that may be inconsistent with the objectives of industrial policies.

Similar problems with administered prices exist for other critical segments of the economy. In many cases, the monopoly power of public enterprises fails to support broader development goals. For example, high telecommunications costs limit the broad-based application of information technologies, placing some industries at a competitive disadvantage. This issue is properly a current focus of government policy, with the government having granted in December 2005 a license allowing a second phone company to operate in competition with Telkom. This initiative, in turn, should support the aim of the ASGISA initiative to target "Business Process Outsourcing" as one of its "immediate priority" sectors.

Cross-subsidization within different units of the parastatals is a separate matter of concern with administered pricing in parastatals. For instance, users of freight rail services effectively subsidize the transport of long-distance passengers, increasing the overall costs of transporting goods. In some cases, such cross-subsidization might be a useful mechanism for achieving a particular social objective—e.g. universal electrification. However, the institutional structure that currently exists for coordinating administrated prices and socio-economic goals is weak and fragmented (Storer and Teljeur 2003).

It is important to recognize that blanket solutions, such as privatization, are likely to fail to resolve these problems. Many of these industries are "natural monopolies" that require regulation regardless of who owns the assets. In others, the existence of economies of scale and barriers to entry suggests that monopolistic pricing would persist even after privatization. It is equally important to recognize that these enterprises have a significant role to play in fostering industrial development in South Africa. There is no guarantee that an unregulated market approach to coordinating industrial activities will be more efficient than an approach embracing stronger state intervention (Chang 1994).

Problems with pricing are not limited to the parastatals. Other pricing practices can raise the costs to sectors along a domestic supply chain. Consider the example of "import parity pricing" in the South African steel industry. It is common for the price of locally produced steel to be set at the international price plus tariff and transportation costs. In addition, a premium for faster delivery times for domestically sourced steel is frequently added to the price. In effect, this practice means that domestic prices reflect the cost of importing steel from abroad, not the actual costs of production in the local steel industry (Chabane et al. 2003).[16]

This system of price determination sets up a situation in which steel producers have an incentive to avoid exporting, since they can sell at a much higher price to domestic producers. However, it raises the costs to downstream producers of a critical industrial input and reduces their competitiveness. Downstream producers effectively subsidize the domestic steel industry. This arrangement not only has important consequences for the development of these downstream sectors, but also has implications for employment. Steel production tends to be much more capital-intensive relative to the downstream activities.

This discussion of pricing arrangements in South Africa illustrates some of the significant barriers to realizing the benefits of generating dynamic linkages between sectors and capturing the efficiency gains of better coordination. If industrial policy is to succeed in South Africa, these practices and similar impediments must be transformed and new approaches established to support industrial development objectives. The specific reforms will vary on a case-by-case basis, but the individual reforms should be crafted within a more general framework to support a broad-based industrial development strategy for employment creation.

Targeting Sectors with Low Employment Multipliers

Motor vehicles

The Motor Industry Development Programme (MIDP) arguably represents the most successful example of a targeted industrial strategy to date in the post-apartheid era. The goals of the MIDP were to further develop the domestic automobile industry, to expand industry exports and global integration, to take advantage of economies of scale, and to maintain the affordability and quality of motor vehicles for the South African market. The primary policy tools designed to achieve these ends were carefully targeted export and investment incentives linked to import duty credits and rebates (Barnes, Kaplinsky, and Morris 2003; Department of Trade and Industry 2003, 2004).

By exporting completely built-up automobiles and motor vehicle parts, firms earn duty credits that allow them to import completed vehicles and components tax-free. The domestic market is not large enough to allow firms to simultaneously produce a wide variety of models and take advantage of economies of scale. Therefore, increasing exports and significantly reducing the number of models produced domestically allowed South African production to become more efficient. The duty credits allowed firms to import models not produced locally at lower prices than would otherwise be the case. This arrangement reduces some of the costs of the MIDP, which are primarily borne by South African consumers (Barnes, Kaplinsky, and Morris 2003). However, it is important to recognize that South African consumers almost certainly pay more for motor vehicles under the MIDP than otherwise, and that the extent to which the savings from import duty credits are passed onto the final consumer is very much debatable (Kaplan 2003).

The results of the MIDP are impressive relative to the performance of other South African manufacturing sectors. As of 2003, exports have increased at an average annual rate of 33 percent since the MIDP was introduced in 1995 (Department of Trade and Industry 2004). Production for the domestic market has also increased, although at a significantly slower rate. The motor vehicle industry is notable in that its share of value added, relative to other sectors of the South African economy, increased during the 1990s (Barnes, Kaplinsky, and Morris 2003).[17] The industry's trade deficit, although still negative, has fallen since 1995, meaning that the sector requires a diminished share of the country's foreign exchange to continue to operate.

In addition, there is some evidence of growing diversification within the motor vehicles sector, an outcome that has evaded most South African manufacturing sectors since the democratic transition (Department of Trade and Industry 2003). Nevertheless, it is important to recognize that the motor vehicle industry still cannot be characterized as being composed of extremely diverse activities. For example, two product types account for the majority of exported motor vehicle components: catalytic converters and leather seats (Kaplan 2003).

The auto industry's job creation record is also noteworthy. Employment in many manufacturing sectors has fallen since the democratic transition (Kaplan 2003). However, employment in the motor vehicle sector has bucked this trend, growing by an estimated 8.1 percent from 1999 to 2003 (Department of Trade and Industry 2004). It is important to recognize that these employment gains are extremely small relative to the magnitude of South Africa's unemployment problem. Nevertheless, the industry's record in retaining and expanding decent employment opportunities cannot be dismissed lightly, given the overall job-creation performance of South African manufacturing.

The motor vehicle sector provides an important example of how a targeted industrial strategy using a handful of policy instruments can have a significant impact on economic development in South Africa. However, the MIDP is the only working example of a targeted industrial strategy at this time.[18] There is no reason why similar interventions could not be crafted for other strategic sectors of the economy, if the costs, benefits, and sustainability of such policies are carefully analyzed (Barnes, Kaplinsky, and Morris 2003).

Capital goods

Despite some domestic production and the export of certain types of machinery, South Africa remains heavily dependent on imported capital goods. For example, according to the country's input-output tables, nearly all—i.e. 96 percent—of the office equipment used in production is imported. Given South Africa's large and growing tertiary sector, this is a sizeable market for goods with potentially strong upstream and downstream linkages. With the notable exception of the building and construction industries, South Africa continues to depend on imports for many other categories of investment goods. Although these industries are not highly labor-intensive, they possess significant job-creating potential. Their employment–output ratios are comparable to those of the motor vehicle industry and the linkages to sectors throughout the economy are well established. Developing the capacity to produce certain categories of capital and investment goods for the domestic and export markets would reduce import dependence, expand access to export markets, and create new linkages with other sectors of the South African economy.

South Africa is well positioned to become an important supplier of capital goods to the African continent in general and the southern African region in particular. Already the country has been an important provider of some types of investment goods to neighboring economies. For example, the top ten destinations for South African exports of medium and heavy commercial vehicles, an important category of capital goods, include Zimbabwe, Angola, Mozambique, Zambia, Malawi, and Tanzania (Department of Trade and Industry 2004).[19] The further development of the South African capital goods industries would help develop stronger economic linkages between the economies of Africa as envisioned by the NEPAD strategy.

One potential problem with the development of an expanded domestic capital goods industry using traditional import-substitution techniques is that, as the exposure of the domestic firms to global competition diminishes, the prices of investment goods could rise as their quality falls. This could have important implications for the country's overall industrial development and its competitiveness in capital goods markets. Therefore, it is important to identify specific products in which South Africa could develop a core productive competency and to design policy to allow firms to inexpensively import capital goods that will not be produced domestically.

Within the context of an employment-targeted program for South Africa, the overarching idea to emphasize with respect to the motor vehicles and capital goods industries is that there are two sides of an important reality: that neither of these sectors should be targeted for accelerated expansion on the basis of their employment multipliers; but that there are other grounds on which they should be targeted. It will clearly be crucial over the next decade for the South African economy to continue enhancing productivity and the capacity to produce import-competing capital goods. This is so, even as policymakers also remain focused on employment creation. Indeed, implementing an effective employment-targeted program should actually enable policymakers to strengthen their efforts to advance a broader economic policy agenda precisely because they can pursue these other issues without appearing to neglect the imperatives of job creation and poverty reduction.

NOTES

1. Trades by registered brokers in their own names are exempt from the tax.
2. The primary way through which the tax might affect the non-wealthy would be indirectly, through the additional costs incurred in managing pension funds.
3. Would this tax raise interest rates on bonds, including government bonds, with bond issuers simply passing on the increased costs they have incurred with the tax? If this is so, then it is possible that the revenue that the government would bring in through the tax would simply move back out of the Treasury coffers through higher interest payments. This is a question that was raised by a Treasury official at a seminar we presented in March 2005 in Pretoria. It is of course true that the tax would raise transaction costs for secondary bond traders, though not for the primary issuers, such as the government. But the tax is also intended to provide a more stable financial environment by reducing the level of speculative noise trading. If the tax succeeds even modestly in creating a more stable financial environment, this would have the counter-effect of lowering the level of risk in the market, and thereby reducing long-term rates. For more discussion on this and related issues, see Pollin, Baker, and Schaberg (2003).
4. In the 2005 Medium-Term Budget Policy Statement, the Treasury reported on the status of this proposal, writing "some complex issues with regard to existing mineral rights holders and a possible review of certain income tax issues related to the mining sector require attention. It is envisaged that this revised draft Bill will be released for comment during 2006," (p. 46).
5. This is the CPIX inflation rate, which is the full-basket CPI rate exclusive of changes in interest rates on mortgage bonds.
6. See T.T. Mboweni (2002), "The Objectives and Importance of Inflation Targeting," *Business Day*, Nov. 13, 2002.
7. The rise in food prices put significant downward pressure on the real earnings of working people. Although South Africa produces most of the food it consumes, food commodities are increasingly traded on international markets and the food distribution networks dominated by oligopolistic firms, providing a transmission mechanism between exchange rates, food prices, and domestic living standards.
    The Reserve Bank responded to the decline in the exchange rate and subsequent increase in inflation by raising real interest rates. However, the Reserve Bank intentionally did not raise rates to the level necessary to achieve its inflation target. Indeed, the Reserve Bank responded

more moderately to this inflationary episode than it did to similar inflationary pressures in the recent past, before the inflation targeting regime was implemented. The Bank was concerned that raising the interest rates in order to meet the inflation target would have a more detrimental effect on the domestic economy than the rise in inflation above the target range.

8. This is the standard deviation of the rate of change of the exchange rate.

9. Amdsen's evaluation of the centrality of development banking and credit allocation policies for achieving development is consistent with a wide range of additional recent research, including that of Mkandawire on Africa (1999), Wade (1990) and Chang (1994) on East Asia, and Padin (2003) on Puerto Rico. More skeptical perspectives are presented in Ganesh-Kumar, Sen, and Viadya (2002) on India, and the multi-country study by Galindo and Micco (2004).

10. The data on the IDC, DBSA, and Land Bank are all from the most recent annual reports of these institutions.

11. We wish to thank Kuben Naidoo of the National Treasury for his assistance in enabling us to find the relevant data for this issue as well as to interpret the data appropriately.

12. These other potential influences include 1) the initial level of GDP; 2) the share of investment spending in GDP; 3) the share of government spending in GDP; 4) the fiscal deficit; 5) the level of overall health, as measured by life expectancy; 6) the international economic environment; 7) the effects of natural disasters; and 8) the effects of wars.

13. Epstein (2002) presents a wide-ranging perspective on this issue as it pertains specifically to South Africa.

14. See Saad-Filho (2004) for an extensive overview on the issue, in particular as it relates to advancing a pro-poor policy framework.

15. Different perspectives on the Nordic experiences are presented in Calmfors (1993), Pekkarinen, Pohjola, and Rowthorn (1992), Marshall (1994), and Iversen, Pontusson, and Soskice (2000).

16. Import parity pricing has come under increasing scrutiny in conjunction with the practices of Mittal Steel South Africa, which holds a near-monopoly over the South African steel market, with a roughly 80 percent market share. *Engineer News Online* reported on 3/22/06 about the hearing of the Competition Tribunal on Mittal's practices. According to *Engineering News*, "a steel-market expert from MEPS International, which currently develops steel-focused reports covering 19 countries as well as a series of Web-based price indices, stated that he had never before come across a market where IPP was employed as the basis for setting domestic selling prices." By contrast, Peter Fish suggested that, in the markets MEPS analysed, domestic selling prices were set through a process of negotiation between the producers and consumers based on the prevailing circumstances of the market at the time. His statement contradicts the prevailing assertion by the South African steel industry as well as other resources-based industries that import-parity pricing is international best practice. When pushed by chairperson Dr. David Lewis as to why Mittal Steel South Africa's pricing computation "was odd," given that its near-monopoly status made it rational for Mittal to price "just below" what an importer could charge, Fish responded by saying "I suppose, it is odd because I have never seen it." The outcome of this Tribunal investigation remains undecided at the time of writing.

17. One of the reasons for the rise in rankings in terms of value-added of the motor vehicle industry is the relatively poor performance of other manufacturing sectors. The motor vehicle industry still relies heavily on imported inputs. Therefore, improvements in value-added under the MIDP, although probably positive, are probably not as large as the substantial export growth would lead one to believe (Kaplan 2003).

18. Clothing and textiles represent the only other sector in which a targeted industrial strategy is claimed to exist in South Africa. However, this strategy has not been successful and there are questions about the long-run viability of an export-oriented garment sector in South Africa given the removal of quotas in January 2005. For more detailed discussion, see Kaplan (2003).

19. The other four countries in the list of top ten destinations for medium and heavy commercial vehicle exports are the U.S., the U.K., Germany, and France.

Appendix 1: Sources of Employment Data and Employment Elasticity Estimate

EMPLOYMENT DATA

Employment data in South Africa are derived from two sources: 1) household surveys, such as the October Household Surveys and the Labour Force Surveys; and 2) enterprise surveys, such as Survey of Employment and Earnings. These two sources are not strictly comparable. They differ in their coverage, methodology, and focus. Moreover, they produce strikingly different estimates of the change of employment over time in South Africa. This has helped fuel debate, and spread confusion, around the question of whether South Africa has experienced "jobless growth" or a reasonable record of job creation in recent years.

Long-run trends in South African unemployment are difficult to measure with any certainty. Reasonable household surveys that measure unemployment for all South Africans date back to just 1993. Since that time, the survey instruments have undergone many changes that make unemployment rates from year to year not strictly comparable. The annual October Household Survey was operable until 1999 after which time it was replaced by the biannual Labour Force Survey (LFS). Since 2000, the drawing of new samples, changes in the nature of the questions asked, and improvements in data collection raise some concerns about the strict comparability of employment numbers and unemployment rates from year to year.[1]

A much longer time series on employment in South Africa is available—the estimates of employment generated by enterprise-based surveys, such as the Survey of Employment and Earnings. However, there are important limitations in the historic quality of this survey data. The enterprise-based surveys not only exclude agricultural employment and the informal economy, they also, until recently, had not attempted to incorporate newly emerging sectors.[2] In addition, they tend to be biased towards large-scale enterprises. The increase in subcontracting in South Africa has important implications for employment data from enterprise surveys. Growth in subcontracted labor can be counted as a net loss of jobs, although in reality employment has simply shifted to firms not covered by the survey.

Those who believe that South Africa has experienced "jobless growth" base their arguments on the enterprise-survey data. Using this data, it can be shown that, in the sectors and firms covered by the surveys, there has been a net loss of jobs as output expanded. In terms of the traditional industrial base of formal employment in South

Africa, there apparently has been an overall pattern of jobless growth. However, this is only part of the story.

The new LFSs have much broader coverage than the enterprise surveys. They are household surveys and therefore sample the workers themselves, not workplaces. Therefore, the LFSs include informal and agricultural employment. Moreover, they are also more likely to capture other types of employment that the enterprise surveys might miss—such as employment in newly emerging industries. However, as mentioned above, the LFSs have not yet produced a reliable long-run time series to accurately gauge employment trends.

Despite these problems, researchers have used the household surveys to assess changes in employment. A comparison of the October Household Surveys and the Labour Force Surveys suggests that employment has grown significantly in South Africa over the past 10 years. Much of this employment growth occurred in the informal economy. Therefore, South Africa as a whole does not appear to have experienced "jobless growth," although the composition of employment has undergone dramatic changes.

Eventually, future improvements in both the household and enterprise surveys should help minimize these problems. However, the discrepancies pose a significant challenge for researchers analyzing employment policy and trends in South Africa. There is no easy solution to this problem.

In this report, we assume that the Labour Force Survey represents the most complete picture of the current level and composition of employment in South Africa. Therefore, whenever possible, we use the LFS numbers as a base from which we assess the current situation and make predictions of the future path of employment growth. However, despite its limitations, the enterprise survey data has two advantages over the household data. First, it is the only source of data on long-run trends in employment. Second, it is easier to use the enterprise data to analyze employment within detailed industrial sectors—for example, when using the input–output model described in this report.

When circumstances warrant, we use the enterprise survey data in our analysis, recognizing that it represents an imperfect, second-best approximation of the real employment situation in the country. Since the survey data tends to underestimate employment, the estimates we produce—for example, estimates of employment multipliers—should be taken as conservative estimates. Furthermore, improvements in the Survey of Employment and Earnings (SEE) after 2001 introduced a structural break in the series. Therefore, we do not use enterprise-based estimates beyond 2001 in this report.

ESTIMATION OF EMPLOYMENT ELASTICITY

1. Data

As noted above, time series data on employment for South Africa are problematic. These estimates use the SEE time series data from 1967 to 2001 (Statistics South

Africa) for total non-agricultural employment. These figures are based on enterprise surveys. The sample of enterprises surveyed is flawed and therefore these estimates will not fully capture the reality in South Africa. For example, the surveys may not accurately capture developments in new sectors and industries or changes in the employment relation (e.g. the growth of subcontracting in South Africa). Nevertheless, this data represents the only time series data on employment available for South Africa prior to 1995 (without resorting to speculative extrapolations).

Real value added for non-agricultural sectors of the South African economy (that is, total value added minus the value added of the agricultural sector) was used to measure real output.

All data were taken from the Reserve Bank website. The time series is quarterly, running from 1967:1 to 2001:4. After 2001 there is a structural break in the employment data.

2. Characteristics of the variables

Both output and employment were expressed in natural logarithms. Both variables have a unit root and are integrated of the first order. Cointegration tests of the two variables were inconclusive and not robust—some specifications suggested a cointegrating relationship, while others reject this possibility.

Estimate of the simple equation

log(employment) = c + b*log(output)

was unhelpful. There was evidence of strong autocorrelation of the error terms. A dynamic specification of the model addressed the autocorrelation problem. However, the level of employment was almost entirely explained by its lagged values, suggesting enormous inertia. The aggregate impact of output in the simple specification was negative.

Because of the inconclusive nature of the cointegration tests and the problems associated with the dynamic model expressed in levels, the model was estimated in first differences.

3. Estimates

The estimated model was

dlog(employment) = c + b*dlog(output) +d*dlog(employment)t-1.

The dynamic specification was necessary to address problems of autocorrelation.

The employment elasticity of output was estimated for three different time periods. The results are:

1967:1 to 2001:4. Elasticity=0.28
1980:1 to 2001:4. Elasticity=0.25
1990:1 to 2001:4. Elasticity=0.09 (coefficient not significant),

with reported elasticities representing the long-run elasticity estimates generated by the dynamic model.

The very low and insignificant coefficient for the last time period is consistent with the "jobless growth" patterns observed during this time in the SEE data. These trends are not apparent to the same degree in other data sources (e.g. the Labour Force Surveys that have been conducted in recent years).

NOTES

1. In particular, whether individuals classified themselves as "economically active" or not might have changed from sample to sample and with the nature of the questions asked. For example, a new sample was drawn in September 2001 in which a higher proportion of respondents might have classified themselves as "not economically active." This may account for a portion of the increase in the unemployment rate in that particular Labour Force Survey.
2. In particular, critics argue that the most recent incarnation of the enterprise-based employment survey, the Survey of Employment and Earnings, failed to capture important changes in rapidly expanding sectors, such as information technology. Since 2002, changes in how firms are sampled have attempted to correct these problems of non-representative employment statistics.

Appendix 2: Macroeconomic Policy Factors and Private Investment in South Africa

1. BACKGROUND

Empirical studies have identified a number of key determinants of the rate of private investment in the South African economy. We summarize the key findings from the literature in Table A2.1 in this appendix (all the results discussed in this appendix are presented in Tables A2.1–A2.7 on pp. 150–157). The key factors that drive investment include domestic demand (the "accelerator" effect), the cost of capital, profitability and relative returns to investment in physical capital, and indicators of uncertainty and instability. We explore further the determinants of investment by focusing on the factors that are most directly related to macroeconomic policy. Macroeconomic policy may affect investment through the cost of capital. We decompose the cost of capital to investigate the factors that are most pertinent in driving private investment. We explore the interest rate and exchange rate channels of the impact of monetary policy on investment as well as the effects of fiscal policy on investment through public investment, taxation, and government domestic borrowing. The objective is to shed light on strategies for increasing private investment.

2. THE EMPIRICAL MODEL, THE DATA, AND ESTIMATION METHODOLOGY

The analysis is based on an empirical investment model designed to allow us to estimate the effects of macroeconomic policy variables, controlling for other determinants of investment demand. The policy variables explored are: the interest rate (the lending rate), the real interest rate differential with the U.S., the corporate tax rate, the real exchange rate (both the level and variability of the exchange rate[1]), public investment, and government domestic borrowing. The model controls for the following determinants of investment demand: the "accelerator" effect proxied by the growth rate of the industry's and sector's real GDP; unit labor costs; profits; and the cost of capital.

For an industry or sector i, the cost of capital is calculated as follows:

$$coc_{it} = (ppi_{it} / p_{it}).(R_t - \pi_t + \delta_{it})/(1-\tau_t),$$

where ppi is the producer price index, p is the GDP deflator, R is the nominal interest rate, π is the inflation rate, δ is depreciation rate, and τ is the corporate tax rate. Real profits are obtained by deducting the real wage bill from real value added:

$$profit_{it} = va_{it} / p_t - w_{it} * L_{it},$$

where va is real value added, w is real earnings per employee, and L is employment.[2]

The analysis is based on the following dynamic investment model:

$$(I/K)_{it} + a_0 + a_1(I/K)_{i,t-1} + a_2 POL_{it} + \beta'X_{it} + v_i + \varepsilon_{it},$$

where I/K is the ratio of investment to beginning-of-period capital stock; POL is an indicator of macroeconomic policy; X is a vector of other determinants of investment demand; v_i is an industry- or sector-specific effect; and ε is a white-noise error term. To handle the fixed effects, various methods may be used. The regressions on industry data are instrumental-variable estimates with two-way fixed effects (that is, including yearly effects). In the regressions on manufacturing subsectors we use the two-step GMM estimation procedure.

We use data on the nine major industries and 27 sub-sectors of the manufacturing sector for the period 1970–2001.

3. KEY REGRESSION RESULTS

One of the most consistent empirical results is the positive effect of demand on investment. The accelerator effect is robust to alternative specifications and estimation techniques both in industry data and in manufacturing sector data. The results suggest that an increase in the growth rate of GDP from 3 percent to 4.5 percent would result in a 1 percent increase in investment.

Profitability is positively related to investment. Note that this result casts doubt on findings in some micro-level studies that suggest that high profitability in African private sectors has not generated high investment (e.g., Bigsten et al. 1999). This result is worth investigating further.

The cost of capital has a negative effect on investment, but the result is not robust to alternative specifications. In the industry regressions (not reported here for reasons of space), the effect of the cost of capital is significant in the static model (not including the lag of the dependent variable), but insignificant in the dynamic model. In the manufacturing sector regressions, the cost of capital enters negatively and significantly.

As a next step in the analysis of the effects of the cost of capital, we decompose the cost of capital variable into its policy components—monetary policy (the interest rate and inflation) and fiscal policy (the corporate tax rate). This allows us to make inferences with regard to policies that may help stimulate private investment.

Effects of monetary policy factors

The real lending rate has a negative effect on investment, with an estimated elasticity of -0.07 at the economy-wide level and -0.05 in the manufacturing sector. The nominal lending rate has a negative effect on investment, with an estimated economy-wide elasticity of -0.26 and -0.18 in the manufacturing sector. Inflation has a negative effect on investment; the estimated elasticity is -0.29 at the economy-wide level and -0.12 in the manufacturing sector.

Both the short-term and long-term interest rate differential between South Africa and the U.S. have a negative and significant effect at the economy-wide level, although the effect is insignificant in the manufacturing sector (results not reported here). Note that the estimated economy-wide investment elasticities of the interest rate differential (-0.015 for the short-term differential and -0.037 for the long-term interest rate) are smaller than those for the real and nominal interest rate.

The real exchange rate has a positive effect on investment, with an elasticity of 0.43 at the economy-wide level and 0.29 in the manufacturing sector. The positive effect of the real exchange rate on investment may be due to the fact that a significant portion of production factors (equipment and machinery) are imported, so that an appreciation of the exchange rate reduces the cost of imported inputs and the overall cost of production.

To further investigate the effect of the exchange rate on investment, we include an interaction term between the real exchange rate and a dummy for export orientation (high or low) for the 27 manufacturing sub-sectors. The results show that, among export-oriented sub-sectors, exchange rate appreciation discourages investment.

The results show that exchange rate variability has a negative effect on investment. This supports the view that stabilization of the exchange rate is an important component of strategies for encouraging private investment.

Fiscal policy factors

The corporate tax rate has a negative effect on investment. However, this effect is not robust to alternative specifications of the investment equation. Moreover, the estimated elasticity of investment with respect to the tax rate is very small: -0.002 for the industry regressions and -0.003 for the manufacturing sector.

The results indicate that public investment crowds-in private investment. However, government borrowing from the domestic markets has a negative effect on investment, even controlling for the effects of government debt on investment that operate through inflation and the interest rate. The results suggest that there are important limitations to government's ability to stimulate private investment by increasing public investment that is funded by domestic borrowing. The positive effects of public infrastructure accumulation on private investment may be offset by the crowding-out effects of government borrowing.

Macroeconomic instability

It is worth reiterating the results for inflation and exchange rate variability. These two variables are proxies, along with perhaps the debt overhang variable, for macroeconomic uncertainty. The results for these indicators suggest that macroeconomic uncertainty is a deterrent to investment.

Table A2.1 Determinants of Private Investment—Selected Empirical Evidence

Factor	Fedderke (2004)	Fielding (1997)	Mlambo and Nell (2000)	Heintz (2000; 2002)
Sample period; data; methodology	1970–97; panel data; 27 manufacturing sectors; panel data analysis	1946–92; aggregate (distinguishing between traded and nontraded capital); Time series analysis	1960–94; aggregate; Time series analysis	1970–93; 7 industrial sectors; panel data analysis
Demand; capacity; output		Proxy: change in real GDP at factor cost; Result: positive effect; Elasticity = +0.91 (nontraded); +1.07 (traded)	Proxy: change in real output; Result: positive (small) effect; Elasticity: 0.0001	Proxy: sector value added; Result: positive effect; Elasticity: +0.014
Macroeconomic uncertainty	Proxy: expected change in output; Result: positive effect (largest effect); Elasticity = +0.75	Proxy: number of strikes; Result: negative effect on traded capital; Elasticity: -0.09 (traded)	Variability of macroeconomic environment; Proxy: inflation; terms of trade, budget deficit; debt; Results: all significant	
Political uncertainty	Proxy: weighted average of 11 indicators of repression; Result: negative effect; Elasticity = -0.06			Proxy: combination of prison population, detentions, strikes; Result: negative effect (= factor effect); Elasticity: -0.027
Rate of return (level and uncertainty of return)		Proxy: combination of variability of returns and cost of capital and industrial unrest; Result: negative effect on nontraded capital; positive effect on traded capital; Elasticity = -0.49 (nontraded); +0.35 (traded)		Proxy: profit rate; Result: positive effect; Elasticity: +0.027

Table A2.1 (cont) Determinants of Private Investment—Selected Empirical Evidence

Factor	Fedderke (2004)	Fielding (1997)	Mlambo and Nell (2000)	Heintz (2000; 2002)
User cost; interest rate	Proxy: real interest rate + depreciation rate + corporate tax rate; Result: negative but insignificant Elasticity = 0	Proxy: real interest rate; Result: negative effect; Elasticity = -1.36 (nontraded); -1.14 (traded)	Proxy: real interest rate; Result: negative effect; Elasticity = 0.008	Proxy: real interest rate +; depreciation + tax rate Result: negative but insignificant; Elasticity = 0
Labor costs; wages	Proxy: real wage; Result: insignificant; Elasticity = 0	Proxy: aggregate real wage bill; Result: positive (nontraded); Elasticity = +2.50	Proxy: unit labor cost; Result: negative effect; Elasticity: -0.009	
Government investment	Proxy: public investment; Result: crowding–in; Elasticity = 0.04	Proxy: public investment; Result: positive effect; Elasticity = +0.44 (nontraded); +0.36 (traded)	Proxy: public investment; Result: positive effect; Elasticity: +0.37	Proxy: public investment; Result: positive but insignificant; Elasticity = 0
Finance and credit	Proxy: change in operating profits; Result: insignificant; Elasticity = 0	Proxy: credit to the private sector; Result: insignificant; Elasticity = 0	Proxy: domestic credit; Result: positive effect; Elasticity: +0.0003	
Trade liberalization; exchange rate	Proxy =(exports+imports) / value added; Result: insignificant; Elasticity = 0		Proxy: real exchange rate; Result: negative effect; Elasticity: -0.0001	
Fiscal policy		Proxy: (1 – effective tax on capital income $= 1 - \tau$); Result: negative (nontraded capital); Elasticity = +2.28	Proxy: budget deficit; Result: negative effect of bond-financed deficit (no effect of money-financed deficit); Elasticity: -0.067	

Source: Fedderke, J.W., 2004; Fielding, D., 1997; Heintz, James, 2000;. Heintz, James, 2002; Mlambo, K. and Kevin Nell, 2000.

Table A2.2 Industry Regression Results—Effects of Monetary and Fiscal Policy Factors (instrumental-variable two-way fixed effects estimates)

	Real interest rate (1)	Nominal interest rate (2)	Short-term interest differential with U.S. (3)	Public investment/ GDP (4)	Government domestic debt/GDP (5)	Exchange rate variability (6)
Lagged investment	0.526	0.526	0.526	0.526	0.526	0.526
	(0.00)	(0.00)	(0.00)	(0.00)	(0.00)	(0.00)
Output growth	0.039	0.039	0.039	0.039	0.039	0.039
	(0.06)	(0.06)	(0.06)	(0.06)	(0.06)	(0.00)
Lagged output growth	0.046	0.046	0.046	0.046	0.046	0.046
	(0.02)	(0.02)	(0.02)	(0.02)	(0.02)	(0.00)
Profit	0.0003	0.0003	0.0003	0.0003	0.0003	0.0003
	(0.01)	(0.01)	(0.01)	(0.01)	(0.01)	(0.01)
Real unit labor costs (change)	0.015	0.016	0.015	0.015	0.015	0.015
	(0.64)	(0.64)	(0.64)	(0.64)	(0.64)	(0.64)
Corporate tax rate (change)	-0.100)	-0.425	-0.021	-0.049	-0.370	0.058
	(0.00)	(0.00)	(0.80)	(0.69)	(0.00)	(0.56)
Real interest rate	-0.170					
	(0.00)					
Nominal interest rate		-0.175		-0.056	-0.203	
		(0.00)		(0.25)	(0.04)	
Inflation		-0.262		-0.157	-0.307	
		(0.00)		(0.00)	(0.00)	
Interest rate differential			-0.203			
			(0.00)			
Public investment				0.415		
				(0.01)		
Government domestic debt					-0.099	
					(0.04)	
Exchange rate variability						-0.198
						(0.00)
R-sq within	0.850	0.85	0.850	0.85	0.85	0.85
R-sq between	0.99	0.99	0.99	0.98	0.99	0.990
R-sq overall	0.86	0.86	0.86	0.86	0.86	0.86
F-test for fixed effects	7.05	7.05	7.05	7.05	7.05	7.05
	(0.00)	(0.00)	(0.00)	(0.00)	(0.00)	

Notes: Sample: 9 industries, 1972–2001, N=256 observations; the dependent variable is gross investment as a percentage of capital stock. The numbers in parentheses are the p-values.

Table A2.3 Industry Regression Results—Effects of the Exchange Rate (instrumental-variable two-way fixed effects estimates)

	Real exchange rate (1)	Exchange rate variability (2)
Lagged investment	0.526 (0.00)	0.526 (0.00)
Output growth	0.039 (0.00)	0.039 (0.00)
Lagged output growth	0.046 (0.00)	0.046 (0.00)
Profit	0.0003 (0.01)	0.0003 (0.01)
Real unit labor costs (change)	0.015 (0.64)	0.015 (0.64)
Corporate tax rate (change)	0.116 (0.29)	0.058 (0.56)
Real exchange rate	0.046 (0.00)	
Real exchange rate variability		-0.198 (0.00)
R-sq within	0.85	0.85
R-sq between	0.99	0.99
R-sq overall	0.86	0.86
F-test for fixed effects	7.05 (0.00)	7.05 (0.00)

Notes: Sample: 9 industries, 1972–2001, N=256 observations; the dependent variable is gross investment as a percentage of capital stock. The numbers in parentheses are the p-values.

Table A2.4 Estimated Elasticities from Industry Regressions

Variable	Table (equation)	Partial effects	Elasticities
OUTPUT (SUM)	2 (1)	0.085	0.019
Profit	2 (1)	0.0003	0.02
Unit labor costs (growth rate)	2 (1)	0	0
Real interest rate	2 (1)	-0.170	-0.067
Nominal interest rate	2 (2)	-0.175	-0.264
Inflation	2 (2)	-0.262	-0.293
Corporate tax rate (change)	2 (1-5)	0 to -0.425	0 to -0.003
Short-term interest rate differential	2 (3)	-0.203	-0.015
Exchange rate variability	3 (2)	-0.198	-0.182
Public investment/GDP	2 (4)	0.415	0.282
Government borrowing	2 (5)	-0.099	-0.350

Notes: Tables 2-3; elasticity $=(dy/dx)\ (x/y)$. A value of 0 means that the partial effect or the elasticity is not statistically significant at the 10% level.

Table A2.5 Manufacturing Sector Results – Monetary and Fiscal Policy Factors (dynamic specification – GMM two-step results)

	Cost of capital (1)	Real interest rate (2)	Policy components of cost of capital (3)	Public investment (4)	Government domestic debt/GDP (5)	Exchange rate variability (6)
Lagged investment	0.547	0.577	0.608	0.633	0.561	0.513
	(0.00)	(0.00)	(0.00)	(0.00)	(0.00)	(0.00)
Output growth	0.034	0.03	0.025	0.033	0.037	0.043
	(0.00)	(0.01)	(0.01)	(0.00)	(0.00)	(0.00)
Lagged output growth	0.033	0.016	0.029	0.033	0.047	0.041
	(0.00)	(0.04)	(0.00)	(0.00)	(0.00)	(0.00)
Real unit labor costs	-0.052	-0.039	-0.036	-0.018	-0.034	-0.033
	(0.00)	(0.09)	(0.12)	(0.43)	(0.18)	(0.06)
Cost of capital	-0.048					
	(0.07)					
Real interest rate		-0.19				
		(0.03)				
Nominal lending rate			-0.186	-0.274	-0.139	
			(0.08)	(0.02)	(0.26)	
Inflation			-0.273	-0.159	-0.324	
			(0.02)	(0.28)	(0.03)	
Corporate tax rate (change)		-0.046	-0.215	-0.283	-0.324	
		(0.66)	(0.03)	(0.00)	(0.01)	
Public investment				0.886		
				(0.02)		
Government domestic debt					-0.229	
					(0.04)	
Exchange rate variability						-0.065
						(0.00)
First-order autocorrelation	-3.3	-3.13	-3.4	-3.44	-3.29	
	(0.00)	(0.00)	(0.00)	(0.00)	(0.00)	
Second-order autocorrelation	-1.27	-1.23	-1.19	-1.13	-1.21	
		(0.2)	(0.22)	(0.23)	(0.25)	(0.23)

Note: Sample: 27 sub-sectors of the manufacturing sector; N=756.

Table A2.6 Manufacturing Sector: Exchange Rate, Exchange Rate Variability, and Export Orientation (dynamic specification–GMM two-step results)

	Real exchange rate (1)	Exchange rate: level + variability[a] (2)	Trade orientation: high exports (3)
Lagged investment	0.536	0.588	0.560
	(0.00)	(0.00)	(0.00)
Output growth	0.048	0.002	0.052
	(0.00)	(0.01)	(0.00)
Lagged output growth	0.030	0.002	0.042
	(0.00)	(0.02)	(0.00)
Real unit labor costs	-0.002	-0.018	-0.017
	(0.85)	(0.93)	(0.39)
Real exchange rate	0.050	0.298	0.082
	(0.00)	(0.00)	(0.00)
Exchange rate variability		-0.012	
		(0.04)	
(Exchange rate)[a]			-0.066
(high exports dummy)[b]			(0.00)
First-order	-3.240	-3.760	-3.430
autocorrelation	(0.00)	(0.00)	(0.00)
Second-order autocorrelation	-1.280	-0.630	-1.210
	(0.20)	(0.53)	(0.23)

[a] Logarithmic specification.

[b] High exports dummy = 1 if the sector is classified as having high export orientation.

Table A2.7 Estimated Elasticities from Manufacturing Sector Regressions (Tables 5–6; elasticity = $(dy/dx)(x/y))$

	Table (equation)	Partial effects	Elasticities
Output (sum)	4 (3)	0.054	0.01
User cost of capital	4 (1)	-0.048	-0.085
Unit labor costs	4 (1)	-0.052	-0.35
Real interest rate	4 (2)	-0.190	-0.049
Nominal interest rate	4 (3)	-0.186	-0.178
Inflation	4 (3)	-0.273	-0.190
Exchange rate variability	5 (2)	-0.065	-0.044
Corporate tax rate (change)	4 (2,3,5)	0 to -0.324	0 to -0.001
Public investment	4 (4)	0.886	0.387
Government borrowing	4 (5)	-0.229	-0.552

Note: a value of 0 means that the partial effect or the elasticity is not statistically significant at the 10% level.

NOTES

1. A proxy for the variability of the real exchange rate is calculated as the absolute value of the deviation of the annual value from the average of the previous three years. A drawback of this proxy is that it assumes symmetry of the effects of exchange rate instability on investment (appreciation vs. depreciation). Regressions with the actual difference yield an insignificant coefficient.
2. We do not have data on value added by sub-sector in the manufacturing sector. Therefore, this variable is not included in the manufacturing sector regressions.

Appendix 3: Estimation of Consumption Function for South Africa

Household consumption primarily depends on the long-run disposable income of households, adjusted for changes in inflation and the price level. Household consumption cannot increase at a faster rate than disposable income for an extended period of time without triggering a corrective adjustment. Of course, in the short- to medium-term, individual households that have access to credit can borrow against future expected earnings and increase consumption above the level that can be sustained by their immediate incomes. In South Africa, rotating savings and credit arrangements (e.g. stokvels) can also allow for short- and medium-term consumption smoothing among poorer households. However, debt payments (or payments into the stokvels) will reduce the discretionary income that indebted households can dedicate to consumption in the future. Therefore, we expect to find a long-run relationship between consumption and disposable income in South Africa.

Household disposable income is taken from the series published by the Reserve Bank of South Africa. Sources of disposable income include wages and salaries, income from property and investments, and transfers (grants and subsidies) from the government. Taxes and fees are subtracted from household income to derive an estimate of disposable income.

Payments on household debt are not included in the calculation of disposable income. Fluctuations in debt payments can have a significant impact on the discretionary income households have at their disposal. For example, households with variable interest rate bonds on their houses or flats can experience rapid changes in their discretionary income when interest rates rise and fall. The size of the debt payments, adjusted for inflation, depends on two variables: the real stock of debt and the nominal interest rate.[1] Data on the total debt stock of households is not readily available. Therefore, we will use the nominal lending rate in South Africa to estimate the impact of non-discretionary debt payments on consumption.

In the short- to medium-term, as noted above, interest rates have a substitution effect, as well as an income-effect, on the consumption of households with access to credit. The lower the interest rates, the more likely households will be to substitute current consumption for future consumption (i.e. they borrow to consume more now).

Unexpected inflation can also affect a household's consumption. If prices rise suddenly, a household can be expected to reduce consumption in the short run. In the long run, inflation should only have an effect on household consumption if it reduces discretionary income. If incomes do not keep pace with increases in the price level, real incomes will fall and we would expect consumption to be reduced. If real incomes remain constant, high inflation can have a positive effect on consumption if it reduces the value of the debt stock and, hence, the value of real debt payments. However, this positive impact on the stock of debt will likely be offset to a significant degree by the increase in the inflation premium reflected in the nominal lending rate.

In the aggregate household consumption function that we estimate, consumption depends on real disposable income, the nominal interest rate, and the inflation rate:

$$C = C(Y, r, ð),$$

in which C is real household consumption; Y is real disposable income; r is the nominal lending rate; and ð is the inflation rate. All variables are taken from the Reserve Bank of South Africa, with the exception of the nominal lending rate, which comes from the IMF's *International Financial Statistics* database.

Statistical tests show that C, Y, and r are non-stationary.[2] Furthermore, cointegration tests reveal the existence of one cointegrating relationship among the variables. This suggests that a long-run equilibrium relationship exists between household consumption, disposable income, and the nominal interest rate. However, no long-run relationship exists between consumption and the inflation rate.

Because of the possible existence of a long-run cointegrating relationship between three of the four variables in the consumption function, an error-correction model will be used.

The econometric model estimated is:

$$dln(C) = á + ã[ln(C)_t - ô_1ln(C)_{t-1} - ô_2ln(C)_{t-2} - ô_3ln(Y)_t - ô_4ln(r)_t]$$
$$+ â_1dln(C)_{t-1} + â_2dln(C)_{t-2} + â_3dln(Y)_t + â_4dln(r)+_{t-1}$$
$$+ â_5ln(ð)_t + â_6ln(ð)_{t-1} + â_7ln(ð)_{t-2}$$

The symbol "d" represents the first difference of the variable in question and "ln" the natural logarithm. Because the equation is estimated in logarithms, the coefficients of the model can be interpreted as elasticities (more details on elasticities are given below).

The estimated model is (t-statistics appear in parentheses):

$$dln(C) = -0.002 - 0.7[ln(C)_{t-1} - 0.81ln(C)_{t-2} - 0.08ln(C)_{t-3} - 0.13ln(Y)_{t-1} + 0.02ln(r)_{t-1}]$$

(-0.5) (-4.2)   (11.2)   (1.3)   (4.8)   (-4.2)

$$+ 0.6dln(C)_{t-1} + 0.3dln(C)_{t-2} + 0.13dln(Y)_t - 0.04dln(r)+_{t-1}$$

(3.8)   (3.8)   (5.1)   (-2.3)

$$- 0.004ln(ð) - 0.002ln(ð)_{t-1} + 0.006ln(ð)_{t-2}$$

(-1.8)   (-0.9)   (2.5)

The cointegrating relationship (presented above in italics) is well-behaved in terms of the adjustment to a long-run equilibrium and the stationarity of the residuals.

Economic estimates of the responsiveness of consumption to other economic factors are frequently expressed as elasticities. An elasticity is simply the percentage change in consumption associated with a one percent change in one of the determinants of consumption. For example, if the income elasticity of consumption were one, then a 1 percent increase (decrease) in income would be associated with a 1 percent increase (decrease) in consumption. Likewise, an interest elasticity of consumption of -0.5 means that a 10 percent *increase* in interest rates results in a 5 percent *decrease* in consumption.

The model produces the following long-run elasticity estimates of consumption:
       income: 1.2 (not statistically different from 1.0, as predicted by theory)
       nominal lending rate: -0.2

Short-run elasticities from the first-difference relationships are:
       income: 0.13 (contemporaneous), 0.91 (overall)
       lending rate: -0.04 (contemporaneous), -0.28 (overall)

Cumulative inflation effects on consumption:
       contemporaneous period: -0.0039
       one-period lag: -0.0065
       two-period lag: -0.0007 (not significantly different from zero).

NOTES

1. Nominal debt payments would be calculated as the stock of debt times the nominal interest rate. Real debt payments are therefore the real stock of debt (the stock of debt divided by the current price level) multiplied by the nominal interest rate.
2. Augmented Dickey-Fuller tests suggest that these variables are first-order integrated.

Appendix 4: Input–Output Model and Employment Multipliers

The Input–Output (I-O) model used to estimate the employment and output multipliers used in the report was derived from the 2000 Supply and Use Tables constructed by Statistics South Africa. The South African supply table shows the value of products supplied in 153 different product categories by 94 industrial categories. The South African use table shows the value of industrial output used by product category (95 categories) and industry (94 categories). The use table also contains the final demand for products by product category. Import supply and export demand are included in the supply and use tables, respectively.

An I-O table shows the value of domestic output supplied by industry X and used by industry Y. Industry X and industry Y can refer to the same industrial category. The I-O table also reports the final demand for domestically supplied output by industry. A standard I-O table can be constructed from the South African supply and use tables. To do this, the product categories of the two tables have to match. Therefore, the 153 product categories in the supply table had to be consolidated to match the 95 product categories in the use table.

The full I-O table is too large to reproduce conveniently in this appendix. However, we can reproduce a small section of the I-O table to illustrate its construction:

	Use		
	Agriculture	Gold mining	Coal
Supply			
Agriculture	1931.5	13.9	24.3
Gold mining	2.3	1.5	21.5
Coal	4.3	5.5	13.9

Note: R millions.
Source: Input–Output Table 2006.

From the table, it is easy to read off the linkages between industries. For example, the domestic agricultural industry supplied R1,931.5 million in output for use by enterprises within the agricultural industry itself. Coal mining and related industries supplied R5.5 million in output to gold mining.

Often, I-O tables are not expressed in monetary values, but rather in coefficients that represent a fraction of the total value of output produced by that industry. Each cell in the I-O table would be converted into a fraction that represents the value of inputs supplied by industry X as a fraction of the total output produced by industry Y. In order words, the I-O table would be transformed to show the amounts supplied and used by the various industries in order to produce one rand of output.

An I-O model uses the basic I-O table described above to draw conclusions about the interrelationships between the various industries that comprise an economy and to describe how industrial output might respond to various external changes. Most commonly, I-O models are used to describe how industrial output and employment respond to changes in final demand for an industry's output or for a category of expenditure (e.g. household consumption or fixed capital investment).

The standard I-O model is expressed as follows:

$$x - Ax = d,$$

in which

x is a vector of total demand for industrial output (total demand = industry demand + final demand);
A is the I-O coefficient matrix described above; and
d is a vector of final demand for each industry's output.

In essence, the expression for the I-O model represents a simple accounting relationship: total demand for domestic industrial output (x) less the industrial uses for domestic output (Ax) must equal the final demand for domestic output (d).

However, we are often interested in how total industrial output responds to changes in final demand. Therefore, the I-O model must be solved for 'x':

$$x = [I-A]^{-1}d$$

in which I represents the identity matrix. The inverse matrix $[I-A]^{-1}$ is often referred to as a "Leontief Inverse."

Output multipliers can be derived directly from the Leontief inverse matrix. The coefficients in the matrix show how industrial output responds to a R1 increase in the final demand for the products of any of the industries—taking into account the interconnections between the various industries and leakages due to imports. For example, a R1 million increase in the demand for agricultural goods in South Africa clearly will have a direct impact on agricultural output, but it will also have indirect impacts on all those industries that supply the agricultural industry with products used in production. These industries, in turn, will demand inputs from other industrial sectors, and so forth. The output multipliers derived from the I-O model take into account all these interconnections.

The basic I-O model described above can be extended to include feedback effects that impact final demand. Increases in output also increase the value added that industries generate. A portion of this value added is distributed to households in the form of salaries and wages. This household income, in turn, is spent on consumption—a component of final demand. Therefore, increases in industrial output can also affect final demand. To capture these dynamics, the basic I-O model described above has to be extended to include the household sector and value added in the core I-O coefficient matrix. I-O models that include the household sector are often described as "endogenous household models."

Employment multipliers can also be computed using the I-O models described here. In order to estimate employment effects, we need to know the number of jobs per unit of output (e.g. R1 million of output) for each industrial sector. These employment-output ratios can then be used to transform the Leontief inverse matrix to express multipliers in terms of employment instead of output. In this report, the employment-output ratios for each industrial sector were estimated using 2000 industrial employment data from the Trade and Industrial Policy Secretariat (TIPS) database.

Unless otherwise noted, all output and employment multipliers discussed in the body of the report were calculated using an endogenous household I-O model and the employment data from the TIPS database. It should be noted that the employment data are derived from the enterprise surveys of Statistics South Africa and therefore refer to formal employment only. In addition, enterprises in certain sectors of the South African economy, particularly new firms and small- and medium-sized formal enterprises, are likely to be underrepresented in the survey data for 2000. Therefore, the employment multipliers generated by this methodology are conservative estimates of overall employment effects.

Appendix 5: Securities Transaction Taxes Around the World as of 2002

Table A5.1 Securities Transaction Taxes Around the World as of 2002

COUNTRY	STOCKS	CORPORATE BONDS	GOVERNMENT BONDS	FUTURES	DETAIL
Argentina	0.60%	0.60%	0.60%	0.60%	Tax of 0.6% on all financial transactions approved by legislature March 2000
Australia	0.30%	0.15%	—	—	Reduced twice in 1990s; currently 0.15 each on buyer and seller
Austria	0.15%	0.15%	—	—	Present
Belgium	0.17%	0.07%	0.07%	—	Present
Brazil	0.3% [0.38%]	0.3% [0.38%]	0.3% [0.38%]	—	Tax on foreign-exchange transactions reduced from 2% to 0.5% 1999. Tax on stocks increased and on bonds reduced June 1999
Chile	18% VAT on trade costs	18% VAT on trade costs	—	—	Present
China	0.5% or 0.8%	[0.1%]	0	—	Tax on bonds eliminated 2001, higher rate on stock transactions applies to Shanghai exchange
Colombia	1.50%	1.5%	1.50%	—	Introduced June 2000
Denmark	[0.5%]	[0.5%]	—	—	Reduced in 1995, 1998, abolished effective Oct. 1999
Ecuador	[0.1%]	1.0%	—	—	Tax on stocks introduced 1999, abolished 2001. Tax on bonds introduced 1999
Finland	1.60%	—	—	—	Introduced January 1997; applies only to trades off HEX (main electronic exchange)
France	0.15%	See note	—	—	Present
Germany	[0.5%]	0.4%	0.2%	—	Removed 1991

168

Table A5.1 (cont.) Securities Transaction Taxes Around the World as of 2002

COUNTRY	STOCKS	CORPORATE BONDS	GOVERNMENT BONDS	FUTURES	DETAIL
Greece	0.60%	0.60%	–	–	Imposed 1998; doubled in 1999
Guatemala	3.00%	3.00%	See note	–	Present
Hong Kong	.3% + $5 stamp fee	[0.1%]	[0.1%]	–	Tax on stock transactions reduced from 0.6% 1993; tax on bonds eliminated Feb. 1999
India	0.50%	0.5%	–	–	Present
Indonesia	0.14% + 10% VAT on commissions	0.03%	0.03%	–	Introduced 1995
Ireland	1.00%	–	–	–	Present
Italy	[1.12%]	–	–	–	Stamp duties eliminated 1998
Japan	[.1%], [0.3%]	[0.16%]	–	–	Removed April 1999
Malaysia	0.50%	0.5%	015%[.03%]	0.0005%	Present
Morocco	0.14% + 7% VAT on trade costs	7% VAT on trade costs	7% VAT on trade costs		Present
Netherlands	[0.12%]	[0.12%]	0	–	1970–90
Pakistan	0.15%	0.15%	–	–	Present
Panama	–			–	Stamp duties eliminated Jan. 2000
Peru	18% VAT on trade costs	18% VAT on trade costs	–	–	Present
Philippines	[0.5%] + 10% VAT on trade costs	–	–	–	VAT present

169

Table A5.1 (cont.) Securities Transaction Taxes Around the World as of 2002

COUNTRY	STOCKS	CORPORATE BONDS	GOVERNMENT BONDS	FUTURES	DETAIL
Portugal	[0.08%]	[0.04%]	[0.008%]		Removed 1996
Russia	0.8% on secondary offerings + 20% VAT on trade costs				Present
Singapore	0.05% + 3% VAT on trade costs	—	—	—	Reduced 1994, eliminated 1998; VAT present
South Korea	.3%[.45%]	.3%[.45%]	—	—	Reduced 1996
Sweden	[1%]	—	—	—	Removed 1991
Switzerland	0.15%	0.15%	0.15%	—	Present; 0.3% on foreign securities, 1% on new issues
Taiwan	.3%[.6%]	0.1%	—	0.05%	Reduced 1993
United Kingdom	0.50%	—	—	—	Present
Venezuela	0.5% [1%]	-	-	-	Reduced May 2000
Zimbabwe	0.45% VAT on trade costs	-	-	-	Present

Notes: [...] indicates former tax rate. Sources ambiguous as to whether tax applies to bonds in France and government bonds in Guatamala. Austria, Belgium, Finland, Germany, Italy, Japan, Mexico, Portugal and Spain also impose VAT-type taxes on commodity futures trades.

Sources: *The LGT Guide to World Equity Markets* (London: Euromoney Publications, 1997); *1994 Handbook of World Stock and Commodity Exchanges* (London: Blackwell Finance, 1994); *Oppenheim Securities Markets Around the World* (New York: John Wiley & Sons, 1988); *OECD Financial Market Trends* (Paris: OECD, 1993); *Trends* (Security Industry Association, August 18, 1994); *Taxation of Stock Transfers in Various Foreign Countries* (Washington: Law Library of Congress, 1989); *Tax Notes International and World Tax Daily* (www.taxbase.org); IBFD, International Bureau of Fiscal Documentation (www.ibfd.nl); *The Salmon Smith Barney Guide to World Equity Markets*; *Dow Jones Interactive*; *PriceWaterhouseCoopers Guides to Doing Business*.

Appendix 6: South Africa Monetary Policy Alternatives: VAR-Based Simulation Models

In this appendix, we present details of the data, procedures, and estimates underlying the monetary policy simulation results presented in the body of the report. The appendix reports on the following components of our study:

1. The objectives of the analysis and an overview of the techniques used;
2. The data used in the study;
3. A presentation of the estimations and simulations of monetary policy experiments; and
4. A presentation of the estimations and simulations of credit policy changes.

1. MONETARY AND CREDIT POLICY EXPERIMENTS

Our study proposes a set of interconnected policy and structural changes designed to generate significant increases in employment in South Africa over a 10-year period. It is crucial to generate a set of plausible estimates to indicate how much employment our policies can generate, and what side benefits and costs might be associated with our policy suggestions in order to assess their economic feasibility and desirability.

Rather than try to create a very large—and therefore possibly highly complex and obscure—policy model to incorporate all the policies we are suggesting, we have decided to build a series of smaller models designed specifically to assess one or a few aspects of our overall program. We believe this approach yields much more transparent and focused results, perhaps at the expense of some checks for consistency across models and issues.

In this appendix, we describe the models we used to assess the impacts of our proposed changes in monetary and credit policy on the macroeconomy. To do this, we have implemented a set of techniques widely used in monetary policy analysis: vector autoregression (VAR) simulation models (see, for example, Aron and Muellbauer, 2002; Bernanke 1986 and Bernanke et al. 1997; Leeper and Zha 2003; Stock and Watson, 2001; Walsh 2003). This approach uses a minimum number of assumptions about the structure of the economy to estimate a small, simplified model of the macroeconomy. Based on that estimation, we simulate the model with changes in various policy tools and estimate the impact of those changes in policy on the economy. We do this by estimating the difference between the baseline path of economic variables such as inflation and economic growth, and the path these variables take under the new (hypothetical) settings of the monetary policy tools. The difference between these is taken to be the "impact" of the policy change on the economy.

In this appendix we describe two such models. The first focuses on the impact of changes in the South African Reserve Bank monetary policy's rule on exchange rates, inflation and economic growth. The goal is to estimate the effect of different interest rate settings on economic growth, inflation and exchange rate variability. The second model, using the same basic techniques, estimates the impact of private credit growth on economic growth and inflation. Both models incorporate some important exogenous variables as well.

Before describing the estimates and the simulations, we first discuss our data variables and sources.

2. DATA

All data are either originally quarterly data or have been transformed into quarterly data from monthly data.

Prime rate: The "prime rate" is the "prime lending rate." It tracks closely the changes in the repurchase (or "repo") rate, which is the main tool of monetary policy. The reason we use the prime rate rather than the repo rate is that it has a longer data series. Source: IMF International Financial Statistics (IFS) South Africa (hereafter IFS), lending rate.

Exchange Rate: The nominal rate relative to the U.S. dollar. Our measure is the four quarter rate of change of the rand, measured so that an increase means an increase in the rate of depreciation of the rand. Source: IFS.

Inflation Rate: We use the CPIX variable, as calculated by Aron and Muellbauer. This is the consumer price level, excluding mortgage interest. We use the four-quarter rate of inflation. Source: http://www.csae.ox.ac.uk/resprogs/smmsae/datasets.html.

GDP Growth: The four quarter rate of growth of real GDP. Source: South African Reserve Bank (http://www.reservebank.co.za/).

US T-bill: The three-month U.S. Treasury Bill rate. Source: IFS.

Private Credit: The four-quarter rate of growth of private credit created by all monetary institutions; monthly data transformed to quarterly data. Source: South African Reserve Bank (http://www.reservebank.co.za/).

Table A6.1 Stationarity Tests

Variable	Stationary (significance level)	Intercept	Intercept and Trend
Exchange Rate Change	Yes (5%)	Yes	No
Credit Change	Yes (5%)	Yes	No
Growth	Yes (1%)	No	Yes
Inflation	Yes; I(1) (1%)	Yes	No
Prime	Yes; I(1) (1%)	Yes	No
U.S. T-Bill	Yes; I(1) (1%)	Yes	

Terms of Trade: Four-quarter change in the terms of trade. Source: South African Reserve Bank (http://www.reservebank.co.za/).

Stationarity Tests on Variables

All of the variables were tested for stationarity using the Augmented Dickey-Fuller tests. Table A6.1 shows the results.

For the estimates that follow, we report on results using the growth variable (of real GDP). We have also done the estimates with detrended GDP growth, and the results are roughly the same. We report on the non-detrended variable because of greater ease of interpretation.

3. VAR ESTIMATES OF MONETARY POLICY

Using some of the data discussed above, we estimated a VAR model with four endogenous variables (prime, exchange rate change, inflation and growth) and one exogenous variable (U.S. Treasury Bill), over the period 1989, first quarter (1989.1) to 2004, fourth quarter (2004.4), with 4 quarter lags. We then estimated the impulse response function using the Choleski decomposition, with the following ordering (prime, change in exchange rate, inflation, growth). We tried the results with different orderings and the results did not seem very sensitive to the reorderings. A positive shock in the prime reduces economic growth, has a modest, cyclical impact on inflation, and is associated with increased variability in the exchange rate.

Figure A6.1 presents the impulse response functions from this model. This model was then transformed into a simulation model to be used for monetary policy experiments.

Simulation Results

The goal of the simulation exercise is to estimate the impacts of a medium- to long-term decline in the prime lending rate on exchange rate variability, inflation, and growth. In order to estimate these effects, we undertook the following steps:

*Figure A6.1 Accumulated Response to Cholesky One Standard Deviation
Innovations (± 2 Standard Errors)*

Accumulated Responses Are over 10 Quarters

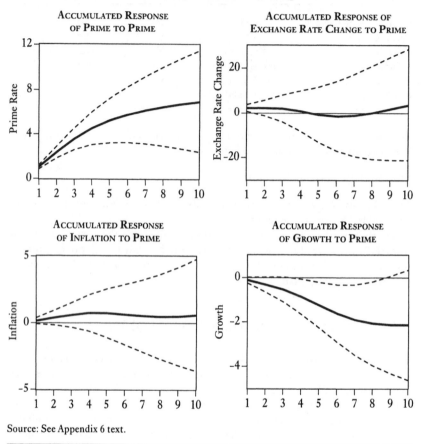

Source: See Appendix 6 text.

1. We solved the estimated VAR model, using a dynamic simulation, over the period
   1994.1 – 2004.4. We call the results of this dynamic simulation the "baseline"
   results. We use these baseline estimates in combination with data generated by
   "policy experiments" to estimate the impacts of changing the prime lending rate
   in the steps described below.

   As seen in Figure A6.2, the baseline estimates, when compared to the actual
   data, capture basic trends in the data for the most part, but do not do a good job of
   tracking all turning points. Unfortunately, this is a common problem in such models.

Figure A6.2 Baseline Estimates from VAR Model Versus Actuals 1994.1–2004.4

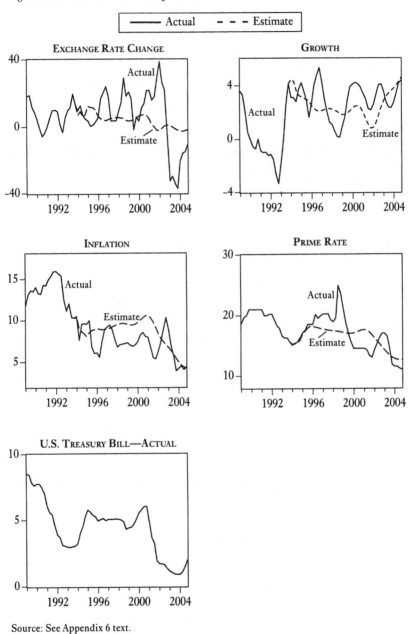

Source: See Appendix 6 text.

2. The next step is to create alternative scenarios in which the prime lending rate is adjusted according to a different monetary policy than that which prevailed in practice. In this respect, we report on two alternative scenarios:

   a. lowering the prime rate so that it remains one point below the baseline scenario for five years; and

   b. lowering the prime rate so that it remains four percentage points below the baseline for five years.

A One-Point Drop in the Prime Rate

Figure A6.3 shows the model's estimated impact of a one-point drop in the prime rate below the baseline on inflation, growth, and exchange rate variability for the period 2000.1 to 2004.4. Figure A6.4 shows the difference between the baseline and the simulated monetary policy change.

Table A6.2 (p. 179) presents the numerical summary of the main effects of this policy experiment. According to these results, real GDP growth is estimated to increase by approximately 0.15 percentage points as a result of the drop in the prime by one percentage point below the baseline. Inflation increases by 0.2 percentage points on average. The exchange rate depreciates by up to 1.5 percentage points more during the period.

Simulation II: Reduce the Prime Rate by Four Percentage Points, 2000.1–2004.4

In this simulation, we estimated the impacts of lowering the prime rate by four percentage points and holding it there over the period, 2000.1 to 2004.4. Figure A6.5 describes the impacts by showing the difference from the baseline. The Figure A6.5 results show that GDP growth goes up on average by about 0.6 percent for the 2001–04 period (about 0.5 percent on average for the whole five-year period), inflation increases by about one percentage point on average, and the exchange rate changes become more variable.

These are the results reported in the text. Of course, it is important to keep in mind the limitations of estimates such as these. We will discuss those in somewhat more detail towards the end of this appendix.

3. CREDIT AND MONETARY POLICY

As we discuss in the text, our plan for generating more employment in South Africa includes reallocating credit to employment-oriented investments, as well as increasing the quantity of credit to some extent. Because of limited degrees of freedom, among other problems, we cannot simply add a credit variable to our VAR. Moreover, because ours is an aggregative model, we cannot use the same VAR model to estimate the effects of credit reallocation. Instead, we estimate the effects of increases

Figure A6.3 Simulation of a One Percentage Point Reduction in Prime Rate, 2000.1–2004.4

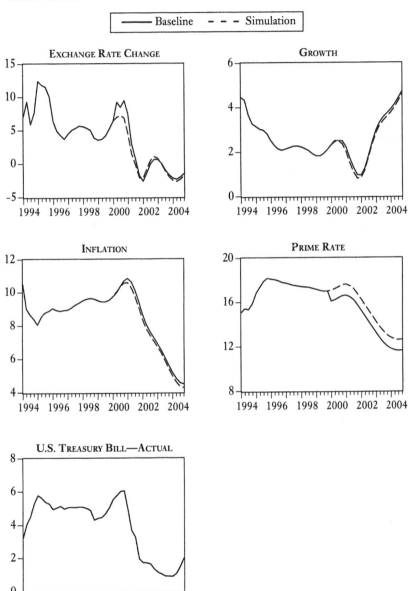

Source: See Appendix 6 text.

Figure A6.4 Estimated Deviations off of Baselines from One Percentage Point Decline in Prime Interest Rate, 2000.1–2004.4

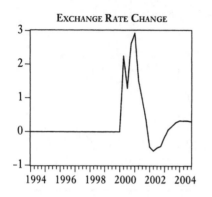

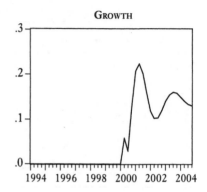

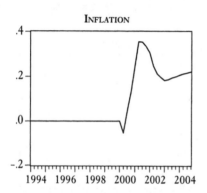

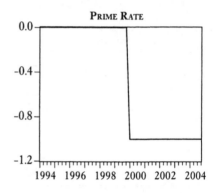

Source: See Appendix 6 text.

Table A6.2 Impact of a One Percentage-Point Drop on Growth, Inflation and Exchange Rates

	2000	2001	2002	2003	2004
Exchange Rate Change	1.54	1.44	-0.48	0.09	0.32
Growth	0.05	0.20	0.11	0.15	0.14
Inflation	0.03	0.32	0.24	0.19	0.21
Prime Rate	-1.00	-1.00	-1.00	-1.00	-1.00
U.S. T-Bill	0.00	0.00	0.00	0.00	0.00

Source: VAR-based simulation, as described in text.

Table A6.3 Impact of Four Percentage-Point Decline in Prime Rate

	2000	2001	2002	2003	2004
Exchange Rate Change	6.16	5.74	-1.91	0.35	1.29
Growth	0.22	0.79	0.44	0.61	0.55
Inflation	0.12	1.29	0.96	0.76	0.85
Prime Rate	-4.00	-4.00	-4.00	-4.00	-4.00
U.S. T-Bill	0.00	0.00	0.00	0.00	0.00

Source: VAR-based simulation as described in text.

in private credit growth on the economy first by using so-called "Granger causality tests" and then by using a different, smaller VAR model and simulation exercises in some respects similar to the ones we used for interest rate policy.

First we should say a word about our choice of a credit variable. We have chosen the growth of private credit as our credit variable primarily because we expect that our credit policies described in the body of the text will largely result in increases (and reallocations) of private credit, rather than public credit.

Granger Causality Tests

We conducted a battery of Granger causality tests. Table A6.4 presents the results.

The Granger tests indicate that changes in credit affect growth and inflation, but no other relations are statistically significant.

Credit VAR and Simulation

To pursue these relationships further, we built a small VAR with private credit growth as one of the three variables, with the other two endogenous variables being inflation

Figure A6.5 Impact of Four Percentage Point Drop in Prime Interest Rate
Relative to Baseline, 2000.1–2004.4

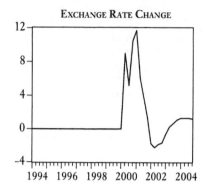

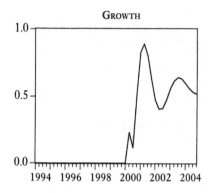

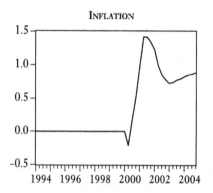

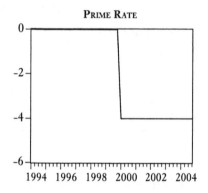

Source: See Appendix 6 text.

Table A6.4 Granger Tests of Effects of Credit Expansion on Macro Variables

Variable relationship	Does it Granger Cause? (at 10% Level)
Credit Growth cause Economic Growth?	Yes
Economic Growth Cause Credit Growth?	No
Credit Growth Cause Inflation?	Yes
Inflation Cause Credit Growth?	No
Credit Growth Cause Exchange Rate Change?	No
Exchange Rate Change Cause Credit Growth?	No
Credit Growth Cause Prime Rate?	No
Prime Rate Cause Credit Growth?	No

Table A6.5 Impact of Increased Credit Growth (5%) and Lower Prime Rate (by 2%)

	2001	2002	2003	2004
Private Credit	5.00	5.00	5.00	5.00
Terms of Trade	0.00	0.00	0.00	0.00
Growth	0.71	1.37	1.48	1.45
Inflation	-0.56	-1.77	-2.12	-1.98
Prime Rate	-2	-2	-2	-2
U.S. T-Bill	0.00	0.00	0.00	0.00

and real GDP growth. As exogenous variables, we used the U.S. T-Bill rate to control for the impacts of foreign financial factors, the terms of trade facing South Africa to control for foreign-related price factors, and the prime rate. We put the prime rate as an exogenous variable because of the lack of evidence from the Granger tests that the prime rate was associated with the credit variable. We also did this to save on degrees of freedom.

Figure A6.6 shows the basic accumulated impulse response functions from this model.

The impulse response functions show that private credit growth is positively related to real economic growth, and, in turn, more rapid economic growth is positively associated with more rapid growth in private credit. The most surprising results in these estimates is the negative relationship between private credit growth and inflation: higher growth in private credit is associated with lower inflation, quite contrary to normal expectations. This relationship appears to make a reappearance in the policy experiment simulations reported presently.

Based on this VAR model, Figure A6.7 shows the simulated impacts of a five percentage point increase in private credit growth *plus* a two percentage point decline in the prime rate, relative to the baseline, for a five-year period, 2000.1 to 2004.4.

Figure A6.6 Accumulated Responses to Cholesky One Standard Deviation Innovations (± 2 Standard Errors)

Accumulated Responses Are Over 10 Quarters

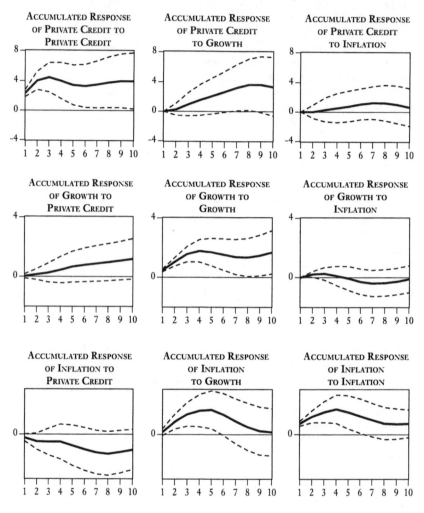

Source: See Appendix 6 text.

*Figure A6.7 Impact of five Percentage Point Increase in Private Credit Growth
and Two Percentage Point Reduction in Prime Interest Rate
(deviations from baseline)*

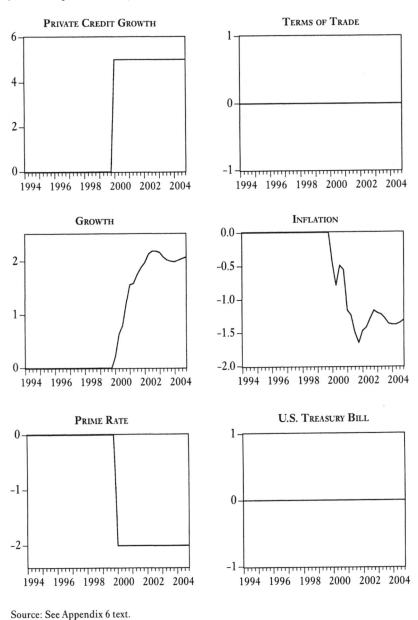

Source: See Appendix 6 text.

The simulation estimates, in the example used in the text, that real GDP growth would rise by about 1.5 percentage points from the baseline, say from 3–4.5 percent. It further predicts that inflation would fall. Without fully believing that inflation would actually fall in these circumstances, we think the results still suggest that large increases in inflation rates resulting from these policies are unlikely to occur.

In other simulations, not reported, we added the exchange rate changes to the VAR as an endogenous variable. The combined policy of lowering the prime rate and expanding private credit is not estimated to have a large effect on the exchange rate variability, greater than what we saw above.

In short, these results suggest that combining private credit growth with lower interest rates can be an effective means of raising economic growth without causing enormously difficult problems of increased inflation or exchange rate depreciations and instability.

Caveats

A number of cautions are necessary in interpreting these results. First of all, the degrees of freedom at our disposal are very limited because of the short period since the end of apartheid, which was obviously a major structural change. Second, it is well known that VAR models are highly simplified models of the economy because by requiring many degrees of freedom, they are limited in the number of endogenous variables they can incorporate. In addition, the simulation model is highly imperfect: it misses many important fluctuations and turning points in the data. As a result, it will only give a very rough guide to the impact of policy experiments. Hence, all the results in this appendix should be seen only as indicative.

Bibliography

Ahmed, Faisel (2004) "Determinants of Interest Rates in South Africa," manuscript, International Monetary Fund.

Amsden, Alice (2001) *The Rise of 'The Rest': Challenges to the West from late-industrializing economies*, Oxford: Oxford University Press.

Aron, Janine and Muellbauer, John (2000) "Financial Liberalization, Consumption, and Debt in South Africa," Working Paper Series 2000-22, Center for the Study of African Economies.

Aron, Janine and Muellbauer, John (2002) "Interest Rate Effects on Output: Evidence from a GDP Forecasting Model for South Africa," IMF Staff Papers, special issues.

Aron, Janine and Muellbauer, John (2005) "Monetary Policy, Macro-Stability and Growth: South Africa's Recent Experience and Lessons," *World Economics* (http://www.world-economics-journal.com/).

Aron, Janine, Muellbauer, John, and Smit, Benjamin (2004) "A Structural Model of the Inflation Process in South Africa," Working Paper Series 2004-08, Center for the Study of African Economies.

Arora, Vivek (2004) "Sovereign Spreads in South Africa," power point presentation at OECD Conference on How to Reduce Debt Costs in Southern Africa, Johannesburg, March 25–26, 2004.

Baker, Dean (2003) "Tobin Taxes: Are They Enforceable?" in Weaver, James, Dodd, Randall, and Baker, Jamie eds. *Debating the Tobin Tax: New Rules for Global Finance*, Washington, DC: New Rules for Global Finance Coalition, pp. 101–08.

Ball, L. and Sheridan, N. (2003) *Does Inflation Targeting Matter?*, IMF Working Paper No. 03/129.

Barnes, Justin, Kaplinsky, Raphael, and Morris, Mike (2003) "Industrial Policy In Developing Economies: Developing Dynamic Comparative Advantage In The South African Automobile Sector," Paper presented at the TIPS and DPRU Annual Forum 2003, Johannesburg, South Africa.

Barro, Robert J. and Lee, Jong-Wha (2000) "International Data on Educational Attainment: Updates and Implications," CID Working Paper no. 42 (http://www.cid.harvard.edu/ciddata/ciddata.html).

Bell, Trevor and Cattaneo, Nicolette (1997) "Foreign Trade and Employment in South African Manufacturing Industry," Occasional Report 4, Employment and Training Department, International Labour Office, Geneva.

Bernanke, Ben S. (1986) "Alternative Explanations of the Money-Income Correlation," Carnegie-Rochester Conference Series on Public Policy, Autumn, pp. 49–100.

Bernanke, Ben S., Gertler, Mark and Watson, Mark (1997) "Systematic Monetary Policy and the Effects of Oil Price Shocks," *Brookings Papers on Economic Activity*, 1, pp. 91–157.

Bernanke, Ben S., Thomas Laubach, Adam S. Posen, and Frederic S. Mishkin (1999) *Inflation Targeting: Lessons from the International Experience,* Princeton, NJ: Princeton University Press.

BIG Financing Reference Group (2004) *Breaking the Poverty Trap: Financing a Basic Income Grant in South Africa,* Johannesburg: Economic Policy Research Institute.

Bigsten, A., Collier, A.P., Dercon, S., Gauthier, B., Gunning, J.W., Isaksson, A., Oduro, A., Oostendorp, R., Pattillo, C., Söderbom, M., Sylvain, M., Teal, F., and Zeufack, A. (1999) "Investment in Africa's manufacturing sector: a four country panel data analysis." *Oxford Bulletin of Economics and Statistics,* 61 (4), 489–512.

Blinder, Alan S. (1998) *Central Banking in Theory and Practice,* Cambridge, MA: MIT Press.

Bruce-Brand, A. M. (2002) "Overview of Exchange Controls in South Africa," Statement to the Commission of Inquiry into the Rapid Depreciation of the Exchange Rate of the Rand, Reserve Bank of South Africa.

Bruno, Michael (1993) *Crisis, Stabilization, and Economic Reform: Therapy by Consensus,* Oxford: Clarendon Press.

Bruno, Michael (1995) "Does Inflation Really Lower Growth?" *Finance and Development,* September, pp. 35–38.

Bruno, Michael and Easterly, William (1998) "Inflation Crises and Long-Run Growth," *Journal of Monetary Economics,* 41, pp. 3–26.

Burdekin, Richard C.K., Denzau, Arthur T., Keil, Manfred W., Sitthiyot, Thitithep, and Willett, Thomas D. (2004) "When Does Inflation Hurt Economic Growth? Different Nonlinearities for Different Economies," *Journal of Macroeconomics,* 26, pp. 519–32.

Calmfors, Lars (1993) "Centralization of Wage Bargaining and Macroeconomic Performance," *OECD Economic Studies,* No. 21, Winter, pp. 161–91.

Casale, Daniela, Muller, Colette, and Posel, Dorrit (2004) "'Two million net new jobs.' A reconsideration of the rise in employment in South Africa, 1995–2003," *The South African Journal of Economics,* 72 (5), December, pp. 978–1002.

Cassim Rashad, Onyango, Donald, Skosana, Zola, and van Seventer, Dirk (2003) "A Review of the Changing Composition of the South African Economy," Report prepared for the 10-Year Review Project, Office of the Presidency.

Chabane, Neo, Machaka, Johannes, Molaba, Nkululeko, Roberts, Simon, and Taka, Milton (2003) "10 Year Review: Industrial Structure And Competition Policy," Report prepared for the 10-Year Review Project, Office of the Presidency.

Chang, Ha-Joon (1994) *The Political Economy of Industrial Policy,* New York: St. Martin's Press.

Corbo, Vittorio, Landerretche, Oscar, and Schmidt-Hebbel, Klaus (2001) "Does Inflation Targeting Make a Difference?" *Central Bank of Chile Working Papers, No. 106.* http://www.bcentral.cl/Estudios/DTBC/doctrab.htm.

Davies, Rob, and van Seventer, Dirk Ernst (2006) "An Economy-wide Impact Assessment of the Economic Infrastructure Investment Component of the Accelerated & Shared Growth Initiative (ASGISA)," forthcoming Working Paper, Political Economy Research Institute, University of Massachusetts-Amherst.

Deininger, Klaus and Squire, Lyn (1999) "Measuring Economic Inequality: A New Dataset Measuring Income Inequality," The World Bank Group http://www.worldbank.org/research/growth/dddeisqu.htm.

Department of Labour for South Africa (2003) *Growth and Development Summit 2003,* Pretoria: Chief Directorate of Communication, Department of Labour.

Department of Trade and Industry (2002) "Accelerating Growth And Development: The Contribution Of An Integrated Manufacturing Strategy," Pretoria: Department of Trade and Industry.

Department of Trade and Industry (2003) "Current Development in the Automotive Industry 2003," September, Pretoria: Department of Trade and Industry.

Department of Trade and Industry (2004) "Current Developments in the Automotive Industry 2004," Pretoria: Department of Trade and Industry.

Dooley, Michael P. (1995) "A Survey of Academic Literature on Controls over International Capital Transactions," NBER Working Paper, No. 5352.

Dornbusch, Rudiger and Fischer, Stanley (1991) "Moderate Inflation," National Bureau of Economic Research Working Paper 3896.

Easterly, William and Sewadeh, Mirvat (2002) "Global Development Network Growth Database," http://www.worldbank.org/research/growth/GDNdata.htm.

Edwards, Lawrence (2001a) "Globalisation and the Skill Bias of Occupational Employment in South Africa," *South African Journal of Economics,* 69(1), pp. 40–71.

Edwards, Lawrence (2001b) "Trade and The Structure of South African Production, 1984–97," *Development Southern Africa,* 18(4), pp. 471–91.

Edwards, Lawrence and Golub, Stephen (2004) "South Africa's International Cost Competitiveness And Exports In Manufacturing," *World Development,* 32(8), pp. 323–1339.

EM-DAT: The OFDA/CRED International Disaster Database www.em-dat.net Brussels, Belgium: Université Catholique de Louvain.

Epstein, Gerald (2002) "Employment-Oriented Central Bank Policy in an Integrated World Economy: A Reform Proposal for South Africa," University of Massachusetts-Amherst: Political Economy Research Institute, Working Paper #39, http://www.umass.edu/peri/pdfs/WP39.pdf.

Epstein, Gerald and Schor, Juliet (1992) "Structural Determinants and Economic Effects of Capital Controls in OECD Countries," in Banuri, T. and Schor, J., eds. *Financial*

Openness and National Autonomy: Opportunities and Constraints, Oxford, England: Clarendon Press, pp. 136–161.

Epstein, Gerald, Grabel, Ilene, and Jomo, K.S. (2005) "Capital Management Techniques in Developing Countries," in Gerald Epstein, ed. *Financialization and the World Economy*, Northampton, MA and Cheltenham, UK: Edward Elgar.

Fallon, Peter and Lucas, Robert (1998) "South African Labor Markets Adjustment and Inequalities," Discussion Paper 12, Informal Discussion Papers on Aspects of the Economy of South Africa, The World Bank Southern Africa Department.

Farrell, G. N. (2001) "Capital Controls and the Volatility of South African Exchange Rates," South African Reserve Bank, Occasional Paper No. 15, July.

Fedderke, J.W. (2004) "Investment in Fixed Capital Stock: Testing the Impact of Sectoral and Systemic Uncertainty," *Oxford Bulletin of Economics and Statistics*, 66 (2), pp. 165–187.

Fedderke, J.W. and Vaze, P. (2001) "The Nature Of South Africa's Trade Patterns by Economic Sector and the Extent of Trade Liberalization During the Course of the 1990s," *South African Journal of Economics*, 69(3), pp. 436–73.

Fielding, David (1996) "Consumer Expenditure in South Africa: A Time Series Model," *Applied Economic Letters*, 3, pp. 385–389.

Fielding, David (1997) "Aggregate Investment In South Africa: A Model With Implications For Political Freedom," *Oxford Bulletin of Economics and Statistics*, 59 (3), pp. 349–369.

Galindo, Arturo and Micco, Alejandro (2004) "Do State Owned Banks Promote Growth? Cross-Country Evidence for Manufacturing Industries," *Economic Letters*, 84, pp. 371–76.

Ganesh-Kumar, A., Sen, Kunal, and Vaidya, Rajendra R. (2002) "Financial Markets, Financial Intermediaries, and Investments in India," *Journal of International Development*, 14(2): pp. 211–28.

Gelb, Stephen (1996) "Inflation: inertia, indexation, and incomes policy," mimeo prepared for Department of Finance, 1996.

Gelb, Stephen (2004) "The South African Economy: An Overview, 1994–2004," Typescript, EDGE Institute and University of Witwatersrand, Johannesburg.

Gelb, Stephen and Black, Anthony (2004) "Foreign Direct Investment in South Africa," in Meyer, K. and Estrin, S., *Investment Strategies in Emerging Markets*, Northampton, MA and Cheltenham, UK: Edward Elgar.

Ghosh, Atish and Phillips, Steven (1998) "Warning: Inflation May Be Harmful to Your Growth," *IMF Staff Papers*, 45 (4), pp. 672–86.

Ghosh, Jayati (2003) "Exporting Jobs or Watching Them Disappear? Relocation, Employment and Accumulation in the World Economy," in Ghosh, J. and Chandrasekhar, C.P., *Work and Well-Being in the Age of Finance*, New Delhi: Tulika Books, pp. 99–119.

Gleditsch, Nils Petter, Wallensteen, Peter, Eriksson, Mikael, Sollenberg, Margareta, and Strand, Håvard (2002) "Armed Conflict 1946–2001: A New Dataset," *Journal of Peace Research* 39(5), pp. 615–37.

Grabel, Ilene (2004) "Trip Wires and Speed Bumps: Managing Financial Risks and Reducing the Potential for Financial Crises in Developing Economies," United Nations Conference on Trade and Development (UNCTAD), G-24 Discussion Paper, No. 33, November.

Griffith-Jones, Stephany and Fuzzo de Lima, Ana Teresa (2004) "Alternative Loan Guarantee Mechanisms and Project Finance for Infrastructure in Developing Countries," Typescript, Institute of Development Studies, University of Sussex, February.

Heintz, James, (2000) "Political Unrest, Distributive Conflict, and Investment: The Case of South Africa," Paper presented at the PERI workshop on Investment in Africa, October.

Heintz, James, (2002) "Political Conflict and the Social Structure of Accumulation: The Case of South African Apartheid," *Review of Radical Political Economics*, 34(3), pp. 319–326.

Heintz, James and Pollin, Robert (2003) "Informalization, Economic Growth and the Challenge of Creating Viable Labor Standards in Developing Countries," Political Economy Research Institute Working Paper Series, #60.

Heintz, James and Pollin, Robert (2006) "Informalization, Economic Growth, and the Challenge of Creating Viable Labor Standards in Developing Countries," in Kudva, Neema and Beneria, Lourdes eds. *Rethinking Informalization*, Cornell University Open Access Repository, http://hdl.handle.net/1813/3716.

Heston, Alan, Summers, Robert, and Aten, Bettina (2002) *Penn World Table Version 6.1*, Center for International Comparisons at the University of Pennsylvania (CICUP), October.

Hirsch, Alan (2004) "South Africa's Development Path and the Government's Programme of Action," typescript, Office of The Presidency Policy Coordination and Advisory Services.

Hirsch, Alan (2005) *Season of Hope: Economic Reform under Mandela and Mbeki*, Scottsville, SA: University of KwaZulu-Natal Press; and Ottawa, Canada: International Development Research Centre.

Hoogeveen, Johannes G., and Ozler, Berk (2004) "Not Separate, Not Equal: Poverty and Inequality in Post-Apartheid South Africa," manuscript, Washington, DC: World Bank.

IMF (2003) *South Africa: Selected Issues,* IMF Country Report, No. 03/18, January.

IMF (2004) *South Africa: Selected Issues,* IMF Country Report, No. 04/379, December.

IMF (2006) Direction of Trade Statistics. Database/CD-ROM. April 2006. Washington, DC: International Monetary Fund.

Inter-American Development Bank (2003) "Guarantee Disbursement Loans (GDLs) with Sovereign Guarantee: Pilot Program to Provide the Option of Disbursing Loans in the Form of a Guarantee," typescript, March.

Iversen, T., Pontusson, Jonas, and Soskice, David, eds. (2000) *Unions, Employers, and Central Banks*, Cambridge, UK: Cambridge University Press.

Jacobson, Tor, Per Jansson, Anders Vredin, and Anders Warne (1999) "A VAR Model for Monetary Policy Analysis in a Small Open Economy," mimeo.

Kaplan, David (2003) "Manufacturing Performance and Policy in South Africa: A Review," Paper presented at the TIPS and DPRU Annual Forum 2003, Johannesburg, South Africa.

Kaplan, Ethan and Rodrik, Dani (2001) "Did the Malaysian Capital Controls Work?" February KSG Working Paper No. 01-008. http://ssrn.com/abstract=262173.

Khan, Azizur (2004) "Growth, Employment and Poverty: An Analysis of the Vital Nexus Based on Some Recent UNDP and ILO/SIDA Studies," Paper presented at the UNDP International Policy Conference on Strengthening the Employment Nexus Between Growth and Poverty Reduction, Brasilia, Brazil, January 11–12, 2005, UNDP International Poverty Centre.

Khan, Mohsin S. and Senhadji, Abdelhak S. (2001) "Threshold Effects in the Relationship Between Inflation and Growth," *IMF Staff Papers*, 48:1, 1–21.

Leeper, Eric M. and Zha, Tao (2002) "Empirical Analysis of Policy Interventions," NBER Paper, No. 9063.

Leeper, Eric M., and Zha, Tao (2003) "Modest Policy Interventions," *Journal of Monetary Economics,* 50, pp. 1673–1700.

Lewis, Jeffrey D. (2001) "Policies to Promote Growth and Employment in South Africa," Discussion Paper 16, Informal Discussion Papers on Aspects of the Economy of South Africa, World Bank Southern Africa Department.

Li, Wenli (1998) "Government Loan, Guarantee, and Grant Programs: An Evaluation," *Economic Quarterly,* Federal Reserve Bank of Richmond, 84(4), pp. 25–51.

Liebbrandt, Murray, Levinsohn, James, and McCrary, Justin (2005) "Incomes in South Africa Since the Fall of Apartheid," Working Paper 11384, Cambridge, MA: National Bureau of Economic Research.

Maisel, Sherman (1973) "Improving Our System of Credit Allocation," in Federal Reserve Bank of Boston, *Credit Allocation Techniques and Monetary Policy*, Proceedings of a Conference held at Melvin Village, New Hampshire, pp. 15–30.

Marshall, Mike (1994) "Lessons from the Experience of the Swedish Model," in P. Arestis and M. Marshall, eds. *The Political Economy of Full Employment*, Northampton, MA and Cheltenham, UK: Edward Elgar, Chapter 10.

Mboweni, T.T. (2002) "The Objectives and Importance of Inflation Targeting," *Business Day*, Nov. 13, 2002.

McCord, Anna (2004a) "Policy Expectations and Programme Reality: The Poverty Reduction and Labour Market Impact of Two Public Works Programmes in South Africa," London: Overseas Development Institute.

McCord, Anna (2004b) "Public Works and Overcoming Under-Development in South Africa," manuscript delivered at UNDP, HSRC, & DBSA Conference on "Overcoming Under-development in South Africa's Second Economy," October.

McCord, Anna and van Seventer, Dirk (2004) "The Economy-Wide Impacts of the Labour Intensification of Infrastructure Expenditures in South Africa," typescript presented at DPRU, TIPS & Cornell Conference on African Development and Poverty Reduction, the Macro-Micro Linkages, October.

Meth, Charles (2006) "What Was the Poverty Headcount in 2004? A Critique of the Latest Offering from van der Berg et al.," manuscript, South African Labour and Development Research Unit (SALDRU), University of Capetown, April.

Milesi-Ferretti, Gian Maria (1998), "Why Capital Controls? Theory and Evidence," in Eijffinger, S. and Huizinga, H., eds. *Positive Political Economy: Theory and Evidence*, Cambridge: Cambridge University Press, 1998, 217–47.

Mkandawire, Thandika (1999) "The Political Economy of Financial Reform in Africa," *Journal of Internaitonal Development*, May/June, pp. 321–44.

Mlambo, K. and Nell, Kevin (2000) "Public Policy and Private Investment in South Africa: An Empirical Investigation," in Elbadawi, I. and T. Hartzenberg, eds. *Development Issues in South Africa*, New York: St. Martin's Press, pp. 80–109.

Mlambo, K. and Oshikoya, T.W. (2001) "Macroeconomic Factors and Investment in Africa," *Journal of African Economies*, 10 (2) (Supplement), pp. 12–47.

Mondi, Lumkile (2006) "Targeted Employment Programs: The Case of the Industrial Development Corporation of South Africa," Santon: The Industrial Development Corporation of South Africa, April.

National Treasury, Republic of South Africa (1996) *Growth, Employment and Redistribution*, June, Pretoria.

National Treasury, Republic of South Africa (2004) *Medium Term Budget Policy Statement*, Communications Directorate, National Treasury, www.treasury.gov.za.

National Treasury, Republic of South Africa (2005) *Medium-Term Budget Policy Statement 2005*. October 25, 2005. Pretoria: National Treasury.

Padin, Jose A. (2003) "Puerto Rico in the Post War: Liberalized Development Banking and the Fall of the 'Fifth Tiger,'" *World Development*, 32(2), pp. 281–301.

Pekkarinen, P., Pohjola, M., and Rowthorn, B. (1992) *Social Corporatism: A Superior Economic System?* New York: Oxford University Press.

Phillips, Sean (2004a) "Expanding Employment in Public Works in South Africa," ILO: ASIST, Bulletin No. 18, September 2004, http://www.ilo.org/public/english/employment/recon/eiip/asist/bulletin/bul-18/bul-18.pdf.

Phillips, Sean (2004b) "The Expanded Public Works Program," typescript, National Department of Public Works, Government of South Africa.

Pollin, Robert (1993) "Public Credit Allocation through the Federal Reserve: Why It's Necessary; How It Should Be Done," in R. Pollin, G. Dymski, and G. Epstein, eds. *Transforming the U.S. Financial System: Equity and Efficiency for the 21st Century,* Armonk, NY: M.E. Sharpe, pp. 321–354.

Pollin, Robert (1995) "Financial Structures and Egalitarian Economic Policy," *New Left Review,* 214, November/December, 26–61.

Pollin, Robert (1997) "Financial Intermediation and the Variability of the Saving Constraint," in R. Pollin ed., *The Macroeconomics of Saving, Finance and Investment,* Ann Arbor, MI: University of Michigan Press, pp. 309–366.

Pollin, Robert (2003) Entry on "Savings," in J. King, ed., *Elgar Companion to Post-Keynesian Economics,* Edward Elgar, pp. 304–08.

Pollin, Robert (2006) "Globalization and the Transition to Egalitarian Development," in Boyce, James, Cullenberg, Stephen, Pattanaik, Prasanta, and Pollin, Robert, eds., *Human Development in the Era of Globalization: Essays in Honor of Keith B. Griffin,* Northampton, MA: Edward Elgar, pp. 211–38.

Pollin, Robert and Luce, Stephanie (1998) *The Living Wage: Building a Fair Economy,* New York: The New Press.

Pollin, Robert and Zhu, Andong (2006) "Inflation and Economic Growth: A Cross-Country Non-linear Analysis," *Journal of Post Keynesian Economics,* forthcoming. Available at http://www.umass.edu/peri/pdfs/WP109.pdf.

Pollin, Robert, Baker, Dean, and Schaberg, Marc (2003) "Securities Transaction Taxes for U.S. Financial Markets," *Eastern Economic Journal,* 29(9), Fall, pp. 527–58.

Rodrik, Dani (2004) "Rethinking Growth Policies in the Developing World," manuscript, October, Harvard University.

Saad-Filho, Alfredo (2004) "Pro-Poor Monetary and Anti-Inflation Policies: Developing Alternatives to the New Monetary Policy Consensus," a report commissioned by the United Nations Development Program, typescript, Department of Development Studies, School of Oriental and African Studies, University of London.

Selvanathan, E.A. and Selvanathan, Saroja (2003) "Consumer Demand in South Africa," *The South African Journal of Economics,* 71(2), 325–344.

Standing, Guy, Sender, John, and Weeks, John (1996) *Restructuring the Labour Market: The South African Challenge,* Geneva: International Labour Office.

Statistics South Africa (2005). "Labour force survey, 2005." Statistical Release P0210. July 2005, Pretoria: Statistics South Africa.

Stock, James H. and Watson, Mark W. (2001) "Vector Autoregressions," *Journal of Economic Perspectives,* 15(4), Fall, pp. 101–115.

Storer, David and Teljeur, Ethel (2003), "Administered Prices," Paper presented at the TIPS and DPRU Annual Forum 2003, Johannesburg, South Africa.

United Nations Conference on Trade and Development (2002) *Trade and Development Report 2002,* Geneva.

United Nations Conference on Trade and Development (2004) *World Investment Report: The Shift Toward Services,* New York and Geneva.

USAID (2005) "Overview of USAID Partial Credit Guarantees," http://www.usaid.gov/our_work/economic_growth_and_trade/development_credit/index.html.

van der Berg, Servaas, Burger, Ronelle, Burger, Rulof, Louw, Megan, and Yu, Derek (2006) "Trends in Poverty and Inequality since the Political Transition," Development Policy Research Unit Working Paper 06/104, University of Stellenbosch, March.

van Seventer, Dirk (2001) "The Level and Variation of Tariff Rates: An Analysis of Nominal and Effective Tariff Rates in South Africa for the Years 2000 and 2001," Paper presented at the TIPS Annual Forum 2001, Johannesburg, South Africa.

Wade, Robert (1990) *Governing the Market: Economic Theory and the Role of Government in East Asian Development*, Princeton, NJ: Princeton University Press.

Walsh, Carl E. (2003) *Monetary Theory and Policy,* 2nd Edition, Cambridge, MA: MIT Press.

World Bank (2003) *World Development Indicators*, Washington, DC, CD-ROM.

Index

About the Authors

Robert Pollin (Project Director) is Professor in the Department of Economics and founding co-director of the Political Economy Research Institute at the University of Massachusetts-Amherst. He received a Ph.D. in Economics from the New School for Social Research in New York City in 1982. His research centers on macroeconomics, conditions for low-wage workers in the U.S. and globally, and the analysis of financial markets. His recent books include *Contours of Descent: U.S. Economic Fractures and the Landscape of Global Austerity* (Verso, 2003); *The Living Wage: Building a Fair Economy* (with Stephanie Luce, The New Press, 1998); and the edited volumes *Human Development in the Era of Globalization* (with James Boyce, Stephen Cullenberg, and Prasanta Pattanaik, Edward Elgar, 2006 and *The Macroeconomics of Saving, Finance, and Investment* (University of Michigan Press, 1997). He writes and consults extensively throughout the United States on the viability of "living wage" policies. Parallel to his work in South Africa, he is also directing a UNDP-sponsored project on employment promotion and poverty reduction in Kenya. He has worked previously with the UNDP in Bolivia, the Joint Economic Committee of the U.S. Congress, and as a member of the Capital Formation Subcouncil of the U.S. Competitiveness Policy Council.

Gerald A. Epstein is Professor of Economics and a founding Co-Director of the Political Economy Research Institute (PERI) at the University of Massachusetts, Amherst. He received his Ph.D. in Economics from Princeton University in 1981. He has written articles on numerous topics including the political economy of central banking, capital management techniques, international credit relations, and multinational corporations. He has worked with the United Nations Development Program in the areas of Pro-Poor Macroeconomic Policy and Human Development Impact Assessments of Trade Policies, and with UN-DESA on developing alternatives to inflation targeting monetary policy. Epstein's current research focuses on employment oriented macroeconomic and trade policies. He is the editor or co-editor of several books, including *Globalization and Progressive Economic Policy* (Cambridge University Press, 1998, with Dean Baker and Robert Pollin), *Capital Flight and Capital Controls in Developing Countries* (Edward Elgar, 2005) and *Financialization and the World Economy* (Edward Elgar, 2005).

James Heintz is Associate Research Professor and Associate Director at the Political Economy Research Institute, University of Massachusetts-Amherst. He received his Ph.D. in Economics from the University of Massachusetts in 2001 and an MS in Economics in 1992 from the University of Minnesota. He has written on a wide range of economic policy issues, including job creation, global labor standards, egalitarian macroeconomic strategies, and investment behavior. In addition to this project in South Africa, he has also worked as an international consultant on projects in Ghana and and Kenya, sponsored by the International Labor Organization and the United Nations Development Program, that focus on employment-oriented development policy. He is co-author, with Nancy Folbre, of *The Ultimate Field Guide to the U.S. Economy*. From 1996 to 1998, he worked as an economist at the National Labour and Economic Development Institute in Johannesburg, a policy think tank affiliated with the South African labor movement. His current work focuses on global labor standards, employment income, and poverty; employment policies for low- and middle-income countries; and the links between macroeconomic policies and distributive outcomes.

Léonce Ndikumana is Associate Professor of Economics at the University of Massachusetts at Amherst where he teaches courses in macroeconomics, money and banking and African economic development. He received his Ph.D. in Economics in 1996 from Washington University in St. Louis. His research investigates the role of financial systems for domestic investment, the issues of external borrowing and capital flight from African countries, and the politics and economics of conflict and civil wars in Africa. Since January 2006, Ndikumana is on leave at the United Nations Economic Commission for Africa where he serves as Senior Economic Affair Officer in the Economic and Social Policy Division. He also has served as consultant, researcher and resource person for several organizations including the World Bank, UNU/WIDER, ILO, UNCTAD, and the AERC. His work has appeared in *The Journal of Post Keynesian Economics, World Development, The Journal of African Economies, International Journal of Money and Finance, Development and Change, The Journal of Development Studies, International Review of Economics and Finance, The African Studies Review*, and *The Journal of Modern African Studies*. He has also contributed numerous chapters to edited volumes.